Brightest Heaven of Invention

BRIGHTEST HEAVEN

OF

INVENTION

a Christian guide to six Shakespeare plays

Peter J. Leithart

canonpress
Moscow, Idaho

Published by Canon Press
P.O. Box 8729, Moscow, ID 83843
800.488.2034 | www.canonpress.com

Peter J. Leithart, *Brightest Heaven of Invention:*
A Christian Guide to Six Shakespeare Plays
Copyright © 1996 by Peter Leithart.

Cover design by David Dalbey.
Printed in the United States of America.

Library of Congress Cataloging-in-Publication Data

Leithart, Peter J.
  Brightest heaven of invention : a Christian guide to six Shakespeare
plays / Peter J. Leithart.
      p. cm.
  Originally published in 1996.
  A study guide to Shakespeare for Christians.
  ISBN-13: 978-1-885767-23-3 (pbk.)
  ISBN-10: 1-885767-23-4 (pbk.)
  1. Shakespeare, William, 1564-1616—Criticism and interpretation.
2. Shakespeare, William, 1564-1616—Religion. 3. Christianity and
literature. 4. Christianity in literature. I. Title.
  PR3011.L45 2006
  822.3'3-dc22

                                    2006031654

12 13 14 15 16 17 18   13 12 11 10 9 8

O for a Muse of fire, that would ascend
The *brightest heaven of invention*,
A kingdom for a stage, princes to act
And monarchs to behold the swelling scene!

Prologue, *Henry V*

Table of Contents

Acknowledgments

For three school years, from 1992-1995, I had the privilege of teaching Shakespeare to junior high and high school students at Heritage Academy, a home school ministry sponsored by the church of which I was then pastor, the Reformed Heritage Presbyterian Church of Birmingham, Alabama. I had learned Shakespeare in high school and as an English major in college, but it was not until I began to teach his plays that I came to appreciate his unequalled brilliance as poet and observer of human life, as well as the deeply Christian worldview embodied in his plays. Awesome is today a much-abused word, but in its original sense it fits perfectly Shakespeare's literary achievements. I became an unabashed fan. Fortunately, my students responded favorably when I tried to share my enthusiasm. It was largely the surprising receptivity and interest of those students and their parents that encouraged me to prepare those original classes for distribution to a wider audience. Accordingly, and fittingly, this book is dedicated to them, with gratitude.

Thanks also are due to the Session of Reformed Heritage Presbyterian Church, for giving me leave and encouragement to study and teach what are unconventional subjects for a contemporary pastor.

Thanks to Doug Jones of Canon Press, for his interest in this project, and to whomever it was who invented e-mail, without which communications would have been far more difficult.

Thanks, finally, to my family, for their patient endurance of several years of wild and whirling words in the form of quotations, quizzes, random snatches of speeches, and interpretations good and bad. I especially thank my wife, Noel, and my children Woelke, Lindsey, Jordan, and Sheffield, all of whom helped me check citations and quotations and thereby made this a more accurate book than it could otherwise have been.

Introduction:
A Christian Approach to Literary Study

On Reading Literature

Christians have often had a difficult time with the study of literature. Fiction has been seen as a seductive distraction from the serious business of holy living. Poetry's rich language has been viewed as a means of promoting beautiful falsehoods. Drama has been condemned for depicting immorality and violence, for tempting audiences to lust and anger. So, in writing a study guide to Shakespeare for Christians, I must first address the question, why study literature at all? Why should the Christian spend time with novels or plays or short stories? Shouldn't we be concerned with "real life," with edifying the Church and building God's kingdom, with witness and worship?

Christians who have warned of the dangers and seductions of literature have a point that ought not be ignored. Literature can indeed become a temptation and a distraction from true piety and service to God. Anything in this world can be abused, of course, but it does seem that language and literature are particularly susceptible to abuse and particularly suited to seduce. We are, after all, made in the image of the God whose name is Word. Since language is one of man's greatest glories, it is also potentially one of his most dangerous pitfalls. Having recognized the danger of abuse, however, we need not conclude that therefore literature has no proper use. For the same reason that language may be used to commit evil, its use in speech and writing is near the heart of what it means to live as a creature in God's image.

In defending the study of literature, it is worth pointing out that Scripture itself is a literary work, and while it is a unique book in being divinely inspired, it also uses a variety of common literary types or genres: poetry, narrative, epistle, prophetic vision. C.S. Lewis rightly pointed out that understanding how literature works can lead to a better understanding of Scripture. Rather than follow this valuable line of thought, however, I want to challenge the assumption that there is a sharp distinction between literature and life. (Here, I am concentrating on narrative literature, literature that tells as story—novels, narrative poetry, drama.) Obviously, there are differences between studying history and studying literature. Far from being sharply opposed, however, humans have a natural tendency to think about our lives in narrative terms. Our lives are story-shaped. Let's think about this with a story, or a bit of one:

Will Lissen and Stuart Tistix met for the first time at a wedding reception. After introductions, Lissen took a sip of champagne and said, "So, Stu, tell me about yourself."

"I'm 5'10" and weigh 175 pounds buck-naked. I wear size 9 ½ shoes. My annual adjusted gross income is $53,560. The mortgage on my house is $69,890 with an interest rate of 7.5%. I own a 1992 Honda Accord with 57,906 miles on it—last I checked—Ha! Ha! I've forgotten the registration number. . . it'll come to me. Oh, and I have an unsightly hexagonal mole on my left shoulder blade that measures 3 cm by 2.65 cm."

Lissen shivered as some indescribable horror flitted through his brain, gulped down his champagne, and, excusing himself with all the grace he could muster, fled toward the cake table. Moments later, still sweating, he found himself at the punch bowl, where he met

Ann Terestin. They exchanged introductions, pleasantries, and found they had mutual friends in the wedding party. "So, tell me about yourself," Lissen said, wincing slightly.

"Well, I was an army brat," Ann said. "I was born in Germany, but my father was transferred every few years, so I've lived all over the place. That was hard, having to make new friends all the time, but it was exciting too. It got me hooked, so I majored in international finance and spent a few years working at the Tokyo stock exchange. When I got married and had kids, though, my husband and I decided we wanted a quieter life, so we settled in a little town in Vermont. My husband runs a local printing shop. Now that the kids are older, we're starting to do some traveling again. We love the Far East. Last summer, we went to China with a Christian mission and took in a crate full of Bibles."

Glancing across the room, Lissen saw Stu Tistix in an animated conversation with Congressman Ira Ess, the brains behind the National Survey of Shoe Sizes. With a feeling of satisfaction and intense gratitude for which he immediately felt guilty, Lissen settled into a long and engrossing conversation with Ann Terestin.

When you ask someone to describe himself, you are expecting to hear a story or a series of stories, not a collection of statistics. Individual identity is bound up with the stories we have lived. Stu Tistix may be Ira Ess's dream citizen, but he has never learned how civilized people answer the question, Who are you? For normal people, the question, Who am I? is inseparable from the question, What is my story?

Giving a narrative shape to the events in our lives is virtually inescapable. Historians are quite conscious that they have to select and arrange facts in order to make sense of a topic. It is literally impossible for them to know much less to record everything. In selecting and arranging the facts of history, they give narrative shape to what they study. What is true for historians is true for each of us who tries to make sense of a complex world. The number of events in the real world is impossible for us to even think about, much less record. If you were prepared to go into enough detail and had a lifetime supply of #2 pencils, you could spend the rest of your life describing what is going on around you while you have been reading the first few pages of this introduction. You would have to record every electrochemical interaction in your brain, all your thoughts, every time you were distracted by recalling the bills that need paying or the pile of dirty clothes in the bathroom hamper. You would have to record every time one of the children came through and interrupted, every time you yawned, looked at your watch, scratched your ear, every time heard a passing car on the street or the borborygmi grumble in your abdomen. To make any sense of what seems to be the bloomin', buzzin' confusion that surrounds us, we need to select and arrange the facts of our existence into a manageable order. And this order turns out, frequently if not always, to be the order of a story.

Our understanding of the world typically takes the shape of a story because we are temporal creatures. That is, we exist in time. In a timeless universe, a painting or photograph would be able to picture the world as it is. But we live in a universe where time is constantly moving, where the present instantly fades into the past and the future becomes present. To depict the way the world is, we need some way to depict the flow of time that is so basic in all our experience. A picture cannot do it; it can give the illusion of movement, but in the end a painting gives a timeless slice of life. But a story is able to depict a temporal flow and change, as are those ways of depicting the world that have derived from literature—film and drama. Music too has a temporal dimension, but its language is too abstract and specialized for most people to use. So, if we want to describe the world, we are pretty much left with telling stories.

There are theological reasons why we think of life as

having a narrative structure. Though everyone naturally arranges the events of his life into a narrative pattern, Christians have particular reasons for doing so. God has a plan—that is, a story—for each one of His children. Strictly speaking, we do not shape the facts of our lives into stories; we try to discern the pattern of the story that God is telling with our lives. The story is built into the web of life; it is not a figment of our imagination. More generally, we believe and confess that history is the story of God's plan for mankind. The whole history of mankind and the creation has a beginning, a middle, and is moving toward an end. The history of the world began with creation and the fall of man; the center of history was the coming of the Son in human flesh to redeem us; and the end will come when Jesus returns. It is not just that we arbitrarily impose narrative patterns on life. Real life is sovereignly shaped and arranged by God into a story. History is not just *His*-story; it is His-*story*.

Thus, it is a mistake to suggest that literature and life are completely different from one another. They are not the same, but they fall into similar patterns. This means that learning narrative literature can enhance our understanding of real life. It is true that the study of literature can be dry, dusty, and completely irrelevant to life, but then some have made the study of the Bible dry, dusty, and completely irrelevant to life. Such is the perverse ingenuity of the human mind. But literary study need not be like this. Although the characters and events of fiction are not real, they can help us to gain wisdom about real people and events. Literature abstracts from the complex events of life (just as we do all the time every day) and can reveal patterns that are like the patterns of events in the real world. Studying literature can give us sensitivity to those patterns. This sensitivity to the rhythm of life is closely connected with what the Bible calls wisdom.

Literature also helps us to discern patterns of character. Literary characters can teach us a great deal about how real people act and think. Literature gives us a kind of shorthand for knowing and describing people. For those who have read

Lewis's *Narnia Chronicles*, if I describe someone as a "Puddleglum," you know what kind of character type I'm talking about. If you know Winnie the Pooh, saying that so and so is more like Piglet than Eeyore will give you a handle on his personality. If you know *Much Ado About Nothing*, and I say that so and so uses the English language like Dogberry, you know he does not speak the king's English. If you know *Macbeth*, and I describe a woman as a "Lady Macbeth," you know it's not a compliment. Saying someone is an "Esau" or a "Judas Iscariot" brings to mind a host of thoughts and associations and can more effectively characterize a person than a long, detailed description.

I have found Shakespeare's plays to be especially helpful—I daresay, edifying—in this respect. Shakespeare was, as Caesar says of Cassius, "a great observer," who was able to look "quite through the deeds of men," able to see and depict patterns of events and character. He understood how politics is shaped by the clash of men with various colorings of self-interest and idealism, how violence breeds violence, how fragile human beings create masks and disguises for protection, how schemers do the same for advancement, how love can grow out of hate and hate out of love. Dare anyone say that these insights are irrelevant to living in the real world? For many in an older generation, the Bible and the Collected Shakespeare were the two indispensable books, and thus their sense of life and history was shaped by the best and best-told stories. And they were the wiser for it.

The Bible as a Master Story

If the argument above has convinced you that studying literature is worthy of a Christian's time and effort, the next question is likely to be how to go about it. How does a Christian approach literature *as a Christian*?

Before offering some thoughts on that question, I should make a couple of qualifications. First, though this is a guide to the study of "serious" or "classical" literature, I have no desire to condemn other, more popular kinds of literature. There is nothing wrong with reading simply for enjoyment. There are certain kinds of literature that would violate Paul's exhortation to think only on things that are lovely, of good report, and true (Phil. 4:8). But nothing in Scripture forbids you to read John Grisham or Tom Clancy because they write exciting stories. If you like reading Eugenia Price's novels or Agatha Christie's detective stories as a diversion, that too is fine. I have nothing against "light reading," which, to my mind at least, is normally preferable to television as a way to use leisure time. Having said that, I would insist that the richer and more profound your reading—if you will, the more "serious" your reading—the more enjoyable it will be.

Second, I offer no suggestions for evaluating literature, for making either artistic or moral judgments. Those kinds of judgments must be made, of course, and there are some good books on how Christians can go about making them. It is also true that evaluation is involved in any act of reading; we can never totally separate knowing facts from making value judgments. The emphasis of my remarks here, however, is how Christians seek to *understand* literature, rather than how we should *evaluate* it. Christians must avoid the danger of forming judgments, especially moral judgments, without really understanding what they are reading. We should not condemn *Macbeth* as occultic and unChristian because witches play a major role; we need to look carefully at how Shakespeare uses the witches in the play, and I will argue that his use is perfectly compatible with a Christian view of life. Some Christians think little of the *Iliad* because it seems to celebrate senseless violence. Before I support that evaluation, I want to make sure that, in fact, the *Iliad* does celebrate senseless violence. Ghosts appear with some frequency in Shakespeare's plays, but the plays are not ghost stories; Shakespeare uses ghosts to make profound points about guilt and the consequences of sin.

It is helpful to compare the study of literature to learning a foreign language. In general, we learn not just by studying individual things but, perhaps more importantly, by comparing one thing to another. We learn a new language not only by studying that language's grammar and vocabulary, but also by making comparisons with a language we already know. As you learn about Latin, you compare its grammar and vocabulary to English grammar and vocabulary. You can remember that *agricola* means "farmer" because you know the word "agriculture"; you can remember that *amo* means "I love" because you link it with the word "amorous." Grammar is learned in a similar way. In English, word order is very important; if you switch the subject and the direct object, you change the sense of the sentence. In Latin, word order is not so important for making sense and has more to do with emphasis and style. In English, case endings are used only with pronouns (who, whom; he, him), but case endings are basic to Latin. When, as a native speaker of English, you learn a new language, English functions as your "master language." You learn the new language by noticing similarities and differences between it and your native tongue.

We can approach learning literature in a similar way. Just as we learn a new language by reference to a "master language" or a "native tongue," so we learn literature by reference to a "master story," a "native story" that we already know. As Christians, our "native story" or "master story" is the story revealed in the Bible, the real life story of God's works in history. In fact, the Bible gives us a several of what I am calling "master stories" or "model stories."[1] Once we have grasped the architecture of these stories, we can make comparisons with other examples of narrative and dramatic literature.

The first of these model stories is the "fall story," which follows basically this sequence of events: God makes a world

---

[1] Far and away the best work on the literary patterns of the Bible is James B. Jordan, *Through New Eyes: Developing a Biblical View of the World* (Nashville, TN: Wolgemuth & Hyatt, 1987). Jordan's more recent work is available from Biblical Horizons, P.O. Box 1096, Niceville, FL, 32588-1096.

and places human beings in it. He gives them instructions about how to behave, but they don't listen and they violate His instructions. Because of their sin, they are punished and their fall into sin leads to a decline. This story can be pictured as a upside down U: the character starts in a low position, is raised higher, but from that height, he descends on account of his sin.

The first and most familiar fall story in the Bible is of Adam and Eve, and it sets the pattern for other fall stories. Adam and Eve were given great privileges and blessings; God instructed them not to eat of the tree of knowledge, but they disobeyed; as a result, they were cursed in various ways. Though this is the most familiar fall story, it is far from the only one. The line of Seth, the "sons of God" fell into the sin of inter-marriage with the heathen (Gen. 6). Because of their sin, God did not merely remove them out of the garden but removed all living things from the world through the flood. Saul's history is a fall story: he was a member of a small and despised tribe; God chose him to be the first king of Israel and raised him to the throne; and for a while Saul was an admirable figure, a great warrior and a good king, whom 1 Samuel subtly compares with the greatest judges of Israel's history. But Saul refused to listen to the Lord's prophet, and eventually the Lord abandoned him. Saul is an Adam whose kingdom is taken from him.[2] The whole history of Israel can be seen as a "fall" story: Israel was elected by God in Abraham, brought into the land, where they abandoned the Lord and went after idols. After calling them patiently to return to Him, the Lord finally drove them into exile. Though they returned, they later rejected their Messiah, and the kingdom was given to another nation (Mt. 21:33-46).

The upside-down U pattern appears in literature outside the Bible, so often that it is one of the basic narrative patterns of world literature. By studying the various fall stories in the Bible, and by comparing literature outside the Bible to these

---

[2] See Jordan's essay on Saul, available from Biblical Horizons.

"master stories," our understanding and appreciation of the
extra-biblical literature will be enhanced. For example, we shall
see that *Macbeth* is a "fall story," which focuses on what comes
to pass when an ambitious man impenitently commits murder. Comparing *Macbeth* to the "master story" in the Bible
leads us to make many fruitful comparisons: Macbeth's murder of King Duncan is something like the original fall of Adam;
Lady Macbeth, who encourages and tempts her husband to
commit murder, is a combination of Eve and the serpent;
just as Adam's sin led to a curse on the earth, so Macbeth's
plunges Scotland into a dark age. Some fall stories will di-
verge significantly from the biblical pattern. Oedipus, for instance, falls because his fate has been unchangeably determined,
not because he sins.

The other "master story" in the Bible tells is a reversal of
the fall. Where the fall story has the shape of an upside-down
U, this other story has a U-shape. We can call this a "redemption story." This is the main story the Bible tells, the main
point of the story of history. Man fell into sin, and became
alienated from God with his whole life under God's curse.
God rescued him from sin, death, and Satan and brought
those who believe into fellowship with the Father, Son, and
Spirit. The redemption story can take a number of forms.
The gospel is an adventure story: Jesus is a Hero who comes
to rescue his people from their enemies. He is the Stronger
Man who binds Satan and plunders His house, and the gospel
is the story of His holy war against Satan and his triumph
over death and sin. When you read an adventure story, as a
Christian you have a built-in model to compare it to. Every
hero in an adventure story is something of a "savior," and all
his opponents have something of the demonic about them.
The gospel is also a Romance. Jesus is the Lover who comes
to rescue His Bride. To put it differently, He comes to recover His unfaithful Bride (cf. Hos. 1-2).

Again, the master redemption story of the Bible can be
compared and contrasted with the stories found in other literature. Though *Macbeth* is in one respect a fall story, it ends

with Malcolm's triumph over Macbeth and the beginning of Scotland's restoration. We will find it useful to compare Macbeth's fall from power to Jesus' triumph over Satan, "the ruler of this world," and to consider Malcolm and Macduff as something like "Christ figures." The death and resurrection sequence that is at the heart of the gospel is brought out in various ways in the works studied in this volume: Hero in *Much Ado About Nothing* goes through a mock death and resurrection; Katherina, the shrew, is killed by the "kindness" of her husband, Petruchio, and emerges as a new creature; Scotland goes through a winter of tyranny under Macbeth, but good king Malcolm comes to renew spring.

Much literature combines these two patterns. Some characters find redemption while others are judged. The *Odyssey* is a good example of this double story line. Odysseus spends the epic trying to get home from the Trojan War, encountering various trials and tests along the way. At home in Ithaca, his wife, Penelope, is beset by suitors who insist that Odysseus is dead, pressure her to marry again, and meanwhile eat Odysseus out of house and home (as Odysseus' son Telemachus describes it). For Odysseus, the story has a redemptive shape, for he returns and is reunited with Penelope. The suitors, by contrast, are slaughtered when Odysseus returns; theirs is definitely a story of fall and judgment. For this type of story too there are biblical models, for the gospel involves not only the redemption of the Bride but judgment of her oppressors.

How to Use This Book

I wrote this book as a guide for junior and senior high school students. Now that it is finished, I find that it is more suitable to the latter than the former, though, with guidance from parents or teachers, I believe junior high students could also use it profitably. It is suitable for both home school and traditional Christian school settings. Home school students in high school should be able to use it as a self-study course.

I do not, however, believe that I have greatly oversimplified, so that the guide may also be useful for adults who are discovering or rediscovering Shakespeare.

I should note that I have not covered some of the topics one normally expects from a book of this sort, such as the dates of the plays, the events of Shakespeare's life, or Elizabethan theater. That information is readily available from encyclopedias or general works on Shakespeare. It might be useful, however, if a student using this guide were given an assignment that would introduce him to these matters.

This book provides several things. First, each chapter is a self-consciously Christian interpretation of one of Shakespeare's plays, organized around one or several main themes. The major organizing theme of each play is reflected in the quotation that serves as the title of the chapter. Within each chapter, there are 4-5 sections that offer a running commentary on the play, showing how the particular themes are developed. At the end of each of these sections are two sets of questions. The "Review Questions" are designed to determine whether or not the student has comprehended the chapter; answers to these questions can be found in the preceding commentary. The "Thought Questions" are based on the commentary but go beyond it, and require the student to consider questions and draw conclusions for which the book provides no explicit answers. Some of the Thought Questions ask the student to interpret a particular passage or sentence in the light of what he has learned; some require the student to apply ideas given in the commentary to matters that are not mentioned there; others prod the student to formulate a Christian view of a particular issue. In some cases, there is a right answer to a Thought Question but in many cases the questions are intended to be fairly open-ended, and the parent or teacher should be willing to accept an answer for which the student can give a convincing rationale, based on the text. At the end of each chapter I have included brief comments on the most readily available video versions of the play and a list of suggested paper topics.

The studies in this volume assume that the student is already familiar with the plots and characters of the various plays. I have not summarized the story nor introduced the characters. Thus, before using this book, the student should acquire some grasp of the play to be studied. This can be done in a number of ways. The parent or teacher may require the student to read the actual play before beginning to use this book. This may not, however, be the most effective way to introduce Shakespeare. Beginning students often have difficulty not only because Shakespeare's language is unfamiliar but also because of the way Shakespeare constructed his plays. He sometimes assumes that readers know something about the events that he depicts, and the plays present the action and necessary background in bits and pieces, and leave the reader or viewer to put things together. Thus, it may be helpful for a student to begin by reading a retelling of the play in straight story form. Charles and Mary Lamb's *Tales from Shakespeare* is the most widely available of these re-tellings, but its language and syntax is such that it is almost as difficult to read as the plays themselves. More readable simplifications are available.

Another way for the student to become familiar with the plot and characters is to view a stage, video, or film version of the play. When I taught Shakespeare, I found video a most helpful tool to awaken my students' interest. Shakespeare has recently taken on new life at the cinema, and there are a number of new films currently under production. In addition, there are a number of fine older Shakespeare films readily available on video. By watching a film, a student will come to realize that Shakespeare's plays are exciting and fun stories, which, if he learns nothing else, helps to break down prejudices and barriers. Of course, all enactments of a play—whether on film or stage—are inevitably interpretations, just as every book is an interpretation. The play itself imposes certain limits on the director, but the director or filmmaker must still make important decisions about how the characters and events will be portrayed, and these decisions are ultimately based on the filmmaker's view of the world. Students should therefore learn to be discerning and critical of the way a film presents a particular play.

Once the student is somewhat familiar with the plot and characters, he is ready to use this book. At this point, the student should be required to read the play itself. I suggest the following sequence of assignments:

(1) The student should read the appropriate portion of the play carefully, whether an act, two acts, or several scenes. There are numerous editions of individual plays, many of them relatively inexpensive, as well as collections. As regards the plays discussed in this text, all but *The Taming of the Shrew* may be found in Bertrand Evans, ed., *The College Shakespeare*, which also includes brief but insightful material on individual plays and on Shakespeare in general.[3]

(2) The student should read the commentary provided in the guide.

(3) The student should answer the Review Questions at the end of the section. The parent or teacher should make sure that the student has answered these adequately before going on to the Thought Questions.

(4) The student should answer the Thought Questions at the end of the section. As noted above, these questions may be difficult to answer precisely, and it may be helpful for the parent or teacher to discuss the answers with the student.

(5) When the student has finished working through each section of the chapter, he may be asked to prepare a paper on one particular aspect of the play. He may use one of the suggested topics or formulate a topic of his own.

---

[3] In this guide, each citation from a play gives the Act, scene, and line numbers, in that order. Thus, 1.3.45 means "Act 1, scene 3, line 45." For most plays, the citations follow the text of *The College Shakespeare*. For *The Taming of the Shrew*, I used the 1982 Oxford Shakespeare edition, edited by H. J. Oliver. Line numbering and text may differ from edition to edition.

Each play is divided into four lessons, each of which, if the student is required to provide written answers to the Review and Thought Questions, could take a week of class time in a home school setting. Assuming that the student will spend 45 minutes to an hour each day on the assignment, I suggest the following schedule for a week:

(1) Monday: read the appropriate scene(s).
(2) Tuesday: read commentary in the guide.
(3) Wednesday: answer Review Questions.
(4) Thursday and Friday: answer Thought Questions.

Each play, following this scheme, would take a month to cover. In a traditional school setting, the assignments could easily be adjusted. I would also encourage teachers and parents to require students to memorize at least thirty lines from each play. Memorization is useful as a mental exercise, but more than that countless writers have attributed some of their skill in language to their early memorization of Shakespeare.

If a student were to use this guide as part of his English curriculum for three years, covering two plays a year, I would suggest something like the following sequence of plays:

Year 1: Taming of the Shrew and Julius Caesar
Year 2: Much Ado About Nothing and Macbeth
Year 3: Henry V and Hamlet

Conclusion

I do not agree with H. Rider Haggard's fictional adventurer, Allan Quatermain, for whom the Bible and Shakespeare were interchangeable authorities. Yet, over the past several years I have discovered Shakespeare to be a stimulating source for reflections on pastoral practice, history, politics, love, and life in general, not even to mention that Shakespeare uses the English language as no human being, before or since, has used language. It is my hope that this volume will open some of the riches of at least a few of his works to a new generation of Christian students.

Cambridge, England
Advent 1996

Section I:

History

Introduction: History

Bertrand Evans has pointed out that history plays account for "nearly half the total of Shakespeare's plays." He wrote ten plays on English history, as well as a number of Roman dramas. Even *Macbeth* and *King Lear*, normally classified as tragedies, are based on historical persons and events.

Though they dramatize historical events, however, we should not expect Shakespeare's histories to read like a high school history text. Shakespeare was a playwright, not a producer of historical documentaries. There are a bewildering number of people and events depicted, but Shakespeare was selective and he portrayed what would best highlight his particular themes. He sometimes made changes of detail for dramatic or thematic purposes. Julius Caesar is killed in the middle of the play that bears his name; the play is not at all a biography of Caesar, and it is about Caesar only in a subtle though very important sense. *Henry V* covers only a brief period of that king's reign, but it is the portion that for Shakespeare best revealed his character and politics. As we look at these two history plays, therefore, we will be examining not only the historical events that lie in the background of the play, but also how Shakespeare selected and arranged events to illustrate important truths about mankind, politics, and history.

Not all the characters in Shakespeare's histories are historical figures. A number of scenes in *Henry V* focus on the friends of the king's youth, Pistol, Bardolph, and Nym. In the two parts of *Henry IV*, Shakespeare created one of his most popular and memorable characters, Sir John Falstaff. The fictional characters in the histories often provide comic relief, but they play a serious role in the drama as well. We will see that the words and actions of the fictional characters in *Henry V* provide a commentary on the king and his French invasion.

The story lines of Shakespeare's histories have important similarities to his tragedies and comedies. *Julius Caesar* has been understood by many as the tragedy of Brutus, and depending on how you read it, *Henry V* can be understood as comedy or as tragedy. From a Christian perspective, as we saw in the Introduction, this similarity between fiction and history is not accidental, for Christianity teaches that God sovereignly shapes the events of history into a beginning, middle, and end. Shakespeare thus had ample warrant to write history in dramatic form, and we have ample warrant to believe that studying his histories will contribute to our understanding of His-story.

The Mirror of All Christian Kings:
Henry V

Henry V focuses on a series of episodes during the Hundred Years' War, which lasted from 1337 to 1453 and involved England and France in a struggle over control of the French monarchy. England had been a major presence in France for several centuries prior to the war. King Henry II (1154-1189) was Count of Anjou, duke of Aquitaine, and also claimed Normandy. During his lifetime he controlled half of what we know as France, and at his death he was buried there. England's claim to the French throne was initiated in earnest by Edward III (1327-1377). Isabella, the daughter of Phillip IV (the Fair) of France, had married Edward II of England, and their son was Edward III of England. Edward III thus laid claim to the French throne through his mother and undertook a military action to made good his claim. During his war with France, Edward won famous victories at Crecy (1346) and Poitiers (1356).

After the death of Edward III, England faced not only war with France but also dynastic disputes at home. You may recall that Henry VIII's break with the Roman Church began because his first wife could not give him a son and he worried what would happen if he died without a male heir to the throne. Edward III had the opposite problem, leaving behind a troubled land because he had too many sons. The rules of succession were fairly fluid in Edward's time.

Normally, the crown passed to the oldest son, and, if he died, to the next oldest, and so on. Ambitious younger sons frequently sought, however, to push past their older brothers. Edward III's oldest son, and the heir to the throne, Edward the Black Prince, was killed fighting in France the year before his father died. Richard, son of the Black Prince, succeeded Edward III, but other parts of the family were ambitious to gain the throne.

Richard II (1377-1399) was only ten years old when Edward III died. For the first part of his reign, he was ruled by his relatives. As he came to maturity, he tried to free himself from the control of his family, and allied himself with certain favorites that gained power at court. Not surprisingly, this made his relatives angry, as they saw their own influence waning. Five Lords of the realm, among them Henry Bolingbroke, brought charges of treason against the favorites. In the event, the Lords Appellant, as they were called, won the case and were able to secure their influence at court. By 1397, however, Richard had regained enough power to move against three of the Lords Appellant. To protect himself, Henry Bolingbroke lodged charges of treason against his former ally, Mowbray. The conflict between these former allies nearly ended in trial by combat but Richard intervened and exiled both men. (This is the situation at the beginning of Shakespeare's *Richard II*.)

Two years later, in 1399, John of Gaunt, Henry Bolingbroke's father, died, and Richard seized his lands. Henry invaded England on the pretext of regaining control of his ancestral lands but in truth he intended to assert his claim to the crown. Later that same year, he was crowned as Henry IV, and Richard II died early the following year under suspicious circumstances. Henry IV's reign had supported battles against the nobles who has supported him in his effort to dethrone Richard. The Mortimers were a special problem. They were descended from Edward III's second son, Lionel, and believed their claim to the monarchy was greater than Henry IV's, whose father, John of Gaunt, was Edward's third son. The Percies, a powerful noble family, also revolted in

1403. Shakespeare's play *1 Henry IV* ends with the battle of Shrewsbury, where Henry Percy (Hotspur) was killed and the Percy rebellion squashed. This is important background to *Henry V*, for Henry V's crown was passed to him by a usurper who was also probably a murderer. At moments, Henry is aware that his claim on the throne of England is defiled with the blood of Richard II (4.1.310-323).

By the time Henry V came to the throne, there were no more serious challenges from rival families. (Edmund Mortimer, in fact, was still alive, but imprisoned throughout Henry V's reign, and his death is portrayed in Shakespeare's *1 Henry VI*.) In the two parts of *Henry IV*, Shakespeare presents the young "Hal" (who would become Henry V) as an idle young man loitering in taverns with drunkards and thieves and showing precious little interest in politics, war or the serious business of ruling. Contrary to Shakespeare's presentation, the real Henry V was highly experienced and ready to assume the throne: he fought with Henry IV against the noble rebels; he sat on the king's council from 1406-11; and he governed Wales and put down a Welsh rebellion. In the opinion of some historians, Henry V came to the throne as one of the best-trained kings in English history. Moreover, because his power was relatively secure at home, Henry V could turn his attention to renewing the English claim to the French crown, and this is what Shakespeare's play is about. Shakespeare compresses events that actually took place over a number of years: The wars described in *Henry V* are those of Henry's first French campaign of 1415, but the play ends with Henry's engagement to the French queen Catherine (spelled Katharine in the play), though this did not take place until 1420, when the Treaty of Troyes was concluded.

After Henry V died prematurely, his son, Henry VI (1422-1461/1470-1471) ascended the throne as king of England and France. Though a pious and good man, his inability to control his nobles led to disaster. During his lifetime, England lost the French crown, due in large part to the heroics of Joan of Arc, and the Wars of the Roses began between two branches of Edward III's family, known as the houses of Lancaster and York. The civil wars finally ended when Henry Tudor, who had ancestors from both of the warring families, defeated King Richard III at Bosworth Field. Henry Tudor became Henry VII (1485-1509), and inaugurated the dynasty that included Henry VIII, Edward VI, Mary I, and Elizabeth I.

Shakespeare wrote a cycle of eight plays about this period of English history. The plays were written in something of a reverse order, beginning with three plays about Henry VI, followed by *Richard III*, whose reign began some years after Henry VI died. These plays cover the beginning and end of the Wars of the Roses. Having depicted the civil wars in the first "tetralogy" (set of four plays), Shakespeare went back to examine the events that led up to the Wars of the Roses. This background was presented in the second tetralogy: *Richard II*, the two parts of *Henry IV*, and *Henry V* (produced around 1598-99). Another English history play, *King John*, written shortly after *Richard III*, portrays an earlier period in English history. Though Shakespeare also wrote at least part of a later play on this period, *Henry VIII*, the play examined here is really the last and most mature of Shakespeare's investigations of English history.

Henry V is the main character not only of this play, but also, as Prince Hal, of the two parts of *Henry IV*. In one common interpretation of these plays, Henry V is the model of the true Christian prince, against whom the other royal characters of the plays are to be measured. Taken together, the second tetralogy depicts the education of the ideal prince. Prince Hal matures into the mean or balance between foolhardy bravery and cowardice; he combines the fun of the tavern with the exertions of the battlefield. This is brought out by his similarities and differences with other characters. On one extreme, Hal is contrasted with Henry Percy, called "Hotspur," and in fact *1 Henry IV* leads up to a duel between Hotspur and Hal. Like Hotspur, Hal is a courageous soldier who displays his mettle in the battle of Shrewsbury.

Hotspur, however, represents the foolhardy extreme; as his name implies, Hotspur is a man who throws caution to the wind, much like Laertes in *Hamlet*. Hotspur is also unbalanced because he hates both music and poetry and cares for nothing but war. He is impatient and he talks too much and too boldly. The Dauphin (Prince of France) in *Henry V* is a comic version of Hotspur, with all the bluster but none of the skill.

At the other extreme is Sir John Falstaff. An old soldier, Falstaff is one of Hal's tavern buddies, with whom he spends countless idle hours. While Hal shares with Falstaff a love of prankish fun, Falstaff is self-serving and cowardly and fights no longer than he sees reason to fight. Falstaff, for instance, pretends to be dead on the battlefield at Shrewsbury. When Hal leaves the scene, Falstaff gets up, finds the body of Hotspur lying on the field (where Hal left him), stabs him, and later claims to have killed Hotspur. By the time *Henry V* begins, Falstaff has fallen out of favor. Immediately after he was crowned, Henry said to Falstaff: "I know thee not, old man" and warned him "not to come near our person by ten mile." Henry's rejection of Falstaff may seem cruel, but, on this interpretation, it is essential if Hal is to grow up into Henry V. To be an effective king, Hal must overcome youthful brashness (represented by Hotspur) and also put aside childish pranks (represented by Falstaff). He must take a stand in the middle ground between cowardice and foolishness, the ground in which true courage is rooted.

Henry V provides evidence that Henry is to be taken as the ideal prince. Much of the evidence comes from the chorus, who calls Henry "The Mirror of all Christian kings" (Prol.2.6). As Henry makes the rounds of the camp on the night before the battle of Agincourt, the chorus describes him as a sun bringing cheer and encouragement to every soldier (Prol.4.28-47). As the play closes, the chorus laments the "small time" of Henry's life, adding "but in that small most greatly liv'd this star of England" (Epilogue, 5-6). Beyond that, Henry's meditations on the burdens of kingship

(4.1.248-302) and his rousing speech before the battle
(4.3.18-67) display a man with both courage and sensitivity
to the pitfalls and dangers of his position.

It is even possible to see in Henry something of a Christ
figure. He is rightful king of France but has been denied the
throne. So, he invades alien territory, conquers it, claims
the throne, and marries the bride to seal the compact. So also
Christ invaded "enemy territory" to bind Satan, to triumph
over the principalities and powers, and to win His bride.
From this viewpoint, the violence of Henry's language begins to sound like the words of biblical prophets announcing
the doom of ungodly kingdoms, or the psalms in which
God's victory over the wicked is celebrated: The righteous
will bathe their feet in the blood of the wicked (Ps. 58:10).
Henry becomes not merely a mirror of all Christian kings
but virtually becomes Christ himself.

If Henry is the ideal prince, his exploits are material for
English nationalist celebration. The climax of the play is the
battle of Agincourt, in which Henry's English army, though
greatly outnumbered, won an almost miraculous victory.
Henry is pious in triumph: "be it death proclaimed through
our host to boast of this or take that praise from God which
is His only" (4.8.121-123). The chorus reiterates this impression:

> You may imagine him upon Blackheath,
> Where that his lords desire to have him borne
> His bruised helmet and his bended sword
> Before him through the city. He forbids it,
> Being free from vainness and self-glorious pride.
> Giving full trophy, signal and ostent
> Quite from himself to God. (Prologue.5.16-22)

Interpreters have often taken passages such as these at face
value and understood *Henry V* as the most "flag-waving" of
Shakespeare's historical plays.

Perhaps, though, this is all too easy. Parallels there may be
between Henry and Christ, but Henry is not Christ. And if

the play may be compared to a dramatic rendition of the English national anthem, there are a more than a few wrong notes and dissonant chords. Even the words of the chorus, who is from head to toe a patriotic Englishman, raise some questions about Henry's character. In his first description of Henry, the chorus invites the audience to watch Henry "assume the port of Mars" (Prol.1.6). Mars! Not the Christian God but the pagan god of war. This makes us wonder to whom Henry is praying when later he calls upon the "God of battles" (4.1.307). The God of the Bible is no pacifist, but neither is He the bloodthirsty Mars of Greek mythology, who delights in sheer mayhem.

According to Harold Goddard's insightful discussion, the chorus in the main expresses the popular view of Henry, of the French invasion, of Agincourt; his descriptions present the Henry V of English mythology. There is no reason, however, to believe that Shakespeare accepted the mythology, and in fact, as Goddard points out, the chorus explicitly distinguishes himself from "our bending author" (Epilogue, 2). Far from joining wholeheartedly in the chorus's praise of Henry, Shakespeare wrote a play that continually raises doubts about Henry's character and the justice of his cause.

So, is Henry the "mirror of all Christian kings" or is he not? Instead of directly answering that question, let us take a moment to think about mirrors. What do you see when you look in the mirror? Your first answer is likely to be, "I see myself" or "I see an image of myself." If we take Shakespeare's image in this way, Henry is being presented as the model Christian king; Christian kings may look at Henry to discover what they are supposed to look like. If we think more about it, however, we realize that what we see in the mirror is precisely the *opposite* of ourselves. My right hand is the mirror-image's left, my left eye its right, and so on. Besides, it is possible to play tricks with mirrors. Mirrors can make things appear that are not really there. I am not suggesting that Shakespeare meant to use the "mirror" image in this double-edged way, but thinking about the double nature of "mirrors" will help us to keep in mind the tensions in the play's presentation of Henry. Shakespeare does not explicitly resolve the tensions that are thus raised but leaves both views before the reader or audience. The greatest interest of the play will be found in the area where the two pictures interact and conflict. And it is there that we shall find the play most profound in the questions it raises about national pride, military aggression, and the true nature of Christian politics.

Lesson One: Act 1

The chorus's prologue that opens *Henry V* provides some insights into Shakespeare's conception of his dramatic art. The chorus asks his audience to "pardon . . . the flat unraised spirits that have dar'd on this unworthy scaffold to bring forth so great an object" (Prol.1.8-11). He knows that the "cockpit" or "wooden O" of a stage cannot "hold the vasty fields of France." How, then, can a play become believable to the audience? According to the chorus, a play requires not only actors on a stage but an audience of sufficient imagination to accept that the few actors on stage are really millions of soldiers and that the "cockpit" is really Agincourt. The gaps between the real events and what appears on stage must be filled in by the minds of the audience: "Piece out our imperfections with your thoughts" (Prol.1.23).

Even at this level, the Prologue is worth several attentive readings and a few moments of thought. The chorus provides some of the most beautiful poetry in the play. But the Prologue was not written as a separate poem about the nature of drama. It introduces an historical play, and it is worth pondering why Shakespeare chose to include it. Shakespeare is, after all, quite capable of getting along without a chorus. In most plays, he simply plunges into the middle of the action without introduction, leaving it to the characters themselves to provide whatever introductions are needed. Suggesting that Shakespeare needed a chorus to remind his readers of the history is not convincing, since for his original audience the exploits of Henry V were neither ancient nor unfamiliar. To understand why Shakespeare used a chorus, we need to look at what the chorus actually says. And when we look, we find that the chorus does not say much of anything, at least nothing that we could not have figured out without his help. Let's look at a larger portion of the prologue to Act 1:

> But pardon, gentles all,
> The flat unraised spirits that have dar'd
> On this unworthy scaffold to bring forth
> So great an object. Can this cockpit hold
> The vasty fields of France? Or may we cram
> Within this wooden O the very casques
> That did affright the air at Agincourt? . . .
> Suppose within the girdle of these walls
> Are now confin'd two mighty monarchies,
> Whose high upreared and abutting fronts
> The perilous narrow ocean parts asunder.
> Piece out our imperfections with your thoughts;
> Into a thousand parts divide one man,
> And make imaginary puissance.
> Think, when we talk of horses, that you see them,
> Printing their proud hoofs i' the receiving earth.
> (Prol. 1.8-27)

In short, "Since we can't fit a whole army into the theater, you're going to have to use your imagination." Nothing really profound here.

The chorus has much the same message at the beginning of Act 2:

> . . . the scene
> Is now transported, gentles, to Southampton.
> There is the playhouse now; there must you sit.
> And thence to France shall we convey you safe
> And bring you back, charming the narrow seas
> To give you gentle pass; for, if we may,
> We'll not offend one stomach with our play.
> (Prol.2.34-40)

"Through the miracle of theater," the chorus is saying, "we will take you across the English Channel, and not one will become seasick." Cute, but neither original nor necessary.

The chorus keeps popping up to tell us, "It's just a play! It's just a play!" But we know that, and Shakespeare knew it, and Shakespeare knew we would know it. So, why does he insist on repeating such a trivial point? The reason, I suspect, is related to the tensions that we noted above. On the surface, Henry is being portrayed as the "mirror of all Christian kings" in the sense of being a model of Christian kingship. He is a king who prays at the beginning of battles and gives glory to God alone at the end. But then there is the chorus telling us over and over that it is, after all, only a play. We know that what we see on stage is an actor playing Henry V; the chorus's insistence on the point suggests we should understand "It's only a play" in another sense. The chorus protests too much, and we end up asking ourselves, Are Henry's piety and sense of justice likewise only an act? Is he perhaps a mirror image of a Christian king in the second sense—in the sense that he portrays the opposite of a Christian king, everything a Christian king should *not* be? Perhaps what we are watching is not only an actor pretending to be Henry V. Perhaps we are watching an actor playing a Henry V who is in turn pretending to be a model for all Christian kings. Perhaps Shakespeare is pretending too, pretending to wave his flag and play the national anthem while exposing with all his warts the complex man beneath the thrice-gorgeous ceremony.

That Henry's piety is at least partly pretense is suggested by the two scenes of Act 1. The play proper begins with a secretive conversation between the Archbishop of Canterbury and the Bishop of Ely. The Archbishop wants the church to support Henry's invasion of France and his claim to the French crown, but the Archbishop's motives are far from purely religious. As he explains to Ely, there is a bill before the House of Commons that would strip all "temporal lands" from the church, that is, lands that are not used for church purposes directly but which provide income. Taking away these lands would remove half of the church's possessions; it would "drink deep" of the church's finances, indeed, as the Archbishop says, "'Twould drink the cup and all" (1.1.20). The two churchmen want Henry on their side in opposition to the bill. In itself, this is a good thing; the church should be protected from seizures by political authorities. Canterbury and Ely, however, protect the church not by righteous protest and opposition, but by playing a political game. In order to encourage Henry to be favorable to their position, they promise to give significant financial support for his French campaign, on the assumption that they stand to lose much more by not getting Henry's help. In short, the church leaders intend to buy Henry's favor by giving him money to invade France. The church's support for Henry's French invasion amounts to little more than a bribe.

In reflecting on Henry's character, Canterbury makes both classical and biblical allusions. He says that Henry can unloose the "Gordian knot" of even the most difficult political issue (1.1.45-47). The reference is to Gordius, king of Phrygia, who tied a knot and prophesied that whoever was able to untie it would be master of Asia. Alexander of Macedon untied it, and, as Gordius had predicted, conquered Asia. Canterbury evidently hopes Henry will be another conqueror like Alexander the Great. (Remember the comparison with Alexander, for it will come up again.) Henry is not only an Alexander, but he is also, in Canterbury's opinion, a new Adam. When he became king, the old Adam was kicked out of him and became a new man (1.1.29). Medieval political thought viewed the king as an image of Christ. Just as Christ is divine and human, so the king was believed to be a man with something like a divine nature. Since the king was anointed with sacred oil, he became in effect a clergyman, a representative of Christ; the man who was king (with a small "k") became linked to the eternal King. It was even possible, on this theory, for the king as man to be considered a traitor to the King as divine and immortal.

As King, he combined the whole realm in his person; the nation was the body of the king as the church is the body of Christ. As man, it was recognized that the king was weak and mortal. This duality will come up again in Henry's meditations on ceremony and kingship during the night before Agincourt.

As often in Shakespeare, a character is described by other characters before appearing himself. The chorus has compared Henry to Mars, and Canterbury has compared him to Alexander and, implicitly, to Christ. The audience therefore has certain expectations when Henry appears in person for the first time in scene 2. What we learn there gives some evidence that he is the ideal king of Canterbury's description. Henry consults the church before going to war because he knows that any war brings bloodshed, and that this blood would be a "sore complaint" against the one who initiates an unjust war. Blood cries out for vengeance, and kings are accountable to prevent the shedding of innocent blood (1.2.9-32). It is thus morally imperative that a king know his cause is right. Otherwise, he will put himself in grave moral danger. Henry seems sincere in asking for the church's opinion about his invasion of France (1.2.96).

Still, beneath the melody on the surface of the scene there is a contrary theme. A more careful reading suggests that in fact Henry is shifting responsibility onto the Archbishop. He tells Canterbury that God knows how many healthy men will die because of "what your reverence shall incite us to" (1.2.20); it is the Archbishop, Henry implies, who "impawns" or pledges Henry to war, and the Archbishop who "awakes our sleeping sword of war" (1.2.21-22). The deaths of soldiers will be the responsibility of "him whose wrongs give edge unto the swords that make such waste in brief mortality" (1.2.26-28), and Henry implies that it is Canterbury who has given edge to his sword. Canterbury takes the hint and accepts the responsibility: "The sin upon my head, dread sovereign" (1.2.97).

There is another false note in Henry's instructions to the Archbishop. He claims to believe that the Archbishop will speak sincerely, that what Canterbury will speak "is in your conscience wash'd as pure as sin with baptism" (1.2.31-32). Perhaps Henry is still too young to the throne to suspect that Canterbury has an ulterior motive but this is hard to accept. Canterbury implies in scene 1 that he raised the possibility of a French invasion in the context of discussing the Commons bill with Henry; at least Henry is fully aware of the bill and of the church's opposition to it (1.1.72-81). He should be aware that Canterbury's support for his plans comes with strings attached. Maybe he is aware of it, and only pretending to believe that Canterbury's motives are holy and pure. Sin, moreover, is not, as Henry says, washed pure with baptism; sin is washed *away* with baptism! Henry makes it sound as if baptism makes sin clean and pure, even though it remains sin. If this is a slip of the tongue, it is an appropriate slip, for what Canterbury will proceed to do is precisely to wash sin, to make an ambitious, unnecessary, and bloody invasion seem pure as snow and clear as the summer's sun.

Though these various hints could be interpreted in a way more favorable to Henry, the same cannot be said of Henry's reaction to the message of the Dauphin, the crown Prince of France. Shakespeare clearly and deliberately sets up the scene to raise questions about Henry's piety. When the messengers ask permission to speak freely, Henry answers, "We are no tyrant, but a Christian king, unto whose grace our passion is as subject as are our wretches fetter'd in our prisons" (1.2.241-243). The Dauphin, however, mocks Henry by sending tennis balls, implying that Henry is so childish that he should occupy his time playing games rather than going to war. Henry understands that the Dauphin "comes o'er us with our wilder days, not measuring what use we made of them" (1.2.266-267). Then Henry's passions, which moments ago he claimed to be subject to God's grace, erupt in a rant that can hardly be equaled for violence:

> But tell the Dauphin I will keep my state,
> Be like a king, and show my sail of greatness
> When I do rouse me in my throne of France. . . .

And tell the pleasant prince this mock of his
Hath turn'd his balls to gun-stones, and his soul
Shall stand sore charged for the wasteful vengeance
That shall fly with them. For many a thousand widows
Shall this mock mock out of their dear husbands,
Mock mothers from their sons, mock castles down,
And some are yet ungotten and unborn
That shall have cause to curse the Dauphin's scorn.
(1.2.273-275, 281-288)

This seems, to put it mildly, an overreaction. To be sure, Henry is, according to the political theory of his day, a representative of God. Any mockery of the King is mockery of the God whom he represents. Perhaps this is the way we should take all of Henry's violent speech throughout the play: As the mirror of all Christian kings, he deeply senses that he is an instrument of God's vengeance. But it must be asked whether Shakespeare really wants us to excuse or approve a man who threatens to kill thousands in revenge for what is really a mild diplomatic joke, and who, having made his threat, places blame on the Dauphin for the coming reign of terror. If a Christian king is one whose passion is subject to grace, Henry is as far from acting like a Christian king as can be.

His reference to the "use" he made of his "wilder days" is chilling. It recalls a speech that Prince Hal makes early in *1 Henry IV*:

. . . herein I imitate the sun,
Who doth permit the base contagious clouds
To smother up his beauty from the world,
That, when he please again to be himself,
Being wanted, he may be more wonder'd at
By breaking through the foul and ugly mists
Of vapors that did seem to strangle him. . . .
So, when this loose behavior I throw off
And pay the debt I never promised,
By how much better than my word I am,
By so much shall I falsify men's hopes;

And like bright metal on a sullen ground,
My reformation, glitt'ring o'er my fault,
Shall show more goodly and attract more eyes
Than that which hath no foil to set it off.
(1 Henry IV 1.2.212-232)

We have all heard about beautiful fashion models who were picked on for their ugliness while in grade school, or professional football players who were too small to make their high school teams. Their beauty or skill when they grow to adulthood is all the more remarkable by contrast with who they were as young people. This is what Hal is speaking about in this passage, except that he has a deliberate plan. Hal has determined to play the role of a rascal in his youth, so that when it comes time for him to assume the throne, his wisdom and good behavior will seem more extraordinary by contrast. Though he is talking about the reformation of his own character, and his plan to put off his "loose behavior," we get the sense that he is also already planning to put off the friends and companions of his youth. It seems that he is thinking not only of his own faults but also of Falstaff and the others when he refers to the "foul and ugly mists" that will evaporate when the sun king chooses to reveal himself. At the very least, this speech reveals Hal as a very calculating young man, a young man who plays roles and makes friends in order to further his own ends, a young man perfectly suited to take on the role of the mirror of all Christian kings.

Is Henry's decision to go to war an act of a Christian king? Even assuming that Henry has a clear and just claim to the throne of France (on which, see below), is it necessary that he press that claim? France was, like England, a Christian nation, governed by a Christian king. Is it just for the "mirror of all Christian kings" to lay waste another Christian country simply for the sake of asserting a claim to the throne? If we cannot attribute Henry's decision to piety, why then does he go to war? The best answer is probably to cite his father's deathbed advice, in which he told Hal to "busy giddy minds

with foreign quarrels" (*2 Henry IV* 4.3.342-343). Henry IV
had spent his entire reign fighting against disgruntled nobility,
and as he died he advised his son how to protect himself
from similar rebellions by uniting the nobility in wars against
foreign enemies. If the nobles can be occupied with fighting
in another country, they will not have the time or energy to
fight against the king, and they will eventually forget their griev-
ances against him. There is an enduring pattern of politics
here, one that modern politicians continue to follow. When a
modern politician is having trouble at home, he will often
find a relatively painless foreign war to get involved in, and
everyone forgets he is such a bad ruler and supports the cause
for the sake of the troops. If you've broken your campaign
pledge by raising taxes, you can always send troops to Iraq
and hope people get so caught up in the fervor of war that
they forget about the IRS for a while. If the press is uncover-
ing evidence that your administration is deeply corrupt, you
can always send troops into Bosnia. Henry's motives for war
in France are as suspect as Canterbury's and Ely's, and have as
little to do with justice and right as theirs.

Canterbury offers a convoluted argument to legitimize
Henry's claim to the French throne, an argument that is anything but "as clear as is the summer's sun" (1.2.86). When he
finally ends his speech, Henry asks the same question all over
again: "May I with right and conscience make this claim?"
(1.2.96). Not one of the peers, not even Henry himself, asks
Canterbury to repeat or clarify his analysis, and it is not because they understood it the first time. None of the lords
understands Canterbury's justification for the invasion—and
they don't care! Even if the case were clear, Shakespeare has
already given us ample reason to distrust Canterbury. His conversation with Ely in scene 1 places a question mark over the
entire discussion in the King's Council. Henry has asked the
clergy for a moral judgment about his claim to the French
throne. The clergymen give their wholehearted support to
the expedition, but having been privy to their earlier

conversation, we know that they do not support it for moral or theological reasons. Canterbury, churchman though he is, is willing to plunge England into a war and to shed rivers of French blood to protect his own turf. Canterbury works on the advice of Henry IV as much as Henry V does; he too wishes to busy giddy minds with foreign quarrels.

Review Questions.

1. Why was England in so much turmoil after the reign of Edward III?

2. How did Henry IV become king?

3. In the two parts of *Henry IV*, Shakespeare developed Prince Hal's character by comparison and contrast with Hotspur and Falstaff. How is Henry V like and unlike each of these?

4. According to the Prologue, what is the work of the audience in a dramatic production?

5. Why does Shakespeare have the chorus keep reminding the audience that they are watching a play?

6. Why do Ely and Canterbury support Henry's invasion of France?

7. How does Canterbury describe the change that has overtaken Henry since becoming king? What is the significance of these descriptions?

8. Why does Henry plan to invade France? Why did his father advise him to get involved in foreign wars?

9. What does the Dauphin send to Henry? Why?

10. How does Henry react to the Dauphin's gift? Is his an appropriate response?

Thought Questions.

1. Some have said that television and movies weaken imagination. If you read a book, you have to "piece out the imperfections with your thoughts," since much is left to our imagination. When we watch a television program everything is shown to us. Do you agree with this? What would Shakespeare say?

2. Genesis 6 says that "the imagination of the thoughts of

man's heart are only evil continually." Does this mean that there is no place for imagination in the Christian life? What place does imagination have in Christianity? Is Shakespeare's view of imagination a Christian one?

3. Ely says, "The strawberry grows underneath the nettle" (1.1.60). What does he mean by this? How does this apply to King Henry? Compare this to Henry's talk about the "use" he made of his wilder days.

4. According to "Salique law," no woman is allowed to succeed to the throne (1.2.38-39). What is Canterbury's argument in support of Henry's claim to the French throne through a female ancestor?

5. What is the significance of Canterbury's mention of Pepin and Hugh Capet (1.2.64-77). How are their circumstances similar to Henry's?

6. What does Henry fear will happen if he invades France? (1.2.136-154). How does Westmoreland support Henry's concern? (1.2.166-173). How does Canterbury finally resolve this concern? (1.2.213-220).

7. How is a kingdom like music? (1.2.180-182). How is a kingdom like a beehive? (1.2.187-204).

8. Edmund Mortimer had a claim to the English throne through a female but had been defeated and imprisoned by Henry IV. How does this fact illumine what is going on in the council? How does this fact affect Henry's claim to the throne of *England*?

9. What does Henry see as the two possible outcomes of his invasion? (1.2.221-233).

10. The Dauphin sends Henry tennis balls, and Henry responds by comparing tennis with warfare (1.2.261-266). Explain the comparison.

Lesson Two: Acts 2.1-3.6

Act 2 opens with a Prologue from the Chorus celebrating Henry's "dreadful preparation" for the invasion of France. In the course of this introduction, he tells that the French have

won three noblemen—Richard, Earl of Cambridge, Henry
Lord Scroop of Masham, and Sir Thomas Grey—to their
side. When the Prologue concludes, we are ready to see a
scene in which the traitors are unmasked. We don't. Instead,
we are taken back to one of Henry's youthful haunts and to
some of the characters—Bardolph, Nym, and Pistol—that
Henry "used" in his youth but has since abandoned. These
characters reappear in several later scenes, and create a contrasting melody line to go with the main theme that follows
Henry's invasion of France. Shakespeare enjoyed depicting
rude characters (Falstaff, Dogberry, etc.) simply for their human and comic interest, but such scenes and characters are
always to be taken as implicit commentaries on the main plot
and characters.

So it is here. We have just witnessed Henry, who had
boasted of his reasonable control of passions, explode in
anger; here we witness a near brawl between Pistol and Nym.
Henry is picking a fight with France over her land; Pistol and
Nym fight over a woman, Mistress Quickly. It is remarkable,
as Goddard points out, how often in the play Henry's out-
bursts are immediately followed by scenes involving Pistol:
here in Act 2; again after Henry's violent pep talk to his troops
before Harfleur, Pistol turns up (3.1-2); again after Henry sends
his men into battle, Pistol takes a French soldier captive (4.3-
4); and just before we see Henry negotiating a peace treaty
with the French, Fluellen forces Pistol to eat a leek (5.1-2).
This happens too often to be accidental, and it clearly does
not reflect well on Henry to be continually compared with
the blustering and dishonest Pistol.

Most importantly, the chorus has just announced that
several of Henry's lords have betrayed him, and immediately
following is a scene in the tavern that is overshadowed from
beginning to end by Falstaff, who is dying in an adjoining
room because "the king has killed his heart" (2.1.92-93).
Here especially we see why Shakespeare placed the tavern
scene between the Prologue and scene 2, in which the traitors are exposed and condemned. Before we look at the

sequence of scenes, it will be helpful to examine the scene in which the traitors are unmasked.

Henry acts cleverly in trapping the traitors, and we can see here that Henry can act like the "mirror of all Christians kings" in the best sense, displaying both mercy and terrifying firmness. The scene begins with Henry deciding to free a soldier who had insulted him: "We consider it was excess of wine that set him on, and on his more advice we pardon him" (2.2.41-43). The conspirators, Scroop, Gray, and Cambridge immediately warn Henry that he should make an example of the offender, lest other soldiers be tempted to become insolent toward their commanders. By insisting on strict discipline and punishment, they condemn themselves, as Henry planned, from their own mouths. When Henry reveals that he knows "their worth," that he knows about their treachery, each of the three appeals for mercy. But Henry is not in a merciful frame of mind:

> The mercy that was quick in us but late,
> By your own counsel is suppress'd and kill'd.
> You must not dare, for shame, to talk of mercy,
> For your own reasons turn into your bosoms
> As dogs upon their masters, worrying you. (2.2.79-83)

We can hardly blame Henry for acting decisively against treachery of this sort. Had the conspiracy been successful, the traitors would indeed have "sold your king to slaughter, his princes and his peers to servitude, his subjects to oppression and contempt, and his whole kingdom into desolation." Henry is being perfectly sincere when he says, "Touching our person seek we no revenge, but we our kingdom's safety must so tender" (2.2.170-175). If there is a time for a king to be angry, it is certainly in such circumstances. But the previous scene puts the treachery in an ironic light. Henry is especially dismayed at Scroop's betrayal:

> What shall I say to thee, Lord Scroop? Thou cruel,
> Ingrateful, savage, and inhuman creature!

Thou that didst bear the key of all my counsels,
That knew'st the very bottom of my soul,
That almost mightst have coin'd me into gold,
Wouldst thou have practic'd on me for thy use—
May it be possible that foreign hire
Could out of thee extract one spark of evil
That might annoy my finger? (2.2.93-102)

On one common interpretation of the play, Henry's rejection of Falstaff was no betrayal but a necessary part of the king's development. We could also note that Henry compares the treason to "another fall of man" (2.2.142). Henry, as an anointed king, is a Christ figure. Treason against the king is like rebellion against God Himself, and the traitors have become Judases. The arrangement of the scenes of Act 2 shows that we have to look at Henry's rejection of Falstaff from a different perspective as well. The pattern is: Falstaff is dying—Henry exposes the traitors—Falstaff dies. We know that Falstaff dies of a broken heart, and we know who broke it. Henry's words to Scroop could nearly have been spoken by Falstaff to Henry.

Medieval Christians thought a lot about war, and developed what today is known as "just war theory." In essence, this theory states that a war is just if it meets two criteria. First, it must have a just cause, that is, one must have a good reason to go to war. We have already seen that Shakespeare raises doubts about this. These questions become sharper when the chorus tells us, at the beginning of Act 3, that King Charles of France had offered Henry his daughter in marriage and also certain dukedoms, but that for Henry "the offer likes not" (Prol.3.29-32). The French king is trying to prevent all-out war, and the war proceeds only because Henry insists that it proceed. One of the basic principles of just war theory, however, is that war must be an unavoidable last resort. A war is just only if there be no just and peaceful way of resolving a conflict. Henry's refusal of Charles's offer confirms that Henry's is not a just cause.

Act 3 raises equally acute questions about the other side

of just war theory: just conduct. A war is just in conduct if, once war is underway, the soldiers observe rules of civility and humanity; they cannot, for example, direct their attacks on innocent people but only on the opposing army. Act 3 is largely about the conduct of Henry's war. Scene 1 opens with Henry's speech before Harfleur, in which tells his troops that in war they must

> imitate the action of the tiger
> Stiffen the sinews, summon up the blood,
> Disguise fair nature with hard-favor'd rage;
> Then lend the eye a terrible aspect. (3.1.6-9)

As Homer's *Iliad* makes apparent, war can transform men into beasts, but even the pagan Homer seemed uncomfortable with the transformation. For Henry it is all to the good. "Mirror of all Christian kings"?

If that speech does not raise questions about the Christian character of Henry's war, his warnings to the governor of Harfleur seem unmistakable:

> I will not leave the half-achiev'd Harfleur
> Till in her ashes she lie buried.
> The gates of mercy shall be all shut up,
> And the flesh'd soldier, rough and hard of heart,
> In liberty of bloody hand shall range
> With conscience wide as hell, mowing like grass
> Your fresh-fair virgins and your flowering infants.
> (3.3.8-14)

If Harfleur continues to resist, Henry says, he will give his soldier's leave to do whatever they will with the living, with no restrictions, with a "conscience wide as hell." In the Old Testament, Israel waged a war of total destruction against the Canaanites. This was not wrong; in fact, it was wrong when Israel failed to destroy a city totally (see Josh. 7; 1 Sam. 15). But God had directly commanded Israel to wage such "holy war," and thus they did not destroy the city with a "conscience wide as hell," but with their consciences bound to obey the Lord. When Israel fought other wars, furthermore, they employed less severe methods (see Deut. 20:10-18). The only possible moral justification for total destruction of a defeated city is a direct command from God. Not only does Henry lack such a directive, but the justice of his war is not, as we have seen, obvious.

On the other hand—yes, there is another hand—this speech is, after all, just words, just extreme rhetoric. Perhaps he means to incite his men to war with powerful images, though he does not mean them literally. He threatens Harfleur so roundly to *prevent* bloodshed; if he can frighten the city into surrender, many will be saved. Later in the act, moreover, Henry condemns to death Bardolph, his old drinking buddy, because he has been caught stealing from a church. Here Henry's comments on the conduct of war seem entirely Christian:

> We would have all such offenders so cut off, and we give express charge that in our marches through the country there be nothing compelled from the villages, nothing taken but paid for, none of the French upbraided or abused in disdainful language. For when lenity and cruelty play for a kingdom, the gentler gamester is the soonest winner. (3.6.113-120)

Here Henry appears to desire not only for a conquest of France but the love and loyalty of the French people.

Harold Goddard points out, however, that even here there are ambiguities. Henry condemns Bardolph without so much as an acknowledgment that they are acquainted. Bardolph is condemned for robbing a church but Henry's entire expedition is funded by what amounts to a bribe from the Archbishop of Canterbury. How is Henry's expedition different from Bardolph's thieving, except in scale and prestige, which lends an air of legitimacy? Even when Henry seems most to be the mirror of all Christian kings, the image is full of shadows.

Review Questions.

1. What does the Prologue to Act 2 lead us to expect in the first scene? What does happen in the first scene?

2. What parallels can be seen between the end of Act 1 and the beginning of Act 2?

3. Why is Falstaff dying? How does this relate to Henry's betrayal by the three lords in 2.3?

4. How does Henry trick the traitors into condemning themselves?

5. Whose treachery most angers Henry? Why? Why is this ironic?

6. What are the two criteria of a just war? How does Henry's war measure up?

7. What does Henry tell his troops as they attack Harfleur? What do you think of this advice?

8. What does Henry say to warn the citizens of Harfleur to stop fighting? What do you think of this warning?

9. Why is Bardolph condemned to death? How is this ironic?

10. How does Henry instruct his troops to conduct themselves in France? Is this sound Christian advice?

Thought Questions.

1. Explain the how Prologue to Act 2 uses the words "crown" (Prol.2.8-11, 20-22) and "guilt" (Prol.2.25-26).

2. What role does Bardolph play in the tavern scene in 2.1? How does this cast some light on the council scene in 1.2?

3. What are Pistol and Nym quarreling about? What kind of character is Pistol? Why do you think Shakespeare called him "Pistol"?

4. In actual history, the conspirators were determined to put Edmund Mortimer on the throne, a man who had a claim to the English crown through a female. How does this throw new light on their conspiracy?

5. Why does Henry say that the demons will boast of Scroop's treachery? (2.2.111-125). How do these words reflect on Henry himself?

6. What does the Dauphin think of Henry? (2.4.14-28).

Whom is the Dauphin really describing? What is the Constable's opinion of Henry? (2.4.29-40).

7. Why does the boy decide to abandon Bardolph, Nym, and Pistol? (3.2.28-57). Does he have good reasons? Whom does the boy remind you of?

8. What kind of man is Fluellen? (3.2.61-155).

9. What is Princess Katharine of France doing while Henry invades? (3.4). Why is this significant? What does she think of the English language?

10. Why do Pistol and Fluellen quarrel? (3.6.21-63).

Lesson Three: Acts 3.7-4.8

From 3.7 to 4.3, the scenes alternate between the French and English camps at Agincourt:

3.7: French Camp
    4.1: English Camp
4.2: French Camp
    4.3: French Camp

Shakespeare invites us to compare the scenes not only through this alternating pattern but also by repeating similar lines from scene to scene. 3.7 opens with the French Constable's words, "Tut! I have the best armor of the world. Would it were day!" (3.7.1-2). The first lines from a group of English soldiers are an inverse echo:

> *Court*: Brother John Bates, is not that the morning which breaks yonder?
> *Bates*: I think it be. But we have no great cause to desire the approach of day.
> *Williams*: We see yonder the beginning of the day, but I think we shall never see the end of it. (4.1.89-94)

In the parallel and contrast of these lines, we have the summary of the condition of each camp. The French are well-rested, numerous, confident. By contrast,

> The poor condemned English
> Like sacrifices, by their watchful fires
> Sit patiently and inly ruminate
> The morning's danger, and their gesture sad
> Investing lank-lean cheeks and war-worn coats
> Presenteth them unto the gazing moon
> So many horrid ghosts. (Prologue.4.22-28)

At line 28, the tone of the Prologue shifts suddenly. With the appearance of Henry, the mood of the English soldiers swings from gloom to cheer. The coming of the king brings new life, joy and refreshment to his weary troops. Henry is described as a sun arising after a gloomy night, bringing comfort and renewed hope, thawing fear as the sun thaws a night-time frost. Here the image of the "sun" is set in a new and meaningful context. Henry is no longer the sun bursting into view from behind foul and ugly mists, nor the sun that will strike the Dauphin blind (1.2.280). He is an image of the true Sun King, whose rays warm and lighten every man. Each soldier receives what the chorus calls, in a phrase resonant with quiet beauty, "a little touch of Harry in the night" (Prologue.4.47).

In this scene, more than anywhere else in the play, Shakespeare gives us Henry as the genuine mirror of all Christian kings. Henry inspires confidence and good cheer by his very presence. He is able to bring out the best in his followers, even in the midst of a very dangerous situation, because he himself shows no sign of fear. He does not lord it over them but greets them with a "modest smile, and calls them brothers, friends, and countrymen" (Prol. 4.33-34). Can this be the same man who urged his men to become tigers at Harfleur, who warned of desolations from an army with "conscience wide as hell"? Yes and no. What cheers the English troops, what makes the king so attractive in this scene, is precisely that he gives us a "little touch of Harry"— Harry the man—and not a touch of Henry, the king and warrior. For one scene at least, Harry stops pretending to be Henry; and it is Harry who turns out to be the true mirror of all Christian kings. Quite literally, Henry lays aside his crown and royal cloak and, putting on the garb of a simple soldier, mingles with his troops. The king becomes flesh and dwells among them.

Yet even here, Shakespeare will not let us rest in the warm presence of the sun. Disguised, Henry visits his troops and initiates a discussion on the various responsibilities of king and soldier in war. Bates and Williams express their desire to be anywhere but Agincourt. Henry responds, "Methinks I could not die anywhere so contented as in the king's company, his cause being just and his quarrel honorable" (4.1.132-134). To which Williams bitterly answers, "That's more than we know" (4.1.135). It is more than the audience and readers know, too. What makes Henry attractive in this scene is that he seems to recognize it is also more than he knows, for he does not respond directly to Williams's comment.

The night before a battle is not, however, the time and place for self-examination or doubt. Things have gone too far forward to turn back now. When Williams suggests that the king will pay dearly if his soldiers die in an evil cause, Henry jumps back into the discussion:

> So, if a son that is by his father sent about merchandise do sinfully miscarry upon the sea, the imputation of his wickedness, by your rule, should be imposed upon his father that sent him. . . . But this is not so. The king is not bound to answer the particular endings of his soldiers, the father of his son, nor the master of his servant; for they purpose not their death when they purpose their services. (4.1.156-169)

As Goddard points out, Henry's logic is faulty. The example he gives does not match the situation. Henry is not like a father who sends his son on a legitimate errand, only to find the son has committed wickedness. This example does not fit because the question is precisely: Is the errand legitimate in the first place? Henry, so ready to lay the burden of

thousands of deaths on the shoulders of Canterbury, resists
shouldering the burden himself.

The debate that Henry has witnessed inspires a profound
soliloquy on the burdens of the office of king (4.1.248-302).
Because the king holds office, he becomes the target of
everyone's criticism, no matter how foolish, and held responsible for everyone's failings. What makes the king's condition
so odd is that he is distinguished from his subjects by only
one thing—"ceremony." Before, in the debate with the soldiers, Henry had said that the king is a man as everyone else is.
That is true, but in another respect the king differs from everyone else. As he reflects alone, Henry recognizes that the
king, unlike other men, is "twin-born with greatness": born
as a man and born anew when coronated as king. What Henry
says here about the burdens imposed by "ceremony" applies
not only to kings but to every holder of office. What separates a pastor from a member of the church? The pastor has
gone through a *ceremony* of ordination. What separates the
President from the citizens of the United States? The President has been inaugurated. "Ceremony" is the paper-thin line
that separates the office-holder from an ordinary man.

What is the power of "ceremony"? On the one hand, it
seems to have a creative power. Ceremony makes a man a
king, and the lack of ceremony keeps a commoner a commoner. On the other hand, ceremony seems to have no power
at all. Because of ceremony, the people of England must bow
the knee to Henry; but if an Englishman came to Henry with
a diseased knee, Henry could do nothing to cure him. Ceremony is nothing but "place, degree, and form." Ceremony
cannot even command true loyalty and love. A coronated king
often drinks poisoned flattery instead of true homage. In the
end, Henry concludes that the only thing that ceremony produces is insomnia: In contrast to his once-born subjects, a
coronated king, burdened with responsibility for all his people,
cannot sleep.

Henry's meditations are interrupted by Erpingham, who

tells him that the nobles have been looking for Henry. Realizing battle is about to be joined, Henry falls into fervent prayer, a prayer that is more a prayer of confession and repentance than a request for victory:

> Not today, O Lord,
> O, not today, think not upon the fault
> My father made in compassing the crown!
> I Richard's body have interred new,
> And on it have bestow'd more contrite tears
> Than from it issu'd forced drops of blood.
> Five hundred poor I have in yearly pay,
> Who twice a day their wither'd hands hold up
> Toward heaven, to pardon blood; and I have built
> Two chantries, where the sad and solemn priests
> Sing still for Richard's soul. More will I do,
> Though all that I can do is nothing worth,
> Since that my penitence comes after all,
> Imploring pardon. (4.1.311-323)

For the first time, Henry indicates that he recognizes the moral tenuousness of his position: a king whose own throne is erected on the blood of Richard II now claims still another crown! He understands that the real danger in the coming battle is that God will avenge the blood of Richard by giving victory to France. Sincere as this prayer certainly is, it ends in despair, as it certainly must. How, after all, can Henry truly atone for the sins of his father without giving up the crown that his father shed Richard's blood to secure? And how can Henry give up his own crown when he is about to battle the French for a second crown? As Goddard points out, Henry's dilemma is similar to that of Claudius in *Hamlet*, who wonders how he can repent when he continues to enjoy the benefits that are the fruit of his sin.

Henry's speech before the battle of Agincourt (4.3.19-67) is among the most famous passages of this play, and rightly so. It is a rousing pep talk. Though preparing for battle, this speech comes as much from Harry as from Henry; as he greeted the men the previous night, he called

them brother, friend, countrymen, and here he promises that
"he today that sheds his blood with me shall be my brother"
(4.3.61-62). Henry turns the impossible odds into a privilege:
the fewer English soldiers, the more honor each will gain.
Though the night before Bates and Williams had yearned to
be in England, Henry says that a day will come when men will
"think themselves accurs'd they were not here, and hold their
manhood cheap whiles any speaks that fought with us upon
Saint Crispin's day" (4.3.65-67).

It is an epic introduction to an epic battle. But the battle
as Shakespeare depicts it is hardly of epic proportions. There
is less here than meets the eye. Historically, Agincourt was
won by the skill of the English archers, whose success in
mowing down rows of French knights marked an important
turning point in the history of war and military strategy. Of
this Shakespeare says nothing. Instead, he portrays what is taking place on the fringes of the battle, but the fringes point to
the central significance of Agincourt and the whole French
invasion. First Pistol—of all people!—captures a French soldier; then the French are shown mourning their shameful loss,
as well they might when their soldiers are falling before the
likes of Pistol; then Exeter reports to Henry about the noble
dead. The most significant scene from the battle is the conversation between Gower and Fluellen. Fluellen has just been
informed that the boys keeping the luggage have been slain,
which, Fluellen objects, is "expressly against the law of arms"
(4.7.2). Gower admiringly tells of Henry's reaction to the
slaughter: "the king, most worthily, hath caused every soldier
to cut his prisoner's throat. O, 'tis a gallant king!" (4.7.9-11).

Of course, if *anything* violates the law of arms, it is killing
captured soldiers in cold blood, but Fluellen's mastery of
military theory fails him here. Instead, he launches onto an
extended comparison of Henry and "Alexander the Pig." The
similarities are not strong: Alexander was born in Macedon,
which begins with an "M," and Henry in Monmouth,
which—great Scott!—also begins with an "M." There are,

moreover, rivers in both cities, and salmon in the rivers (4.7.23-33). All this from one of Henry's chief captains in the middle of the climactic battle of the French campaign! What in heaven's name is going on here?

Shakespeare is having fun, of course. Fluellen is speaking of Alexander the Great of Macedon, but his Welsh accent prevents him from saying "*b*s," so Alexander the Big comes out as Alexander the Pig. But Shakespeare is often at his most insightful when he is having fun. Fluellen's mistake could not be more appropriate. For indeed, Alexander was a pig, gobbling up lands and nations until there were no more to gobble up, until he came to India and wept that there were no more lands to conquer. Fluellen thinks he is complimenting Henry, but in fact he implies, without meaning to, that Henry is as much the pig as Alexander. Alexander was an unabashed imperialist, expanding his rule over other lands purely by force of arms, without even pretending he had any justified claim to any of it. That, in spite of Henry's elaborate efforts to give his war a color of law, is precisely what Henry's war is all about.

There's more. Fluellen recalls another episode in the life of Alexander the Pig:

> *Fluellen*: Alexander, God knows, and you know, in his rages, and his furies, and his wraths, and his cholers, and his moods, and his displeasures, and his indignations, and also being a little intoxicates in his prains, did, in his ales and his angers, look you, kill his best friend, Cleitus.
> *Gower*: Our king is not like him in that. He never killed any of his friends. (4.7.36-43)

Oh, but he did, and Fluellen knows it:

> *Fluellen*: As Alexander killed his friend Cleitus, being in his ales and his cups, so also Harry Monmouth, being in his right wits and his good judgments, turned away the fat knight with the great-belly doublet. He was full of jests, and gipes, and knaveries, and mocks. I have forgot his name.

Gower: Sir John Falstaff.
Fluellen: That is he. I'll tell you there is good men porn at Monmouth. (4.7.47-56)

Falstaff again. Though Fluellen is indifferent to Falstaff, even to the point of forgetting his name, he knows that Henry all but killed him, as Alexander the Pig killed Cleitus. Fluellen has no sooner finished his discourse on Alexander's rages and furies and wraths and indignations than Henry appears, and his first words are: "I was not angry since I came to France until this instant," and he proceeds to order that all present and future prisoners be slaughtered (4.7.58-68). "Mirror of all Christian kings"? Or the very image of "Alexander the Pig"?

Review Questions.

1. What is the atmosphere in the French camp on the night before the battle? What is the atmosphere in the English camp?

2. How does Henry affect the troops as he visits them during the night? Why is Henry called "Harry" in this scene?

3. Why is it significant that Henry borrows Erpingham's cloak and goes disguised through the camp? (4.1.24-27).

4. How is Henry like the sun?

5. What do Bates and Williams discuss? What does Henry contribute to their discussion? Does Henry make good points?

6. What makes Henry different from any other man? What is the power of ceremony? What is the ultimate difference between commoner and king?

7. What kind of prayer does Henry pray before the battle? Why?

8. How does Henry rouse his men to fight valiantly at Agincourt?

9. Is Agincourt a great battle in Shakespeare's depiction? Why or why not?

10. To whom does Fluellen compare Henry? How, in Fluellen's view, are they similar? Explain the ironies of this comparison.

Thought Questions.

1. What is the Dauphin's attitude toward his horse? (3.7.11-45). How do the Constable and Orleans react to the Dauphin's praise for his horse? Do they respect the Dauphin? (3.7.100-136).

2. According to the chorus, the French "chide the cripple tardy-gaited night who, like a foul and ugly witch, doth limp so tediously away" (Prologue.4.20-22). What does this mean?

3. Thomas Erpingham appears very briefly, yet we get a clear picture of him. What kind of man is Erpingham? (4.1.13-34). Do you like him? Why or why not?

4. What is the significance of the name "Alexander Court," who speaks only two lines at 4.1.89-90?

5. What does Henry mean when he says that the king's affections are 'higher mounted' but that 'when they stoop, they stoop with like wing'? (4.1.111-113)

6. Why does Williams say that "few die well that die in battle"? (4.1.149-150). Note: he is not merely referring to the pain of suffering wounds.

7. What point is Henry making when he lists the guilt that soldiers in his army may bear? (4.1.169-180). Does this answer the soldiers' questions about the king's responsibility for sending men to death in an unjust cause?

8. How does the discussion between Henry and Williams end? (4.1.205-239). What does Bates do? How does this compare to the scene in 2.1?

9. Where is Henry during the battle? (see 4.6.4-6).

10. Does Pistol know French? (4.4). Discuss Pistol's misunderstandings of his captive. How does this reinforce the overall impression of Agincourt? How does Pistol's treatment of his prisoner compare to Henry's?

Lesson Four: Act 5

Henry V ends with a wedding. The play is about war, division and conflict, and the wedding is a symbol of union. In a sense, the play has a comic ending. The union of Henry and Katharine signifies the union of France and England, the restoration of harmony among these neighbors. Both the King and Queen of France see the marriage as new start for both kingdoms. Charles sets his hopes on the children that will be born to Henry and Katharine, urging them to

> raise up
> Issue to me, that the contending kingdoms
> Of France and England, whose very shores look pale
> With envy of each other's happiness,
> May cease their hatred, and this dear conjunction
> Plant neighborhood and Christian-like accord
> In their sweet bosoms, that never war advance
> His bleeding sword 'twixt England and fair France.
> (5.2.367-374)

The queen more directly compares marital union and happiness to political harmony:

> God, the best maker of all marriages,
> Combine your hearts in one, your realms in one!
> As man and wife, being two, are one in love,
> So be there 'twixt your kingdoms such a spousal
> That never may ill office, or fell jealousy,
> Which troubles oft the bed of blessed marriage,
> Thrust in between the paction of these kingdoms
> To make divorce of their incorporate league.
> (5.2.377-384)

Overall, the plot of *Henry V* is one of invasion, conflict, victory, resolution. If we have taken Henry as a mirror of Christian kings in the first sense, or as a Christ figure, then this marriage brings hope of a new beginning, a new covenant, a new creation.

Burgundy's beautiful speech makes these hopes for a

new creation explicit. In arranging a treaty between France and England, he has been striving for a renewal of the world. He pleads for a restoration of "gentle Peace," "dear nurse of arts, plenties, and joyful births" (5.2.34-35). France, the "best garden of the world," has become a ruined Eden, and Burgundy hopes for the restoration of Paradise. Burgundy knows full well why France has become a cursed land. In a word, the cause is war. Peace, he says,

> hath from France too long been chas'd,
> And all her husbandry doth lie on heaps,
> Corrupting in its own fertility.
> Her vine, the merry cheerer of the heart,
> Unpruned dies; . . .
> And as our vineyards, fallows, meads, and hedges,
> Defective in their natures, grow to wildness,
> Even so our houses and ourselves and children
> Have lost, or do not learn for want of time,
> The sciences that should become our country,
> But grow like savages—as soldiers will
> That nothing do but meditate on blood —
> To swearing and stern looks, diffus'd attire,
> And everything that seems unnatural. (5.2.38-62)

As so often in Shakespeare, the condition of nature reflects the condition of society. Left unattended on account of the war, France's gardens and fields grow wild; so too do the homes and towns peopled with savages who have been taught nothing but violence and blood. Burgundy hopes that peace will transform France, so that it will again become the best garden of the world.

King Charles, his Queen, and Burgundy all have high hopes for the marriage alliance between France and England, but they are not to be realized. It is worth remembering that France would never have become a ruined garden had it not been for the ravages of Henry's invasion. There would have been no need to restore it if Henry had not chosen to busy giddy minds with foreign quarrels. Much more than the chorus, it seems that Burgundy expresses the moral of the play. Moreover, Shakespeare had already written the three parts of *Henry VI*, the first part of which portrays further wars between France and England. He and his audience knew that the marriage alliance provided only a temporary respite from war, not a new creation or a restoration of Paradise.

In fact, the marriage alliance in which they put their hopes is little more than conquest carried on by other means. Charming as is the courtship scene, Henry's pursuit of Katharine is a continuation of what he began on the battlefield; it is, as Goddard points out, his second Agincourt. Henry cannot get away from military language and metaphors even when he is courting his future wife. He says plainly he is a soldier, and knows only how to speak directly and plainly, no poetry or eloquence included. Before he has spoken ten lines to her, he is calling her "Kate," which suggests a familiarity that is hardly appropriate to a first meeting or a formal courtship. It almost seems as if we have stepped back in time to watch Hal flirt with a tavern maid. At times, there is an almost threatening tone beneath the playfulness, as in this exchange:

> *Katharine*: Is it possible dat I sould love de enemy of France?
> *King*: No, it is not possible you should love the enemy of France, Kate. But, in loving me you should love the friend of France—for I love France so well that I will not part with a village of it. (5.2.176-182)

On this theory, Hitler too was a friend of France.

Alone with Kate, Henry's threats are submerged in gaiety; the tone is light, and the scene is full of Henry's efforts to turn Katharine's hesitations to his advantage, his half-successful attempts to speak and understand French, his jokes at his own expense. When Charles and Burgundy return, the threatening tone becomes more overt, though still sugared over with layers of polite diplomacy. It is perfectly legitimate and good to take advantage of a position of strength, provided you are pursuing a just course. We have seen from the

beginning of the play that Shakespeare doubts the justice of
Henry's war. Here too, his threats serve no just purpose but
only to secure his power over France. Henry, Burgundy, and
Charles engage in a discussion about love, and Henry seizes
on the link of blindness and love:

> *King:* . . . you may, some of you, thank love for my blind-
> ness, who cannot see many a fair French city for one fair
> French maid that stands in my way.
> *French King:* Yes, my lord, you see them perspectively, the
> cities turned into a maid; for they are all girdled with maiden
> walls that war hath never entered.
> *King:* Shall Kate be my wife?
> *French King:* So please you.
> *King:* I am content, so the maiden cities you talk of may wait
> on her. So the maid that stood in the way for my wish shall
> show me the way to my will. (5.2.334-347)

Henry has his eye on the "maiden" cities of France but his
love for the French maid Katharine has blinded him. But she
blinds him only because in gaining her Henry gains the cities
as well. Henry presents Charles with a stark choice: Give Kate
as my wife, along with the cities of France, or I will attack
and rape the "virgin" cities. What can Charles do? His nobility
has been decimated by Agincourt, so he announces his agreement to "all terms of reason." What kind of peace can there
be when, after forcing himself on the maiden cities of France,
Henry forces himself on the King and on the Princess?

The future holds not only further war with France, but
also civil war and unrest in England. Pistol appears in 5.1, and
once again we are invited to see his actions as a commentary
on Henry's French conquest. The Welshman Fluellen has
been wearing a leek in his cap, a tradition in the celebration of
the feast of St. David, the patron saint of Wales. In revenge
for an insult from Pistol, Fluellen beats him until Pistol eats
part of the leek. Pistol vows revenge, and ends with these
words:

> Old I do wax, and from my weary limbs
> Honor is cudgeled. Well, bawd I'll turn,
> And something lean to cutpurse of quick hand.
> To England will I steal, and there I'll steal
> And patches will I get unto these cudgel'd scars
> And swear I got them in the Gallia wars. (5.1.89-94)

Uprooted from his home by the wars, having lost his friends Falstaff and Bardolph as well as his wife, Pistol has nothing much to look forward to when he returns home. He plans to return and carry on a life of theft and deceit. Pistol is a living example of Burgundy's insight that graduates from the school of war are savages.

The chorus closes the play with the reminder that England's future was threatened by worse evils than thieving Pistols. After again singing the praises of Henry, the "star of England," who achieved France, "the world's best garden" and left it to his son, the chorus, like the audience, recalls that this is not the end of the story:

> Henry the Sixth, in infant bands crown'd King
> Of France and England, did this king succeed;
> Whose state so many had the managing
> That they lost France and made his England bleed.
> (Epilogue, 9-12)

Henry V may have gained Eden by arms, but the ultimate result of seizing Eden by violence is another loss of Paradise and further bloodshed to England. To close a "flag-waving" play with a reminder of England's self-inflicted suffering during the Wars of the Roses is, to say the least, unusual: It's as if, just when the national anthem should be coming to its triumphant conclusion, every instrument in the band goes flat.

Review Questions.

1. Why is it significant that this play ends with a wedding? What do weddings signify?

2. What do the French King and Queen hope for from the wedding?

3. How does Burgundy describe the condition of France? What has brought this about?

4. What imagery does Burgundy use? Why is this significant?

5. What benefits, in Burgundy's view, does peace bring?

6. Are the hopes for the alliance realized?

7. How does Henry approach his courtship with Katharine? What does Henry call Katharine during the courtship scene? Why is this important?

8. Why, according to Henry, should France be glad that love is blind? What has love distracted Henry from? Explain how Henry implies the threat of further warfare.

9. What does Pistol plan to do when he returns to England? What does this say about the effects of the war?

10. How does the play end? What does this say about Shakespeare's view of Henry V?

Thought Questions.

1. How does the chorus describe Henry's entrance into London? (Prologue.5.13-24). To whom does he compare Henry? (lines 25-28). How does this fit with other allusions and comparisons in the play?

2. Why did Shakespeare put the scene of Pistol eating a leek next to the scene of the peace negotiations? How is Fluellen's treatment of Pistol similar to Henry's treatment of the French?

3. Why is it significant that Fluellen is Welsh, and cannot speak English properly? (see 5.1.73-84). What other signs are there of ethnic divisions within the English army (see 3.2.58-150). How does this fit with the overall plot of the play?

4. How does the French Queen describe Henry's eyes? (5.2.12-20). How does this relate to Henry's later discussion with Burgundy about love and blindness?

5. According to Burgundy's speech, why does France lie in ruins? What does this say about the relationship of man's labor to the earth's beauty and production? How does this

relate to the description of peace as "nurse of arts"?

6. How does Henry say that France can recover peace? (5.2.68-73). How does this fit with Henry's implicitly threatening statements elsewhere in the scene?

7. Why is it significant that Henry and Katharine speak different languages? Why does Shakespeare include French sentences in their conversation?

8. How does Henry try to convince Katharine that he will not grow uglier as time goes by? (5.2.231-246).

9. Trying to get Katharine to kiss him, against the custom of French girls, Henry tells her that "nice customs curtsy to great kings" and "we are the makers of manners" (5.2.284-287). What does he mean?

10. Shakespeare often uses the phrase "stopping the mouth" to refer to a kiss (see 5.2.286-290). In what two senses does Henry use this phrase?

Video Versions of Henry V

I reviewed two video productions of this play. The older film (1945) stars Lawrence Olivier, who also directed the film, in the title role. It is an excellent color film, with realistic action and settings. The film begins as a stage play at Shakespeare's Globe Theater, and these opening scenes are worth watching for their portrayal of Elizabethan theater. Most of the film is not confined to the stage, however, though the final scenes return to the Globe. Like most films, it highlights the most visually exciting scenes. The battle scene is therefore colorful and dramatic, but it leaves a very different impression from that given in the text of the play.

Kenneth Branagh's recent *Henry V*, his first Shakespeare film, is superb. Branagh is excellent as a young Henry; he has a loud voice, and his broad square face makes him look like a warrior-king. Emma Thompson lights up every scene she appears in, and the courtship scene is especially delightful. In its music, pacing, and sets, it is not at all like a film of a stage play. At times, especially the opening conversation between Canterbury and Ely, the sound is bad and the conversation is hard to follow. Branagh leaves none of the ambiguity that I have suggested is part of the play. This is definitely a flag-waving version. On caution for younger viewers: The action scenes are realistically bloody.

Both films depart from the play at points. Branagh shortens a number of speeches, and removes some of the minor scenes. This flattens out the play a bit; the viewer does not have the constant interplay of different settings and perspectives that the play has. For learning about the basic plot and characters, both films are recommended.

Suggested Paper Topics

1. A historical study of the Hundred Years' War, Henry V, Agincourt, or the Wars of the Roses.

2. A study of Prince Hal as he appears in *Henry IV*, comparing him to the portrayal in *Henry V*.

3. Examine Henry's meditations on kingship (4.1.248-302). How does this speech reflect medieval views of kingship? What role does "ceremony" play in modern politics? What insights into modern politics does Shakespeare provide here? If "ceremony" is what distinguishes a king from a common man, is there as sense in which every king is putting on an act?

4. *Henry V* contains several powerful speeches by the king (before Harfleur; before Agincourt). Examine one or more of these speeches, looking not only at what Henry says but also at how he says it. What effect does Henry want to achieve with his speeches?

5. Is Henry presented as an ideal Christian king?

6. What role does the chorus have in the play?

7. Examine the scenes with Pistol, Nym, and Bardolph. How do these scenes fit into the overall action of the play? Do a character study of one or more of these characters.

8. How does Shakespeare depict the French? Examine the characterization of one French character: the Dauphin, the Constable, King Charles, Katharine.

9. There are a number of scenes where characters either speak wrongly or cannot understand each other because of different languages or accents (Katharine learning English; Fluellen; Pistol and his French captive; the courtship scene). Why are there so many such scenes? What do they have to do with the play?

10. Compare and contrast a pair of characters: Henry and King Charles; Henry and the Dauphin; Henry and Pistol. Note how Shakespeare develops characters by their similarities and differences from other characters.

Alas, Thou Has Misconstru'd Everything:
Julius Caesar

Behind the events and characters of *Julius Caesar* are conflicting ideas of Rome, its past and its future. The historical Brutus and Cassius were struggling to maintain what they believed was a traditional Roman system against Caesar's dangerous innovations. Thus, we cannot understand what Caesar represented to such men without knowing something about the history of Republican Rome. Until 509 B.C., Rome had been subjected to the Etruscans but in that year they overthrew the Etruscan king and became independent. By 250 B.C., they founded the Roman Republic, had become the dominant people of Italy, and were on their way conquering most of what today is Europe.

Americans think of a republic as a system in which the rulers are elected by the people and in which those who make and enforce laws are themselves subject to law. These elements were present in Rome but the Roman Republic differed in important respects from the American system. First, economic distinctions were central to Roman politics. Every citizen of Rome, to be sure, was a member of the General Assembly, but only the nobility or patricians could be members of the Senate and a man gained the status of patrician by having a certain amount of property. The Senate, dominated by the wealthy, elected the consuls who governed the Republic. Later the common people, called plebeians, were allowed to elect tribunes and these were eventually given the right to veto the laws of the Senate. In the final analysis, however, Rome was controlled by the rich patricians, supported by "clients" who promised to vote for their Senator and performed other services, while, in exchange, the Senator would use his position and power to protect his clients.

Another difference between the Roman and American systems lies in the conception of citizenship. In the United States, anyone born within the borders of the country is a citizen, and many people from other countries become citizens as well. Roman citizenship was much more restricted. Although it occurred during the time of the Roman Empire, an event in the book of Acts gives evidence of how highly valued it was. As a Roman soldier prepared to whip Paul, the apostle told him he was a Roman citizen, which, to say the least, was troubling to the soldier (Acts 22:22-29). Various movements arose through the history of the Republic to extend citizenship to everyone in Italy, but through most of the Republican period only residents of the capital city could be citizens.

By the time of Caesar, the Republic had changed considerably. Many of the changes were "growing pains," the result of Rome's expansion over about a century to Sicily, Sardinia, Corsica, Spain, North Africa, and Greece. The plebeians, most of whom were small farmers, were enlisted into the army for wars of conquest, and returned home to continue farming after the war was over. As wars were fought further and further from Italy, many plebeians returned home to find their land had been confiscated for failure to pay taxes. The estates of the rich nobility were growing at the expense of smaller estates. At the same time, the Romans were bringing huge numbers of slaves into Italy, who took over jobs that had previously belonged to the plebeians. As a result, many plebeians, landless and without work, migrated to the capital. In Shakespeare's play, this discontented mob plays an important role.

In 60 B.C., power came into the hands of what is called

the "First Triumvirate," a group of three men—Pompey, Caesar, and Crassus—who together controlled the government of Rome. They were elected consul in succession and agreed not to attack each other but instead to fight together against the enemies of any one. In 56, at Luca, they agreed to split up the widespread holdings of the Republic. Pompey became governor of Spain but remained in Rome; Caesar continued his conquest of Gaul (France); and Crassus was sent to fight the Parthians in the East. This arrangement broke down when Crassus died fighting the Parthians. Up to that time, he had been able to mediate between the more ambitious Pompey and Caesar. Now, with Crassus out of the way, Caesar and Pompey went after each other. Civil war broke out in 49/8 B.C. In 49, the Senate ordered Caesar to disband his army. Since his relations with Pompey were already rocky, Caesar feared Pompey would attack him if he relinquished his army and returned to Rome. Rather than put himself at risk, Caesar, starting with only one legion, defied the Senate and illegally crossed the Rubicon and moved south from Gaul into Italy. At the time, he reportedly said, "The die is cast."

As he marched toward Rome, Caesar gathered troops and support. Because he adopted a policy of clemency, or generosity, toward former adversaries, and because he did not confiscate estates, he won support or at least neutrality from many in Italy. Pompey eventually fled from Rome, so that Caesar entered the capital unopposed. After clearing out pro-Pompey factions in Spain and Gaul, Caesar turned East and fought Pompey at Pharsalus on August 9, 48 B.C., winning a decisive victory despite being greatly outnumbered. Pompey fled to Egypt, where he was killed. Caesar pursued him to Egypt and took the opportunity while he was there to have an affair with the Egyptian queen, Cleopatra. In 46/5 B.C., Caesar defeated Pompey's sons, thereby securing his position as sole ruler of the Republic. He had been appointed dictator in 49 and was reappointed several times afterward. Finally, in 44, he was proclaimed dictator for life, which effectively brought an end to the Republican period of Roman history, and inaugurated the empire.

Julius Caesar was, as such things go, an energetic and wise politician and accomplished many useful things for the city and people of Rome. But the proclamation that declared Caesar a god and his appointment as dictator for life offended many who wanted to restore the old Republican system. On February 15, 44 B.C., at the feast of Lupercalia, Mark Antony offered a crown to Caesar three times, which he refused each time. Many, however, believed he intended to become king, a title that repulsed Roman Republicans (as it would repulse most Americans for a President to take the title of "king"). Shortly after Lupercalia, Cassius approached Brutus about an assassination plot, which they carried out in Pompey's Theater on March 15, 44 B.C. The assassination led to a civil war between the conspirators on the one hand and those who claimed Caesar's mantle on the other. At the battle at Philippi in 42, both Cassius and Brutus committed suicide. With the conspirators out of the way, the victors began to fight among themselves and Octavius eventually emerged as the victor, taking the title of Augustus Caesar.

Shakespeare's *Julius Caesar* begins with the assassination conspiracy, portrays its aftermath, and ends with the battle of Philippi. Though the play bears his name, Julius has comparatively few lines and is killed near the beginning of Act 3. Instead of highlighting Caesar himself, the play concentrates attention on two groups of characters: the conspirators, led by Brutus and Cassius, and their opponents, led by Mark Anthony and Octavius. The play is structured fairly simply:

Acts 1-2: Formation of the conspiracy.
Act 3: Assassination and funeral of Caesar.
Acts 4-5: Civil war, culminating in battle of Philippi

Almost as important as any individual character is the Roman mob. The play begins with a scene on the streets of Rome, and there is conflict between the patricians and the plebeians. Moreover, the response of the people to the funeral orations of Brutus and Antony is at least as important as the speeches themselves. In the last scene of Act 3, Cinna, a poet, is killed by a mob that wrongly assumes he is Cinna the conspirator. Shakespeare knew history well enough to realize that power often flows to the politicians best able to manipulate the passions of the mob, and that, for certain kinds of politicians, mobs are exceedingly easy to control.

Individual characters shape events by influencing the mob, and they influence the mob through rhetoric, by means of speech. This theme is especially prominent in the great funeral orations in Act 3, in which Brutus and Antony exhibit very different styles of rhetoric with very different results. But the political use of language is a more pervasive concern. Throughout the play Brutus describes events in terms favorable to himself and the conspirators. He insists that the conspirators are "sacrificers, but not butchers" (2.1.166), and others announce the assassination as an act of liberation (3.1.78-81). In the events of its latter half, the play raises the question, Does calling a murder an act of liberation make it so? Long before the advent of modern communications, Shakespeare was aware of the centrality of propaganda in political life; he knew that a great deal in politics depends on what labels you use. His insight is as relevant for us as it was in Elizabethan England or ancient Rome. Much of the abortion battle in the United States hinges on the words we use. Call abortion a "procedure" and the baby a "foetus," and it sounds like a harmless operation; how can anyone object to a woman exercising her "free choice"? This is America, after all, the land of the free! Call it "killing" and the baby an "unborn child" or "human being," and the act takes on a very different character. Debates about words may seem merely "symbolic," but such symbols are the very substance of politics.

Julius Caesar also offers important insights into the relation of public and private life, of great historical events and the movements of individual conscience. The assassination of Caesar was a major event in the political history of Rome and of Western civilization, an event of enormous political consequence. Shakespeare, however, is also interested in the little twists and turns of private relations and internal argument that contribute to such great events. Brutus is especially important in this regard. In Act 2, Brutus debates with himself about whether he should get involved with the conspiracy, and this is followed by a discussion with his wife Portia. Great political events emerge from and, in important ways, depend upon these private wrestlings. (In a somewhat similar way, Tolstoy in *War and Peace* depicts important battles of the Napoleonic Wars as consisting of individual mistakes, cowardice, and incompetence.)

Reasons for acting one way rather than another may be good or bad, well-considered or ill-considered. As I note in my study of *Macbeth* later in this book, the pitfalls that surround human action preoccupied Shakespeare. In *Macbeth*, he shows insistently that human actions cannot be without consequences, however much Macbeth wishes they could be. In *Julius Caesar*, the conspirators do not, like Macbeth, wish that they could act without suffering ill effects. Experienced politicians, they know full well their assassination of Caesar will have results. Since no one can know the future, however, the problem for the conspirators is to calculate what those results will be. Thus, the play is full of references to various techniques of divination, of foretelling the future: soothsayers predict disaster, augurers read the entrails of sacrificial animals, characters understand changes in weather and the stars as signs of political events. Other characters try to discern the future with more rational kinds of calculation. Brutus, in the soliloquy in Act 2, tries to anticipate whether or not Caesar will attempt to make himself king and how the new title and position would change Caesar. All of these methods of calculating the future are fallible, and the play is largely about the consequences of wrong decisions and mistakes, mistakes that frequently arise because the characters are overly confident of their own power to control the future.

The most monumental miscalculation in the play is the conspirators' hope that assassinating Caesar will establish a new order of justice and freedom. Assassinations are not always wrong, and can bring relief from tyranny (Judg. 2:15-31). In Nazi Germany, some Christians participated in a conspiracy to assassinate Hitler, having concluded that no justice was possible without a complete overthrow of the system. Most of the assassinations in Scripture are, however, roundly condemned (e.g., 2 Sam. 4:1-12), and most conspiracies in history have failed to deliver what they promised. Even when an assassination becomes a grim necessity, it is important to recognize that it will not usher in a perfect world. For Brutus, however, calling Caesar's assassination an act of sacrifice is not merely a piece of political rhetoric, not just an effective way to speak. He really believes that killing Caesar is an act of religious devotion to the ideals of the Republic and to Rome, a sacrifice that will restore Rome's former greatness. Revolutionaries in the modern world have likewise asserted that man and society can be re-made through violence; they preach a religion of revolution. Shakespeare's play attacks this notion. *Julius Caesar* shows that revolutionaries are no more capable than other men of fully predicting or controlling the events their violence unleashes, and that they are in constant danger of misconstruing everything. And it shows that efforts to establish liberty with the sword not only fail to destroy tyranny, but normally make it a good deal worse.

Lesson One: Act 1

As the first scene opens, Caesar has just returned from defeating Pompey in the civil wars and has been elected consul and dictator for life. Rome is celebrating the feast of Lupercal, a fertility feast designed to renew the fruitfulness of man and nature, as well as celebrating the founding of

Rome. According to legend, the city was founded by Romulus and Remus. Romulus killed Remus when the latter tried to become king. At Lupercal, Caesar is hailed as the one who brings renewed prosperity to Rome. Antony offers the crown to Caesar, as is fitting for a feast celebrating the political origins of the city, but there is also the hint that Caesar, like Romulus, might suffer if he accepts.

The first scene portrays the different political viewpoints of the noble patricians and the common plebeians. Flavius and Marullus, two tribunes, represent the patrician class that favors a restoration of the traditional Republic and fears Caesar is gaining too much power. But the patricians are losing control, as Rome is ruled more and more by popular politicians such as Caesar, who builds power upon alliances directly with the mob. From the patricians' perspective, Rome has become chaotic. Workmen go about without wearing the clothing of their vocation, as they are supposed to do. Clothing indicates identity, status, or place in society, and the fact that the plebeians do not wear their proper clothing is a sign that they are not staying in what the patricians believe is their proper place. The lack of order and harmony is underscored by the tribunes' inability to understand the workmen. The cobbler deliberately confuses the tribunes with puns and jokes (1.1.9-35). How can Rome hope to stand united when Romans no longer speak a common language?

Just as the scene depicts how the patricians are losing their firm grip on the levers of political power, it shows the character of the Roman mob, and why politicians are able to secure power by appealing to it. As Marullus points out, the people rejoiced when Pompey came into the city, and now they celebrate Caesar, who has just defeated Pompey and comes to Rome covered with Pompey's blood (1.1.41-55). Marullus's rebuke is so stinging that the people slink away silently (1.1.65-66), now feeling guilty for celebrating Caesar's victories. The crowd's opinions are molded by whoever happens to be talking at the moment.

The first words out of Caesar's mouth are a request that

Antony touch Calpurnia, Caesar's wife, as he runs in the race of Lupercal. This touch, he hopes, will make barren Calpurnia fertile (1.2.6-9). Though he trusts in the powers of the feast of Lupercal, Caesar refuses to listen to the soothsayer who warns him to beware the Ides (the fifteenth) of March (1.2.12-24). Shakespeare draws a contrast between Caesar's belief in the superstitions of Lupercal and his dismissal of the soothsayer's warning by using a parallel structure in 1.2.1-24:

> Caesar calls out
>> Casca commands silence (music stops)
>>> Caesar calls for Antony and asks him to touch Calpurnia (music begins)
> Soothsayer calls out
>> Casca commands silence
>>> Caesar calls for soothsayer and then ignores his warning

Caesar does not even bother to ask the soothsayer what he should beware of, something that might be worth looking into. In principle Caesar is superstitious, but he lacks discernment to know what superstitions to trust. Later, he will again be faced with a decision about how to evaluate an omen, and he will again make the wrong decision. Caesar miscalculates everything.

Caesar reveals much of his own character in his evaluation of Cassius (2.1.192-214). Caesar is pompous, overly sure of himself, a man who believes his own press releases. He frequently refers to himself as Caesar, not "I," as if the divine person of Caesar were distinct from the frail human Julius. He says he does not fear Cassius, though Cassius is worthy of fear, because he is always Caesar, and Caesar is never afraid. Caesar has become overconfident by surrounding himself with yes-men and flatterers, with "fat men." Fat men are contented, satisfied with their position in society, not inclined to think too much or to want things changed, and as a result fat men are safe to have around (1.2.192-195). Cassius is to be feared not only because he is too thin but because he sees quite through the deeds of men (1.2.203). Caesar knows that Cassius is able to look past his pompous exterior, to discern behind Caesar's play-acting that he has grown soft and weak; Cassius knows that behind the facade of being Caesar and being a god, he is a mere man (1.2.90-131). Caesar, in turn, sees through Cassius. He has an accurate understanding of Cassius's character and the danger he poses but Caesar does nothing with the knowledge he has. He is too impressed with himself as the invincible Caesar. His confidence is not well-founded; again he miscalculates. Immediately after assuring Antony of his invincibility, Caesar asks him to speak into his good ear (1.2.213-214). A more alert man might have listened carefully to the soothsayer, but Caesar is half-deaf. Quite rightly is Cassius amazed that "this man is now become a god" (1.2.115-116).

In contrast to the fat men that surround Caesar, Cassius has a "lean and hungry look" (1.2.194). Nor is he, like Caesar, superstitious. He and Brutus find themselves walking under the grotesquely huge legs of Caesar the "Colossus" and trying to find room within the walls of Rome for more than one man (1.2.135-137, 140, 152-160). "The fault," however, "is not in our stars but in ourselves that we are underlings" (1.2.140-141). Fate has not decreed that all submit to Caesar. Cassius sees Caesar's unrivaled greatness as evidence of Rome's loss of "the breed of noble bloods"; in times past Rome's ancestors "would have brook'd th' eternal devil to keep his state in Rome as easily as a king" (1.2.151, 159-161). Cassius's is an activist view of the world. If Rome's condition is not decreed by the arrangement of stars, then it can be changed. And if Caesar is but a feeble man, he can be overthrown. Cassius has seen this "god" shake with fever (1.2.121), and therefore knows it is possible to "shake" him from his seat (1.2.327). What he cannot know beforehand is how far the shaking of Caesar will shake the whole edifice of Rome "like a thing unfirm" (1.3.3-4).

Cassius feels he has good reason to give Caesar a shake. Antony's offer of the crown at Lupercal brings his concerns to the surface, and he decisively moves ahead to recruit Brutus. Cassius opposes Caesar because he refuses to bow to anyone. Caesar is only a man as Cassius is, so why should he have to give homage to Caesar? There is an underlying bitterness and envy at the end of his speech. It amazes Cassius that a man of "feeble temper," whom Cassius has heard cry out like a "sick girl," should "bear the palm alone." Caesar's insight is correct: Cassius is the kind of man who will "be never at heart's ease whiles they behold a greater than themselves" (1.2.208-209). As in most revolutionary movements, envy is one of the sources of the conspiracy to overthrow Caesar.

In the opinion of the other characters, Brutus's motives and character are quite different from Cassius's. Even at the end of the play, when the conspirators have been defeated, Antony's admiration for Brutus is undiminished:

> This was the noblest Roman of them all,
> All the conspirators, save only he,
> Did that they did in envy of great Caesar;
> He only, in a general honest thought
> And common good to all, made one of them.
> His life was gentle, and the elements
> So mix'd in him that Nature might stand up
> And say to all the world, "This was a man!"
> (5.5.68-75)

This explains why Cassius needs Brutus among the conspirators. Brutus will be the "front man" to bring public support and to lend credibility to the conspiracy. Cassius wants the Romans to think, "If Brutus is involved, it must be a good cause." Anything that the conspirators do amiss will be transformed to virtue by a kind of chemical reaction by Brutus's presence (1.3.157-60).

The portrait of Brutus in action in many ways supports his reputation. His tenderness toward Portia (2.1.233-309) and Lucius (4.3.259-270) confirms Antony's assertion that he is gentle. Brutus himself claims his highest aim is the "general good" (1.2.85). If he joins the conspiracy, it will be for the sake of Rome, not for the sake of Brutus. Indeed, Brutus is so deeply sensitive to Rome's divided condition that he suffers internally what Rome suffers. He confesses that he has been distracted "with passions of some difference" (1.2.40), that he is "with himself at war" (1.2.46). Later, after Cassius's intense recruitment, he muses,

> Since Cassius first did whet me against Caesar,
> I have not slept.
> Between the acting of a dreadful thing
> And the first motion, all the interim is
> Like a phantasma or a hideous dream.
> The genius and the mortal instruments
> Are then in council, and the state of man,
> Like to a little kingdom, suffers then
> The nature of an insurrection. (2.1.61-69)

We cannot imagine that Cassius lost any sleep or that he would have called the assassination a "dreadful thing." Brutus is indeed a man who loves Caesar no less than any man, but loves Rome more (3.2.23).

Brutus's character is more complicated than this, however. Nothing Antony says, not even his eulogy for Brutus, should be taken at face value. Like Caesar, Brutus speaks of himself in the third person, as "poor Brutus" (1.2.46). Cassius is more accurate than he realizes when he compares the two (1.2.142-160). These similarities are initially hidden, and it is Cassius who brings them into the open. Cassius is cunning, shrewd, discerning, lean and hungry—an ideal tempter—and 1.2 portrays the temptation and fall of Brutus. Cassius knows Brutus will not be moved by an outright appeal to envy or ambition. He must appeal to Brutus's higher ideals; he must make honor the subject of his story (1.2.92);

he must show Brutus the tree of knowledge is good for the general. Just as Brutus cannot see his own face except in a glass, so Cassius claims to be a mirror to reveal Brutus to Brutus (1.2.66-78). First, he shows that in his heart Brutus wants to stop Caesar, something that Brutus will hardly admit to himself. Brutus protests that Cassius is seeking in him "that which is not in me" (1.2.65), but Cassius sees quite through Brutus as well as he sees through Caesar and knows that he is only drawing to the surface fears and plans over which Brutus is already at war with himself. Cassius is also a mirror to Brutus in his flattery; his mirror reflects Brutus's "hidden worthiness." By continually contrasting Brutus's strength and virtue with Caesar's weakness, he appeals to and increases Brutus's sense of his own nobility and honor. Cassius holds up a mirror to Brutus, and Brutus begins to delight in the reflected image. Once he begins to enjoy gazing into the mirror, Brutus is more than halfway to becoming another Caesar.

Cassius knows that Brutus can be molded, seduced, tempted.

> Well, Brutus, thou art noble; yet I see
> Thy honorable metal may be wrought
> From that it is dispos'd. Therefore it is meet
> That noble minds keep ever with their likes;
> For who so firm that cannot be seduc'd?
> (1.2.313-317)

It would be safer if noble Brutus had kept company with other noble men; in the presence of a cunning seducer, nobility is easily manipulated, especially when one already has, as Brutus does, a strong sense of his own nobility. Brutus sincerely holds to the values of the Republic but the ease with which Cassius tempts Brutus shows how hollow and insecure those values are. Cassius uses and manipulates Brutus's virtues as a tool for his own envy and ambition, molding Brutus's honorable metal into the knife that will make the unkindest cut of all.

Review Questions.

1. Outline the history of Caesar's rise to power.

2. What is the focus of Shakespeare's play? Who are the main characters?

3. How does the play highlight the problem of calculating the future?

4. What is the role of the Roman mob? How does the mob figure into the politics of Rome?

5. Compare and contrast Shakespeare's concern with human action in *Macbeth* and *Julius Caesar*.

6. What is going on in Rome in the first scene? Why is this significant?

7. What kind of character is Caesar? Is he superstitious? Is he discerning?

8. Why does Cassius instigate the conspiracy? What kind of character is Cassius?

9. How does Cassius tempt Brutus to get involved? Why does Cassius want Brutus as a conspirator? How is Cassius a "mirror" to Brutus?

10. What hints do we have that Brutus is like Caesar?

Thought Questions.

1. The cobbler says he is a "mender of bad soles" (1.1.13-14). Explain the double meaning of his words. Why does the cobbler say he is leading men in the streets? (1.1.32-35).

2. Flavius says he will pluck feathers from Caesar's wing (1.1.76-79). What does he mean by this? How does he plan to accomplish it?

3. What is Antony's relationship to Caesar? (1.2.9-10; 1.2.190-214).

4. Cassius says he has heard many people wish "that noble Brutus had his eyes" (1.2.62). What does he mean by this? How is this related to Cassius's function as a mirror?

5. What two events does Cassius recount to highlight Caesar's weakness? (1.2.100-131).

6. What happened to Caesar when he refused the crown?

(1.2.245-256). How does this relate to Cassius's description of Caesar? How does it foreshadow what is to come? What does Cassius mean when he says "we have the falling sickness"? (1.2.259; cf. 1.2.151-161).

7. What happened to Marullus and Flavius? (1.2.289-291). Why?

8. What kind of character is Casca? How does Cassius explain his "rudeness"? (1.2.302-307).

9. What does Cassius plan to do to bring Brutus into the conspiracy? (1.2.320-327). How is this parallel to his becoming a "mirror" to Brutus?

10. Describe the conversation between Cicero and Casca in 1.3.1-40. How does it relate to the larger themes of the play?

Lesson Two: Act 2

2.1-2 has the following structure:

1. Gathering at Brutus's house
   2. Brutus and Portia
   2^1. Caesar and Calpurnia
1^1. Gathering at Caesar's house.

The parallels between the two central scenes are obvious: in both, men speak to wives who are worried for them. In both scenes, men are trying to make calculations about what course to follow in the upcoming day. Shakespeare deliberately puts these scenes side-by-side to develop the parallels between Caesar and Brutus that were already subtly presented in Act 1. Brutus, as we have seen, represents the old Republican tradition, the Roman emphasis on honor and service to the common good, and the philosophy of Stoicism, according to which one should live by reason and not by passion. Caesar represents empire, self-promotion, and rule by divine kings. In many ways, they are polar opposites. But Shakespeare's parallel suggests that perhaps they are more alike than anyone realizes. Caesar has begun to believe his propaganda. He acts as if he believes he really is a god. Brutus has been the focus of Cassius's propaganda campaign, and Brutus has begun to believe in his own nobility. He has begun to imagine himself according to the image presented by his mirror.

It is the night before the Ides of March, a stormy night, full of omens and portents, the turbulent weather reflecting the political thunderstorm that is about to break out. Brutus is in an orchard or garden, ruminating on Cassius's temptation. He speaks of Caesar as an "adder" and a "serpent's egg" (2.1.14, 32). This setting and language can hardly be without significance. It recalls the scene of the serpent in the garden in Genesis 3. At this point, Brutus thinks he is being a faithful Adam who, instead of submitting to the serpent, is determined to crush him. As it turns out, Brutus will commit an act that will plunge the world into chaos. Thinking himself a new Adam, he acts like the old. The real serpent is the one who has seduced him. Brutus has begun to be like Caesar, and like Caesar he immediately begins to miscalculate.

Brutus has convinced himself that "it must be by his death" (2.1.10). Are his reasons convincing? Bearing no personal grudge against Caesar, Brutus professes to be acting for the "general," that is, the common good of Rome. He fears that if Caesar is crowned Caesar will be changed. Brutus admits that Caesar is a good Stoic, ruled by reason not passion (2.1.19-21), but Brutus fears what Caesar may become. Caesar has climbed the political ladder, and once at the top he may forget the rungs below, those who have helped him attain to the height, like Brutus and Cassius (2.1.21-27). Brutus concludes it is better to kill him now and prevent this possibility than to let it happen. As an adder is dangerous in the day, so Caesar may be dangerous if he becomes king. It is better to crush a serpent's egg before it hatches than to have to deal with a full-grown snake, especially a serpent that wears a crown.

Every one of Brutus's reasons is phrased as a possibility,

not an actuality. He is anxious about what Caesar "may" become and what he "might" do. He decides to join the conspiracy on the mere *possibility* that Caesar might change. Since Caesar's transformation would happen, if it happened at all, in the future, Brutus can do nothing but speculate about possibilities. All Brutus has to go on are possibilities. But this means that his decision is made on a very weak basis; he determines to play a part in killing a man, overthrowing a ruler, and violently changing Rome's political landscape because the man may change for the worse sometime in the future. On such a basis, one could justify anything.

From a Christian perspective, we should admit that all human calculations of the future are fallible and no more than "possible." We are not completely in the dark, however, since we have God's revelation in the Bible. The Bible is from a God who knows the end and the beginning. Though we do not know the future, God does. The Bible not only tells us certain things that will happen in the course of history but also gives us much instruction that helps us calculate the consequences of our actions. Paul says that we reap what we sow (Gal. 6:-10); Proverbs tells us again and again that laziness will lead to poverty; Jesus promises blessings to the meek, the pure, the peacemakers (Mt. 5:1-12), and warns that those who live by the sword will perish by the sword. Because God's word is sure, we can anticipate to some degree where our deeds will lead. The characters in *Julius Caesar*, however, live in a pagan world and do not have the Bible. Instead of showing a Christian perspective on this question, Shakespeare merely raises the problem and portrays the tragic consequences that follow from miscalculations.

Once he enters the conspiracy, Brutus immediately dominates. Once he has ascended ambition's ladder, he begins to scorn the base degrees by which he did ascend. Brutus becomes everything he feared Caesar would become. (To get the point, read through his speech in 2.1.10-34 thinking how it applies to Brutus.) Brutus persuades the conspirators not to take an oath (2.1.114-140), since they need no more incentive to kill Caesar than the good of Rome. Brutus implies that an oath would mean that their motives are less pure, and he wants only pure, noble, high-minded conspirators. Similarly, he argues that if they kill Mark Antony, their course will seem too bloody, and therefore their plot will seem impure to the populace (2.1.162-191). Brutus imposes his own vision of honor on the conspiracy, and in so doing sets the conspiracy off on what turns out to be a disastrously wrong course.

Brutus does not dominate because he is wiser than the other conspirators. In fact, Brutus's every decision is wrong, especially in regard to Mark Antony. He persuades the conspirators that Antony is nothing more than a limb of Caesar, who will have no life or power once Caesar is dead (2.1.165). Cassius, that lean observer of men, is more accurate in his assessment of Antony: "We shall find of him a shrewd contriver, and you know his means, if he improve them, may well stretch so far as to annoy us all" (2.1.157-160). Cassius is shrewd enough to know a shrewd man when he sees one; Brutus again shows that his sense of honor makes him easy prey, since he assumes that all men are as honorable as he. Cassius bows to Brutus to save the unity of the conspiracy, not because he has been convinced that Antony is harmless. When Cassius speaks of his fear of Antony, Brutus says simply, "do not think of him" (2.1.185). It is as if he said, "I do not fear, for I am always Brutus."

Brutus uses religious language to justify the conspiracy. They are to be "sacrificers, but not butchers" (2.1.166), to "carve him as a dish fit for the gods not hew him as a carcass fit for hounds" (2.1.173-174), to act as "purgers, not murderers" (2.1.180). Sacrifice is a cleansing rite, removing the defilement and evil of the past. At the same time it removes the dirt of the past, sacrifice makes a new beginning. Brutus implies that the assassination of Caesar will bring an end to the old world, defiled by Caesar's ambition and tyranny, and give birth to a new creation of freedom and prosperity. Brutus says, like revolutionaries of all ages from Robespierre to Lenin, that the world can be made new through violent revolution. Violence is a purgative, and bloodshed cleanses the land.

There are several hints the sacrifice will not be effective. Julius has spoken as if the divine being Caesar were detachable from the man Julius. Brutus thinks he knows better:

> We all stand up against the spirit of Caesar,
> And in the spirit of men there is no blood.
> O that we then could come by Caesar's spirit,
> And not dismember Caesar! But, alas,
> Caesar must bleed for it! (2.1.167-171)

Harold Goddard's summary of the logic of this speech is revealing: "(1) The spirit of men contains no blood. (2) We wish to destroy the spirit of Caesar. Therefore (3) we must spill Caesar's blood." As Goddard points out, the argument is completely wrong, for if spirits have no blood, spilling Caesar's blood will have no effect whatever on his spirit. That "come by" in line 169, moreover, is most intriguing. We expect Brutus to say that he wants to "eliminate" the spirit of Caesar, not "come by" it. To "come by" something means to take possession of it, to make it your own, not to get rid of it. Brutus perhaps reveals more than he intends, since his statement suggests that, whatever his stated goals, the result of the assassination will be as much to take possession of Caesar's spirit as to eliminate it. Brutus, more than anyone else, has already begun to "come by" the spirit of Caesar.

Then there is that odd little conversation among Casca, Decius, and Cinna:

> *Decius:* Here lies the east. Doth not the day break here?
> *Casca:* No.
> *Cinna:* O, pardon, sir, it doth, and yon gray lines
> That fret the clouds are messengers of day.
> *Casca:* You shall confess that you are both deceiv'd.
> Here, as I point my sword, the sun arises,
> Which is a great way growing on the south,
> Weighing the youthful season of the year. (2.1.101-108)

As Goddard notes, "These men think they are about to bring a new day to Rome when they cannot even agree as to where the geographical east lies. They promise a new spiritual morning before they have learned where the material sun comes up!" Casca's pointing to the rising sun with his sword is "the political message of the play condensed into a metaphor," since the conspirators believe they can bring a new day for Rome by the edge of the sword.

Scene 2 moves to Caesar's house, where Calpurnia is trying to convince her husband not to go to the Senate. She has dreamed of Caesar's death, and the odd portents during the night confirm her fears (2.2.8-54). There are no comets except at the death of princes. Caesar explains to Decius, sent by the conspirators to fetch him to the Senate, that Calpurnia

> saw my statue,
> Which like a fountain with an hundred spouts
> Did run pure blood, and many lusty Romans
> Came smiling and did bathe their hands in it.
> (2.2.76-78)

Caesar still believes he is invincible, but in deference to Calpurnia he decides to stay home. He is as dismissive of the Senators as Brutus is of the other conspirators. He tells Decius to announce that Caesar stays home because Caesar wants to stay home, adding that Caesar's will should be "enough to satisfy the Senate" (2.2.71-72).

Decius persuades Caesar to come to the Senate by cleverly reinterpreting Calpurnia's dream:

> It was a vision fair and fortunate.
> Your statue spouting blood in many pipes,
> In which so many smiling Romans bath'd,
> Signifies that from you great Rome shall suck
> Reviving blood, and that great men shall press
> For tinctures, stains, relics, and cognizance.
> This by Calpurnia's dream is signified. (2.2.84-90)

Decius thus saves the conspiracy. Knowing that Caesar is flattered most when told that he hates flattery (2.1.202-208), Decius' explanation of the dream confirms Caesar's self-image, that he is the source of life and prosperity to the people of Rome. Hearing Decius' interpretation, Caesar chides Calpurnia: "How foolish do your fears seem now!" (2.2.105). He is too pompous to notice that even on Decius' view, Caesar must die. How, after all, can Romans suck reviving blood from Caesar without killing him? At the same time, Decius's interpretation reflects the conspirator's view of their actions. For Decius, the dream is of Caesar's death, but, like Brutus, he believes this will be a sacrificial death, renewing Rome. Again, the superstitious Caesar ignores warnings, such as Calpurnia's, that merit his closest attention. He is still half-deaf.

Encouraged by Decius's interpretation, Caesar decides to go to the Senate. The scene ends with Caesar sharing wine with Antony and the conspirators: Caesar spends his last hours drinking wine with those who will betray him, while the new day breaks on the point Casca's sword.

Review Questions.

1. What is significant about the structure of Act 2, scenes 1-2?

2. Where is Brutus during his soliloquy? Why is this significant?

3. How does Brutus convince himself that Caesar must die?

4. Does Brutus have good reasons for going ahead with the conspiracy?

5. What happens to Brutus once he joins the conspiracy? Does he make good decisions? How does this relate to hints in Act 1 of similarities between Brutus and Caesar?

6. How does Brutus describe the assassination?

7. Why is it significant that Brutus says that the conspirators are trying to "come by" Caesar's spirit?

8. What was Portia's dream? How did she interpret it?

9. How does Decius interpret the dream?

10. Explain how Decius's interpretation fits with Brutus's view of the assassination.

Thought Questions.

1. What does Brutus ask Lucius in 2.1.1-5 and 2.1.39-43. Why is this significant?

2. How does Brutus suggest the conspiracy hide itself during the day? (2.1.77-85). Why does conspiracy need to hide itself?

3. Why does Metellus think Caius Ligarius will be willing to help in the plot? (2.1.215-217). What does this say about the motivations of the conspirators?

4. What is Brutus's view of oaths? (2.1.114-140). Is this a Christian view?

5. Describe the reasons for and against including Cicero in the conspiracy (2.1.141-153).

6. What is odd about a clock striking three? (2.1.192-193; cf. 2.1.1-5). Why did Shakespeare include this?

7. After Portia insists on knowing what troubles Brutus he agrees to tell her (2.1.304-308). How does she react? (3.4). What does Portia mean by the poignant question, "Dwell I but in the suburbs of your good pleasure"? (2.1.285).

8. What do Caesar's augurers find when they offer the morning sacrifice? (2.2.38-40). How does Caesar interpret this omen? (2.2.41-48). Is this an accurate interpretation?

9. Calpurnia tells Caesar that his "wisdom is consum'd in confidence" (2.2.49). What does she mean? Compare to Artemidorus's suit to Caesar (2.3.5-10).

10. How does Decius entice Caesar into the Senate? (2.2.92-104).

Lesson Three: Act 3

The assassination is carried out in front of Pompey's statue. Caesar, who conquered Pompey, who rode into Rome over Pompey's blood, is killed before his foe's image. Pompey gets revenge. Caesar lived by the sword and therefore dies by the sword; a man of bloodshed is brought to a bloody end. But Pompey's is not the only avenging spirit in this act.

Caesar is killed in the middle of a speech (3.1.35-48, 58-73). In the first portion of his speech, Caesar is talking about how he cannot be moved by flattery, though Decius has just persuaded him with flattery to come to the Senate. In the second part, Caesar expands on this theme by saying that he is as unchangeable as the north star. Stars are symbols of rulers in Scripture and much literature, and among the stars, as Caesar says, there is only one that holds its place, the north star. He is like the north star also in the fact that all other stars rotate around him, the center of the world. Caesar is about to be killed, and a moment before the daggers strike, he is orating on how constant and unchangeable he is. Moreover, he is saying he will never change, but Brutus joined the conspiracy precisely because he feared how a crown might transform Caesar. In his last words, Caesar is unknowingly defending himself against Brutus's fears. Despite its pompousness, Caesar's comparison of himself to the north star is accurate; he is the center around which the Roman world revolves, the cornerstone and pillar of the edifice of empire. Shaking him down endangers the whole.

Once Caesar is dead, the conspirators proclaim "liberty, freedom, and enfranchisement" and "peace, freedom, and liberty" (3.1.81, 110). As we have seen, Shakespeare is very sensitive to the way revolutionaries use rhetoric to make their violence seem virtuous. Like the conspirators against Caesar, the leaders of the French and the Russian Revolutions promised that through the bloody overthrow of the old order they would usher in a new age.

Brutus suggests that the conspirators wash their hands in Caesar's blood (3.1.104-109). It is difficult to see a good reason for this. Possibly, it has something to do with the sacrificial imagery that Brutus uses to justify the assassination. In fulfillment of Portia's dream, Brutus wants the conspirators to bathe in Caesar's reviving blood. Whatever Brutus's motivation, it is a really dumb move. Now the conspirators will appear before the crowd literally covered in Caesar's blood. Unconsciously, Brutus has made it clear that all the conspirators have, in more than a literal sense, blood on their hands.

Now that Caesar is dead, the most serious obstacle standing in the way of the conspirators is Antony, a close friend of Caesar's and the only man in Rome powerful enough to oppose them. Most fateful is the conspirators' decision to permit Antony to speak at Caesar's funeral (3.1.232-42). Cassius fears the effect that Antony might have on the mob. Brutus, however, thinks that he can persuade the people by giving reasons for the assassination. Brutus is still operating on the assumption that Antony is no more than a limb of Caesar. Brutus, moreover, is a Stoic, who strives to be ruled only by reason. He apparently believes that Rome is a Stoic settlement, and fails to recognize that reason sometimes plays little role in politics. Passions are often more important, and the politician who can create, shape, and control the passions of the crowd is likely to wield a great deal of power. Moreover, Brutus lives by a strict ideal of honor and expects Antony to act by the same code. Beyond this, Brutus may hope to win Antony to the side of the conspirators by offering him a role in the funeral and in the new government. It would help the conspirators if they could get Antony, known to be a friend of Caesar, to endorse their action. The assassination would seem less brutal, less motivated by personal hatred.

Brutus may have many reasons for his decision, but he completely underestimates Antony's abilities as a politician. Cassius again is more discerning: "I know not what may fall; I like it not" (3.1.243). Cassius's acknowledgment that he does not know what Antony might do is in marked contrast to Brutus's supreme confidence that he can foresee and control the Roman people. Cassius's ignorance is wiser than the noble wisdom of Brutus. Again, however, Brutus prevails not by persuading Cassius but by ignoring his objections.

Antony agrees to the restrictions placed on his speech; he promises to let Brutus speak first and agrees not to blame the conspirators. Once the conspirators have left Antony alone with Caesar's body, his true intentions are revealed. Brutus had insisted that the conspirators were "sacrificers, but not butchers"; Antony bluntly calls them "butchers" (3.1.255). Over Caesar's body, Antony promises to avenge the murder by stirring up civil strife against Caesar's killers. Brutus had said that the conspirators would "come by" Caesar's spirit by killing his body. Antony is going to make sure that Caesar's spirit does not rest; he intends to unleash Caesar's spirit to avenge himself (3.1.270-275). Antony himself wants to be the one who will "come by" and control the spirit of Caesar.

At the funeral, Brutus's speech turns the people against Caesar (3.2.13-37). He assures them that the assassination was not motivated by hatred of Caesar. While he loved Caesar, he loved Rome more than Caesar and therefore acted to defend Rome from Caesar. He argues that he offended only those Romans who wanted to be slaves, but did not offend any who want to live in freedom. Caesar had to be killed, Brutus argues, because of his ambition. In the abstract, Brutus's is not an ineffective speech. He is both admiring to Caesar, which satisfies Caesar's friends, yet critical of his ambition. He frames the issues so that anyone who admits to being offended by the assassination would be admitting a preference for slavery over freedom. If there is a flaw in Brutus's speech it is that he provides no evidence of Caesar's ambition. How can he? Brutus's decision to join the conspiracy was not based on anything that Caesar had actually done but on his estimation of what Caesar *might* do. This leaves an opening for Antony to refute the charge of ambition. And Antony makes full use of it.

Though Brutus's is a technically competent speech, it fails utterly to achieve its objective. The mob is not an assembly of Stoics; as we know from 1.1, they respond more readily to passion than to argument. Antony's famous speech is more attuned to the audience. His speech (3.2.79-268) must be understood in the context of his soliloquy at the end of 3.1. There, Antony said he would unleash Caesar's spirit with Ate, goddess of strife and war, beside him. Antony's entire speech is intended to unleash the spirit of Caesar by filling the people with outrage at the assassination. He must act with care, however; the people have been swayed by Brutus's speech and Brutus is reputed by all to be an ideal Roman. Antony would be foolish to attack Brutus and the conspirators directly. The crowd wants Brutus to be Caesar (3.2.56), and only after Antony has won the crowd is it safe for him to call the conspirators "traitors" (3.2.203).

For most of the speech, he does not attack the conspirators at all. He repeatedly concedes that "Brutus is an honorable man" (3.2.88, 93, 100, 105, 130, 133), and insists that he is not trying to refute Brutus (3.2.106). By emphasizing this, Antony technically keeps to his agreement that he will not blame the conspirators (3.1.245). There is a huge gulf, however, between what Antony says and what he means. Antony uses a rhetorical device called "litotes," which involves denying what you mean to affirm. Thus, when Antony says, "I come to bury Caesar not to praise him" (3.2.80) he really means that he has come to praise Caesar. When he says, "I speak not to disprove what Brutus spoke" (3.2.106), he really means that he wants to refute Brutus's charge that Caesar was ambitious. All the while, he is providing evidence that Caesar was not ambitious. The whole speech contrasts Caesar's loyalty and kindness as a friend to Brutus's treacherous disloyalty. As the speech progresses, "Brutus is an honorable man" takes on a bitingly ironic edge. By the end of the speech, it is clear that Antony means exactly the opposite of what he says.

Antony also uses Caesar's will and his body to brilliant

effect. By mentioning the will and then refusing to read its contents, and by claiming that hearing the will would enrage the crowd, he brings their curiosity to a pitch of excitement. He uses Caesar's body in a similar way. He delays unveiling it to arouse the crowd's interest, and then by describing in detail the attack of each conspirator, he arouses pity and anger. Antony thus establishes a powerfully emotional relationship with the crowd. When he spoke, Brutus was both physically and emotionally distant from the people; he remained in the "pulpit" and reasoned with them as if he were arguing in the senate. Antony is a more effective agitator. He does not offer rational arguments, but acts the part of the mourner, weeping and reminiscing over Caesar's body. He comes down from the pulpit to stand amongst the people. He appeals to their passions rather than their minds. Through his words he breathes out the spirit of Caesar, transforming the mob into an instrument of Caesar's vengeance.

Clearly, Antony's claim that he is "no orator, as Brutus is" but only "speaks right on" as a "plain, blunt man" is exactly the opposite of the truth (3.2.223-224, 229). He has not been speaking right on at all; everything he says is two-edged, on the surface supporting Brutus but all the while attacking.

In this scene, the reaction and changeableness of the Roman people is as important as the speeches. The people believe and follow whoever has spoken most recently. The same crowd that praised noble Brutus and wanted to make him Caesar determines, after Antony's speech, to burn Brutus's house (3.2.237); those who once would make him king now cry out for his crucifixion. Shakespeare was very skeptical about democracy in the sense of rule by the majority, or direct rule by the people. Shakespeare's depiction of the Roman crowd reinforces the view that only a morally grounded populace can govern itself. Otherwise, a people can be controlled by every effective speaker that comes along.

The crowd is not only manipulable, but is stirred to

murderous irrationality. It is unfortunate that 3.3 is sometimes left out of productions of *Julius Caesar*. This scene is chilling in its depiction of sheer mob madness. Cinna, a poet who has no connection to the conspiracy, is attacked and killed because he happens to have the same name as a conspirator. When he protests that he is not the Cinna who killed Caesar, the crowd simply finds another reason for continuing to kill him: "Tear him for his bad verses!" A crowd such as this does not need reasons for violence. There has been a regression in the crowd's behavior: from being swayed by Antony to acts of random violence. Once the crowd is excited, they will attack anyone on any pretext whatsoever.

Brutus intended the assassination of Caesar to bring freedom, peace, and a renewal of Rome. By the end of the scene, we have the beginnings of a civil war between the conspirators and Antony's followers. Brutus's sacrifice was ineffective; it did not create a new world. Brutus hoped, illogically, to kill Caesar's spirit by killing his body; through Mark Antony, Caesar's spirit, with Ate at his side, has been unleashed and is wreaking vengeance against his murderers and plunging Rome into chaos.

Review Questions.

1. Where is Caesar killed? Why is this significant?

2. What is Caesar saying as the assassins strike him? To what does he compare himself? What is the point of the comparison?

3. What does Brutus tell the conspirators to do with Caesar's blood? Why? What effect does this have?

4. Why does Brutus decide to let Antony speak at the funeral?

5. Does Brutus make a good decision in allowing Antony to speak? How does this fit with larger themes of the play?

6. What does Antony intend to do?

7. What is Brutus's defense for killing Caesar?

8. How does Antony undermine Brutus's defense without violating his agreement?

9. Explain some of the rhetorical techniques that Antony uses to excite the crowd.

10. What does scene 3 say about the people of Rome? What does it say about the success of the conspiracy?

Thought Questions.

1. Why does Caesar refuse to read Artemidorus's petition? (3.1.1-12). How does this fit with what we have already learned about Caesar's character?

2. In what sense do Brutus and Cassius say they have done Caesar a favor by killing him? (3.1.98-103). Compare this to Caesar's words in 2.2.32-37.

3. How does Cassius expect the conspirators to be remembered? (3.1.116-118).

4. Explain the double meanings that Antony gives to "hart" and "deer" in 3.1.204-210.

5. Who will suffer from Caesar's unleashed spirit? (3.1.259-275). Why?

6. What evidence does Antony offer to refute the charge that Caesar was ambitious? (3.2.80-113). Is it convincing?

7. Caesar first wore the mantle in which he died "on a summer's evening, in his tent, that day he overcame the Nervii" (3.2.176-179). Why does Antony mention this? How does his recollection make his speech more effective? How does the tone of this recollection compare to the tone of the speech as a whole?

8. Whose was the "unkindest cut of all"? (3.2.189). Why?

9. According to Antony, who fell with Caesar's fall? (3.2.195-198). Compare to Cassius's comments in 1.2.258-259.

10. Twice Antony compares Caesar's wounds to mouths (3.1.259-261; 3.2.231-236). What is the point of this comparison? Who puts a tongue in Caesar's wounds?

Lesson Four: Acts 4-5

The longest and most important scene of Act 4 is scene 3, the quarrel scene between Brutus and Cassius (4.3.1-122). Brutus has condemned Lucius Pella for accepting bribes from the people of Sardis but Cassius puts in a good word for Pella, thinking that in a time of war small offenses can be overlooked. In response, Brutus accuses Cassius himself of having an itching palm, that is, of accepting bribes. Honorable Brutus asks, how can those who have killed Caesar for the sake of justice take bribes? If the conspiracy becomes corrupted by greed, the conspirators are no better than Caesar. Brutus also says that he asked for gold from Cassius, which Cassius refused to give.

Cassius reacts like a spurned lover. He is astonished at Brutus's attack and offers to let Brutus kill him. This exchange highlights the two characters' different views of friendship. For Cassius, to be a friend is to overlook faults; in biblical terms, love covers a multitude of sins. For Brutus, however, only a flatterer overlooks faults; a true friend is brutally honest. Like Caesar, Brutus says he hates flattery but is easily flattered. Just as Brutus's sense of honor is too tight to overlook faults in a friend, so it is too rigid to adjust to the realities of fighting a war. He cannot ignore even the slightest offense. The quarrel signals the failure of the conspiracy. Brutus and Cassius killed Caesar to bring peace and liberty to Rome. Not only has the assassination produced civil war, but the conspirators are incapable even of keeping peace among themselves.

As it turns out, Brutus's ill temper has been caused by the news that Portia has killed herself (4.3.145-155). This part of the scene is one of the most puzzling in the play. Brutus tells Cassius that Portia is dead, but later in the same scene Messala repeats the news (4.3.186-187), and Brutus acts as if he did not know. The best explanation is that Brutus at first does not want to discuss Portia's death with Messala. When Messala presses him, and tells him that she is dead, Brutus acts the Stoic. He is playing the part of honorable

Brutus, as Caesar before him played the part of the invincible conqueror. Still, Brutus is strangely calm about his wife's death. His sense of honor not only makes him undiscerning, but makes him inhuman.

The whole scene shows that Brutus has become overbearing, refusing to take advice or listen to anyone else. Despite the failure of every one of his decisions, he takes matters into his own hands and cursorily dismisses Cassius's counsel about Philippi. Cassius wants the army to stay put. "Let the enemy find us," is the essence of his advice. This will wear out the opponents, take up energy and resources, while the conspirators' troops rest and recover. Brutus, by contrast, says that the enemy is growing stronger, and that the people around Philippi will join with Antony and Octavius if the battle does not start soon. Meanwhile, the conspirators are growing weaker. Therefore, they should seek battle before they grow too weak or their enemies too strong. Again, Brutus forces a bad decision on Cassius.

Throughout their quarrel, Brutus treats Cassius with contempt. He is a "slight man" 4.3.37), a "madman" (4.3.40), whose anger is useful only for Brutus's "mirth, yea, for my laughter" (4.3.49). Cassius is amazed at this treatment, and hints that, were Brutus not his friend, he would be tempted to kill him (4.3.12-14). Brutus dismisses the threats as well:

> There is no terror, Cassius, in your threats;
> For I am arm'd so strong in honesty
> That they pass by me as the idle wind
> Which I respect not. (4.3.66-69)

These are words that remind us of nothing so much as Caesar's over-confidence in the opening scenes. Pride such as this, no matter how "honorable," is ripe for a fall.

Brutus misunderstands and miscalculates even on minor issues. In the quarrel scene, Cassius says he is an older soldier, but Brutus misunderstands him as saying he is better. Brutus makes out Cassius's faults to be greater than they are, and makes wrong assessments about Cassius's strength of character. Cassius protests against Brutus's accusations, saying that he never denied Brutus gold. In making strategy for the battle, Brutus speaks some of the most famous lines of the play:

> There is a tide in the affairs of men
> Which taken at the flood leads on to fortune;
> Omitted, all the voyage of their life
> Is bound in shallows and in miseries.
> (4.3.216-219)

This passage expresses the same principle as the proverb, "Strike while the iron is hot." From the mouth of Brutus, the words take on a very different significance. A tide there is indeed, but Brutus consistently fails to "take it at the flood." The little scene where Brutus asks his boy servant Lucius about his lost book underscores this pattern of miscalculation and misplacement (4.3.250-252). Brutus cannot even keep track of his reading material.

During the night before the battle, Caesar's ghost appears to Brutus. Curiously, the ghost introduces himself as Brutus's "evil spirit" (4.3.279). Perhaps this means it is an evil spirit that comes to torment Brutus. Or it could refer to Brutus's own spirit, which has become evil. The phrase is ambiguous, perhaps deliberately so. Part of the meaning seems to be that Brutus has indeed "come by" Caesar's spirit. If Caesar's spirit is Brutus's "evil spirit," then it means Brutus is Caesar's double. Brutus said before the assassination that they had to kill Caesar's body to remove his spirit. But Antony unleashed Caesar's spirit as a spirit of revenge, and here again we learn that the spirit of Caesar is not dead. Caesar dies, but Caesarism continues. Caesarism lives on in Brutus himself.

And not only in Brutus. Octavius has been introduced in 4.1, where, with Antony and Lepidus, he is coldly determining the fate of their political enemies and rivals. When Lepidus leaves, Octavius and Antony discuss Lepidus's fate in the same way. In 5.1, Antony and Octavius quarrel about which flank Octavius will attack. Antony wants Octavius to go to the left but Octavius says he will go right. When Antony objects, Octavius insists that his instructions be followed and Antony capitulates. Octavius, though young, is domineering and strong-willed, insistent on making all the decisions. He is clearly the man in control. Whichever side wins the battle, Caesar's spirit will live on—if not in Brutus, then certainly in Octavius. The play is rightly called _Julius Caesar_, for though Julius is killed halfway through, Caesar dominates, in one form or another, the whole play.

As they prepare for battle, Brutus and Cassius have put their differences behind them and bid farewell in a touching scene (5.1.92-125). Brutus says that the day of the battle "must end that work the ides of March begun" (5.1.113). Brutus means that the battle will decide the outcome of the conspiracy once and for all. For Shakespeare, Brutus's words also mean that Philippi inevitably follows from the assassination of Caesar and the unleashing of Caesar's spirit. Philippi, civil war, blood added to blood—all this is the fruit of the violence planted in the original assassination. Brutus and Cassius are about to reap what they have sown.

Cassius commits suicide in 5.3 in a scene that brings to a brilliant climax the miscalculations that have dominated the play. Cassius has sent Titinius to check out the troops in the valley below the hill where he is resting. Pindarus, acting as Cassius's lookout, tells him that Titinius is captured, so Cassius asks Pindarus to kill him, thinking that he has lost the battle and sent Titinius, his friend, to his death. In fact, Titinius has met friendly troops, and returns ready to tell Cassius that the battle is not going as badly as it seems, and that Brutus is actually defeating Octavius (5.3.51-53). He arrives too late; Cassius is already dead. Titinius blames "hateful error," which, as soon as it is conceived, kills its mother (5.3.66-71). His words to the dead Cassius are an epitaph for the whole conspiracy: "Alas, thou has misconstru'd everything!" (5.3.84).

In the end, Caesar's spirit gets his revenge. Cassius is killed by the same sword that killed Caesar; he lived by the sword, and dies by the very same sword. When Brutus discovers Cassius's body, he comments on the continuing power of Caesar: "O Julius Caesar, thou art mighty yet! Thy spirit walks abroad, and turns our swords in our own proper entrails" (5.3.94-96). Brutus's suicide must be seen in this same light. As he kills himself, he hopes that Caesar's spirit will finally be pacified, that Caesar will have his revenge and go away peacefully, and that Rome can finally enjoy peace and freedom (5.5.50-51). With the hindsight of history, Shakespeare knew this was a vain hope. Brutus can no more kill the spirit of Caesar by killing himself than he could by making Caesar bleed. From his earlier appearances in the play, we already know that Octavius is every inch a Caesar. The spirit of Caesar will definitely live on in the first Roman Emperor.

Julius Caesar does not offer a theological critique of the religion of revolution, the myth of that the world can be remade through violence, but instead enacts a crushing practical refutation. Revolutionary violence does not quell the spirit of tyranny, but unleashes it to take ever more virulent forms; further, those who sacrifice kings for the sake of the general can never fully foresee the consequences of their acts. They are constantly in danger of misconstruing everything, and unleashing forces they cannot control. One might, however, make the same point in more distinctly Christian terms. Biblically, the belief that one can remake the world through terror and bloodshed is a heresy. Its most fundamental error is the belief that there is someone other than the Messiah whose death inaugurates a new age. The most penetrating answer to the religion of revolution is the insistence that there is only one sacrificial Victim whose blood revives and whose unleashed Spirit brings not strife but peace. Only those who trust this sacrifice can have confidence that, whatever their mistakes and errors, they will not, in the end, misconstrue *everything*.

Review Questions.

1. What do Cassius and Brutus quarrel about? What is the significance of this quarrel?

2. How does the quarrel scene reinforce the theme of miscalculation?

3. What is Brutus's view of friendship? What is Cassius's?

4. How does Brutus's sense of honor endanger his side in war?

5. Why is it ironic that Brutus speaks of a "tide in the affairs of men"?

6. Why does Caesar's spirit tell Brutus it is "thy spirit"?

7. What kind of man is Octavius? How does Octavius's character reinforce the larger themes of the play?

8. Why does Cassius kill himself? How does Cassius's death fit with the larger themes of the play?

9. How does Brutus's suicide fit with the theme of Caesar's spirit?

10. How does Shakespeare show the fallacy of believing that violent revolution can bring peace and freedom?

Thought Questions.

1. What do Antony and Octavius think of Lepidus? (4.1.12-40). Why is he given a share in their leadership?

2. According to Brutus, what happens when friendship cools? (4.2.18-27). Whom is he speaking about? From scene 3, whose friendship seems to have cooled?

3. To whom does Cassius compare Brutus during the quarrel scene? (4.3.58). How does this fit with the theme of Caesar's spirit?

4. What does Brutus mean by saying, "We, at the height, are ready to decline"? (4.3.215). Explain how these words have a meaning that Brutus does not intend.

5. What happens during the conference before the battle of Philippi? (5.1.27-66). How does this reflect the plot of the entire play?

6. Why does Cassius tell Messala it is his birthday? (5.1.71; see 5.3.23-25).

7. How has Cassius's view of superstition changed? (5.1.71-88). What omen has Cassius witnessed? (5.1.79-88). What is its significance? How does this fit with the themes of the play?

8. What does Brutus say about Cato's suicide? (5.1.100-106). In the light of the rest of Act 5, how are his words significant?

9. Why has the battle gone poorly for the conspirators? (5.3.5). How does this fit with the larger themes of the play?

10. How does Titinius describe the death of Cassius? (5.3.60-65). Compare this to Caesar's dying words, and to the discussion about the dawning of day in 2.1.101-111.

Video Versions of Julius Caesar

I have viewed two video versions of *Julius Caesar*. The more recent production stars Charlton Heston as Mark Antony and Jason Robards as Brutus. The film is in color, the acting is generally adequate, and the action scenes are credible. The greatest flaw is the casting of Robards as Brutus; Robards's flat Midwestern accent works in westerns but he sounds out of place in a Roman drama; I found myself expecting him to pull a six-shooter from underneath his toga. Since Brutus is the central character of the play, this miscasting detracts a great deal. Still, there is nothing objectionable in the film, and it does present the plot of the play.

Far superior is Joseph L. Mankiewicz's 1953 black and white production starring James Mason as Brutus, Marlon Brando as Mark Antony, and a young John Gielgud as Cassius. (It may be worth watching just to see Gielgud with a full head of hair.) Sets and staging are extremely well done; the Roman streets in 1.1 really are crowded and the mob in the funeral scene really looks like a mob. The acting could hardly be better. Mason is a world-weary, melancholy, contemplative Brutus; though not overpowering, Mason is fine. Gielgud and Brando are positively sizzling. Gielgud is an appropriately intense and jittery Cassius; he does have that lean and hungry look, so much so that the viewer, like Caesar, would be more comfortable if he were fatter. Brando, in his first feature film role, has a sure touch. He conveys the smoldering, subterranean danger essential to an opportunist like Antony. You get the sense that you never know what this Antony is going to do next. This *Julius Caesar* is one of the very best Shakespeare films I reviewed for this book.

Suggested Paper Topics

1. Examine one of the major characters: Brutus, Cassius, Antony, Caesar. What motivates him? What is his view of life, of superstition, of politics? If you do a character study of Brutus, examine how his sense of honor is both his greatest strength and greatest weakness. Or, compare and contrast a pair of characters: Brutus and Caesar, Brutus and Cassius, Brutus and Antony.

2. Discuss the role of various kinds of superstition and divination in the play: Caesar's superstitions, the soothsayer, the role of astronomical portents.

3. Research the life of one of the major characters from sources outside the play. How does Shakespeare's characterization compare to the real man? Is his Caesar anything like the real Caesar? Where did Shakespeare get his information about these historical characters?

4. *Julius Caesar* is dominated by male characters, but two important female characters also appear: Portia and Calpurnia. What is their role in the play? How does their presence affect the tone of a play that is occupied with politics and war?

5. Examine the conspirators' use of religious language: sacrifice, purgation, etc.

6. Examine the role played by the Roman mob. What does Shakespeare's play teach about modern populist politics that appeals directly to the people? What danger would Shakespeare see in the modern welfare state, where some people's living depends on hand-outs from the government?

7. Brutus's sense of honor seems to make him easy to manipulate and leads to many bad decisions. Is Shakespeare

saying that honor is inherently weak in the face of evil? What kind of "honor" does Brutus represent?

8. Discuss the role of rhetoric, of how language is used, especially in the funeral scene. What does the play teach about political propaganda?

9. Make a study of Stoic philosophy. How is Brutus a good Stoic?

10. Revise a scene from Julius Caesar using modern politicians as the chief characters. Who would play Caesar? Brutus? Cassius? In what role would Bill Clinton best fit? Newt Gingrich? Ross Perot?

Section II:

Tragedy

Introduction: Tragedy

The easiest rule of thumb for identifying the genre of a particular play is to look at what happens at the end. At the end of a tragedy, especially a Shakespearean tragedy, the stage is heaped with bloody dead bodies. Useful as this is as a rule of thumb, it is necessary to think in more detail about what makes a drama tragic. The earliest and most influential discussion is that of the ancient Greek philosopher Aristotle. In his *Poetics*, Aristotle stated that the most important aspect of tragedy is the structure of the events that are depicted. A tragedy should arouse fear and pity in the audience by depicting a character moving from a condition of prosperity to one of affliction.

These requirements determine what kinds of stories are, in Aristotle's mind, suitable for tragedy. Some stories, though they may involve a movement from prosperity to affliction, do not qualify as tragic stories. If a good man suffers affliction, the audience is left feeling repulsed by the injustice of it all, rather than feeling fearful and piteous. A story of a wicked man moving from prosperity to affliction is not tragic either; the audience will not pity him but will conclude that he got his just reward. (Shakespeare boldly violated this Aristotelian rule in *Macbeth*, where the protagonist is a usurper, murderer, and ultimately a madman.) Tragedy thus requires a character who is neither simply good nor simply evil, but rather one who falls into affliction because of what Aristotle calls a "certain fallibility." Tragic characters should also be men of some standing, for to make a crash large enough for tragedy a man must fall from a great height. Finally, Aristotle states that the best tragedies are those in which a character acts in ignorance and later discovers, to his horror, that his action is gravely evil.

Sophocles's *Oedipus* is one of Aristotle's chief models. Oedipus falls from his position as king because he kills his father and marries his mother. At the time he commits these wrongs, he does not know he is doing so, and is even ignorant of the prophecy. Only later does he discover what he has done. Sophocles's view of tragedy, approved by Aristotle, is closely linked to the Greek idea of Fate, an impersonal force that determines a man's destiny, so that nothing he does, no amount of care or repentance, affects his future. The Greek tragic hero has no freedom to choose or to avoid his tragic end.

Different as Shakespeare's tragedies are from one another, it is fair to suggest some general ways in which Shakespearean tragedy is distinct from Greek tragedy. In Shakespeare's tragedies the main characters are not merely "fallible" as Oedipus was, but commit sins, acts of moral evil. Nor are they ignorant of what they are doing. Macbeth knows exactly what he is doing when he kills Duncan and one does not hire assassins, as Macbeth does to kill Banquo, by accident; though Hamlet kills Polonius by mistake, he *was* in a murderous rage and did intend to kill. In contrast to Greek tragic characters, Shakespeare's operate in a world where human choice and will makes a difference, where grace is operative, and where the possibility of repentance and redemption is real, even if it is not seized. In this sense, Shakespeare's tragedies are profoundly Christian.

As I explained in the Introduction, the Bible serves as the Christian's "master story," and the Christian can interpret literature by comparing and contrasting it with biblical models. One biblical story type is the "fall story," which corresponds to "tragedy" in dramatic literature. In the following chapters, we will examine two of Shakespeare's major tragedies, *Hamlet* and *Macbeth*, focusing on their character as fall stories. We shall thus be looking for reflections of the characters and events that occur in biblical fall stories: forbidden fruit, temptation, serpents, sin, punishment, Adams and Eves. From this angle, Shakespeare's tragedies can be seen as sobering meditations on the origins and consequences of human sin.

The Serpent Now Wears the Crown:
Hamlet

Hamlet is on nearly everyone's list of the greatest works of English and world literature. The complex character of Hamlet and the play have been endlessly studied not only by students of drama and literature, but also by psychologists and others who seek to understand human behavior. Though it is universally admired, it is a difficult play in many ways, and the difficulties are such that some have concluded that the play lacks unity and coherence.

First, there are textual problems. Editors must work from three early texts that vary widely in length and detail. Even the most complete text that can be constructed from the early editions has glaring gaps and apparent contradictions. Some of these contradictions are rather unimportant. The question of Horatio's nationality, for example, has been raised. In the first scene of the play, it is Horatio who knows all about the political situation of Denmark (1.1.79-108), but later in Act 1, he asks Hamlet about a Danish custom with which he is unfamiliar (1.4.7-38). Is Horatio from Denmark or not? Another minor issue is Hamlet's age. He has recently been a student at Wittenberg, and Laertes and Polonius both warn Ophelia about Hamlet's youth (1.3.10-16; 1.3.124). This leads us to envision a Hamlet in his late teens or twenties. Yet, in the final act we learn that Hamlet is thirty years old (5.1.152-160, 174-175).

Not all of the play's problems are minor. If, for example,

Gertrude's marriage to Claudius was incestuous, why were Hamlet and the ghost the only ones to notice? (see 1.2.157; 1.5.42). Why did no one in the King's Council object to the marriage? What did Gertrude know about Claudius's murder of King Hamlet—and when did she know it? Is Hamlet's madness an act or is it real? And, of course, there is the famed question of the prince's "delay" in taking revenge. None of these questions seem easily or fully resolved at the end of the play.

Though there are unanswered questions and gaps in *Hamlet*, there are also clear signs of careful composition. Shakespeare doubles character types (Gertrude and Ophelia are both characterized by Hamlet as unfaithful women; Hamlet and Ophelia both suffer from madness), and even triples some character types (Hamlet, Laertes, and Fortinbras as vengeful sons; Claudius, Polonius, and King Hamlet as fathers). The parallels between the various characters tie together what might have become a maze of subplots. Another indication of the unity of the play is the appearance of the same or similar characters at important junctures. Dead fathers, for instance, keep turning up: Claudius's first speech is about the death of fathers, then the ghost of King Hamlet appears, and later Hamlet kills Polonius and Claudius. One of the most important unifying characters is Fortinbras, the Prince of Norway, who is mentioned at the beginning of the play, appears briefly but importantly in the middle, and turns up again at the very end to have, literally, the last word. Fortinbras, as we shall see, not only provides structural unity to the play, but underlines some of the major themes. (Unfortunately, some productions of Hamlet leave out all references to Fortinbras, a damaging omission.)

Fortinbras's thematic role in the play is connected to the theme of revenge. *Hamlet* is a revenge tragedy, a common dramatic genre in Shakespeare's day. (See the introduction to "Comedy" for a definition of "genre.") In many cultures, family members consider it a duty to take revenge if a member of their family is shamed, hurt, or killed; we can call this belief the "revenge ethic," since it treats revenge as a moral duty. In Genesis 34, for example, we learn that the sons of Jacob slaughtered every male in the house of Shechem because Shechem had raped their sister, Dinah. Importantly, Jacob condemns their action (Gen. 34:30), and Levi and Simeon are deprived of preeminence among their brothers for their role in this plot of revenge (Gen. 49:5-7). Vengeance is not inherently evil, since God Himself is an Avenger, and civil rulers are called to avenge evil (Rom. 12:19; 13:4). But the Bible forbids private individuals from taking vengeance into their own hands. A revenge tragedy focuses on a character who is called upon to avenge some harm done to a family member. Hamlet is the primary avenger in this play, who is urged to kill Claudius in revenge for his murder of Hamlet's father.

From a study of twenty-one such plays written during the sixteenth and seventeenth centuries, Eleanor Prosser concluded that most of them explicitly condemned revenge. Many students of *Hamlet*, however, have argued that Shakespeare supported the ghost's demand for vengeance. Other critics claim that, while Shakespeare himself rejected the revenge ethic, he was depicting a pre-Christian world, a world in which revenge still reigned supreme; thus, they say, in the context of the play, Hamlet was morally required to take revenge. According to Prosser, the vast majority of students of *Hamlet* simply assume that Hamlet is supposed to follow the ghost's instructions.

The play's rejection of the revenge ethic is so obvious, however, that it is difficult to understand how anyone can miss it. Elizabethan England had its faults, but it was sufficiently Christian to reject the blood feud as savage and pagan, and there is abundant evidence in the play that Shakespeare thoroughly rejected the vengeance. First, there is the overall fact that the various revenge plots all end in utter disaster. At play's end, the stage is littered with the bodies of people who have been violently killed. Unless one believes that Shakespeare simply delighted in gore or was appealing to

Elizabethan bloodlust, his point is obvious: those who live by the violence of revenge will die violently. The last scene's condemnation of revenge is made all the more profound by the way vengeful characters fall victim to their own devices. Laertes is killed by the poisoned sword he planned to use against Hamlet; Gertrude drinks the poisoned cup that Claudius intended for his nephew; Claudius himself is poisoned by both sword and chalice; Hamlet, who has been contemplating revenge throughout the play, falls victim to another avenger. The wicked fall into the very traps they set for others (cf. Ps. 7:15-16). Horatio, who acts as the moral standard of the play, summarizes the action in these words:

> So shall you hear
> Of carnal, bloody, and unnatural acts,
> Of accidental judgments, casual slaughters,
> Of deaths put on by cunning and forc'd cause,
> And, in this upshot, purposes mistook
> Fall'n on th' inventors heads. (5.2.389-393)

Revenge, the play makes clear, never brings resolution. Suppose you avenge your father's murder by killing his murderer. Obviously, the series of killings will not stop there. Your father's murderer has a father or son or brother or cousin. In fact, everyone you kill will have some relative, however distant, ready to avenge a wrong. Thus, every avenger inevitably becomes an object of vengeance; everyone who pursues revenge will eventually find himself being pursued. *Hamlet* is clear and insistent on this point: Revenge simply goes on and on, world without end, and only comes to an end either when everyone renounces revenge or when everyone dies. As the Proverb says, "The beginning of strife is like letting out water, so abandon the quarrel before it breaks out" (17:14).

There are signs not only of structural and thematic unity in the play, but also of repeated imagery that reinforces the structural unity of the play. The interrelated imagery of traps, secrecy, and spying is woven throughout. "Poison in the ear," whether literal poison or the poison of tempting words, is an important theme. Imagery of serpents, venom, and gardens recurs. The opposition of appearance and reality—central to much drama—is represented under the imagery of painting, makeup, and acting, and is related to prostitution. Imagery of disease, rottenness, corruption, and death is also prominent. We shall look at Shakespeare's use of some of these images as we go through the play.

Given these indications of unity, one might say that instead of having "contradictions" and "loose ends," the play is full of "mysteries" that serve the overall thematic purposes of the play. On this interpretation, the difficulties are not so much problems to be solved, but devices Shakespeare used to enrich the play and make it more realistic. Holes give the play its depth. In particular, the unanswered questions about Hamlet's motives and character reinforce one of the major themes of the play—the complexity of human nature. The reasons for Hamlet's "delay," after all, are hidden not only from the reader but from Hamlet himself. Hamlet's soliloquies are full of bewildered self-reproach. Shakespeare certainly did not accept the revenge ethic, but Hamlet does, or at least thinks he should, and he takes everything he sees as a rebuke for his failure to take revenge. When the First Player weeps over the fictional Hecuba, Hamlet wonders why he does not feel as strongly about the death of his real father (2.2.582-640). When Fortinbras risks death in Poland for "an eggshell," Hamlet wonders why he cannot act as decisively in taking vengeance against Claudius (4.4.32-66). Hamlet asks himself questions, but never answers them. It is not only readers who cannot understand Hamlet; Hamlet doesn't understand himself.

As Cedric Watts explains it, Shakespeare deliberately avoided providing answers so as to "generate the sense of a deep, inaccessible region in Hamlet's nature." Watts adds that we should not assume "that if a character asks a big question about his own nature, the text is obliged to supply the answer." Instead, "the function of such a question may be to draw attention to the absence of an accessible answer." Hamlet drives home a similar point in the pipe-playing scene with those two irritating spies, Rosencrantz and Guildenstern. When Guildenstern protests that he cannot play the pipe, Hamlet rages:

> You would play upon me; you would seem to know my stops; you would pluck out the heart of my mystery; you would sound me from my lowest note to the top of my compass; and there is much music, excellent voice, in this little organ; yet cannot you make it speak. 'Sblood, do you think I am easier to be played on than a pipe? (3.2.383-90)

According to the Bible, God's mind and ways are impossible for man to understand completely. Since man is made in the image of this God, men and women have profound depths that we will never fully grasp. We not only can never completely know God; we can never completely know ourselves, never completely unravel our tangled motives and desires, never fathom the depth of our own sin. Today, many believe that science will eventually explain everything, including human behavior and thought. In an age dominated by this scientific idolatry, *Hamlet* is a healthy reminder that people are not machines, that there is a mysterious complexity to human nature. *Hamlet* is not only a dramatic exploration of the evils of the revenge ethic, but also a profound meditation on the nature of man.

Lesson One: Act 1

Hamlet opens with a scene on the battlements of Elsinore that sets out the political context for the play. Denmark is, at the outset, literally a nation under siege, a nation preparing for war. Extra guards are on duty, we learn, because Fortinbras, the young prince of Norway, has threatened to invade Denmark. After the ghost appears, Horatio explains the military and political situation:

> Our last king,
> Whose image even but now appear'd to us,
> Was, as you know, by Fortinbras of Norway,
> Thereto prick'd on by a most emulate pride,
> Dar'd to the combat, in which our valiant Hamlet—
> For so this side of our known world esteem'd him—
> Did slay this Fortinbras; who by a seal'd compact,
> Well ratified by law and heraldry,
> Did forfeit, with his life, all those his lands
> Which he stood seiz'd of, to the conqueror; . . .
> Now, sir, young Fortinbras,
> Of unimproved metal hot and full,
> Hath in the skirts of Norway here and there
> Shark'd up a list of lawless resolutes,
> For food and diet, to some enterprise
> That hath a stomach in 't. Which is no other—
> As it doth well appear unto our state—
> But to recover of us, by strong hand
> And terms compulsatory, those foresaid lands
> So by his father lost. (1.1.80-89, 95-104)

Fortinbras wants revenge for King Hamlet's killing of his father, and seeks to recover the lands his father lost to Denmark. Fortinbras is the first of several vengeful sons in the play, and, being the first, he acts as a model for the others.

The political threat from Norway shapes Horatio's interpretation of the ghost's appearance. He says that the ghost "bodes some strange eruption to our state" (1.1.69), and asks if it is "privy to thy country's fate" (1.1.133). Horatio's fears are more specific. He reminds Bernardo and Marcellus that before Julius Caesar was killed, "the graves stood tenantless, and the sheeted dead did squeak and gibber in the Roman streets" (1.1.115-116). The opening of the graves and appearance of spirits foretell not only disruption of the stability of Denmark, but more specifically the death of some prominent leader. Another Caesar, Horatio surmises, is about to fall to another Brutus.

If Denmark's political situation is threatening, Claudius hardly seems to notice it. He seems entirely unmoved by the death of King Hamlet, explaining that "discretion fought with nature" and therefore he has overcome his grief at the death of his brother (1.2.5). He maintains a balance of sorrow and wisdom, following Aristotle's view that virtue is always a "golden mean," a middle way between too much of something and too little. He dismisses the death of Denmark's king in 16 lines, and immediately moves on to something else. He seems equally calm in the face of the threat of Fortinbras. Unlike Henry V, Claudius is not one to spend sleepless nights agonizing on the burdens and dilemmas of kingship.

It is not clear whether Claudius is extremely confident and competent or if he is simply indifferent to his country's peril, more interested in his own pleasure than in protecting his subjects. Evidence for the latter interpretation is found toward the end of scene 2, when Claudius dismisses the council with the promise that he will drink later on; he says that when he drains his cup, the cannons will sound and the heavens will echo with the report of his prowess in drink (1.2.125-128; see 1.4.7-22). Claudius moves through the council's business so speedily because he can't wait to party. In this, he is ironically contrasted with the ghost of the former King Hamlet, which appears on the battlements in armor. The ghost is more prepared for battle than the current king, whose only connection with military matters is his demand that cannons be sounded when he drains a glass of Rhine wine.

Claudius deals with three young men in his opening speech: Fortinbras, Laertes, and Hamlet. We know from the first scene that Fortinbras is seeking vengeance, and the fact that he is linked with Laertes and Hamlet hints at what lies in the future for the other two. Through the play, Laertes and Hamlet will become like Fortinbras, as both seek to avenge their fathers. It is also significant that each of these young men is discussed in relation to a father: Fortinbras wants to recover lands lost by his father to King Hamlet, and Laertes requests permission to return to France with the blessing of his father. Hamlet's situation is defined in relation to two fathers: his dead father the king and his adoptive father Claudius.

The significance of fathers is brought out in Claudius's speech on the death of fathers. Gertrude and then Claudius try to rouse Hamlet from his mourning by reminding him of the commonness of death (1.2.72-73, 87-117). Everyone must die, Gertrude says; the theme of reason is the death of fathers, Claudius agrees. While it is appropriate to give proper mourning to the dead, ultimately one must accept death and get on with life. Claudius's talk of the death of fathers is significant on several levels. First, it is ironic that Claudius should call himself father to Hamlet in the same speech that he emphasizes the necessity for fathers to die. Moreover, as noted in the introduction above, several dead fathers appear in the play. Fathers embody the past, and the death of fathers has to do with the death of the past; Claudius says in effect, "You have to put the past behind you and move on." It will shortly become clear that putting aside one's past is not so easy. Fathers leave behind unfinished business that sons must take up. Dead fathers have a habit of turning up to haunt their children.

In a helpful book called *What Happens in Hamlet*, John Dover Wilson argues that we cannot understand *Hamlet* without recognizing that Claudius is a usurper, who seized the throne that should rightly have passed from King Hamlet to his son. Hamlet clearly considers Claudius a usurper, telling his mother that Claudius is not only a "murderer and a villain" but that he "from a shelf the precious diadem stole and put it in his pocket" (3.4.95, 98-99). Later he tells Horatio that Claudius "kill'd my king and whor'd my mother, popp'd in between th' election and my hopes" (5.2.64-65), his hopes being aspirations to succeed his father as king.

Claudius, for his part, knows that he is a usurper, and this explains why he is so pleased that Hamlet is planning to stay in Denmark, rather than return to the university at

Wittenberg (1.2.112-121). Claudius does not want Hamlet to stay in Denmark because of his affection for his adopted son; he clearly prefers Laertes to Hamlet (1.2.43-49). Rather, Claudius fears that Hamlet will try to take the crown, and therefore wants him to stay at Elsinore so he can keep an eye on him. If he lets Hamlet return to Germany, the prince might be tempted to raise an army and seize the throne that is rightfully his. This is also the background to Claudius's continual attempts to spy on Hamlet. Norway scarcely enters Claudius's mind; the only threat he is conscious of comes from his nephew and son.

In speaking of Fortinbras, Claudius suggests that the young Norwegian prince is trying to take advantage of the death of King Hamlet. Fortinbras, Claudius says, holds

> a weak supposal of our worth,
> Or thinking by our late dear brother's death
> Our state to be disjoint and out of frame. (1.2.18-20)

Claudius's whole demeanor rests on his assumption that in fact Denmark is not "disjoint and out of frame" but strong and secure. He feels safe to spend his time drinking rather than defending the battlements of Elsinore.

Hamlet senses that, on the contrary, "something is rotten in the state of Denmark" (1.4.90), that the "time is out of joint" (1.5.189). Hamlet's first words to his mother include reflections on the relationship of appearance and reality, of what "is" and what "seems." His mother suggests that he "seems" sad, but Hamlet insists that he is not pretending to be sad so that others will pity him. Nor is he making a mere show of his grief at his father's death. In fact, the outward trappings of sadness—his black mourner's clothing, the sad expression on his face—are nothing compared to the depths of pain and sorrow he feels. He is not merely acting a part. The contrast of appearance and reality is basic to much of Shakespeare's poetry and drama, but Hamlet's speech gives an important twist to this common theme. Normally,

appearance is treated as a kind of disguise of reality. That is
how Hamlet takes his mother's use of the word "seems."
Hamlet, however, suggests that his outward appearance is an
accurate expression of his inner state of mind. His appearance is not false, merely limited; in his heart there is a surplus
of sadness that even the suits and trappings of woe cannot express.

Hamlet's consciousness of a possible contrast between
what "is" and what "seems," his consciousness that there are
"actions that a man might play" implicitly challenges the Danish
court. Hamlet is surrounded by an appearance of stability, a show of uprightness, safety, and joy. Claudius is keen
to make it seem that things are under control and that there
is no danger to Denmark that cannot be handled. Hamlet's
mere presence at the court (like the ghost's appearance on
the battlements) is a sign that things are not as fine as everyone pretends they are. Hamlet's presence as a mourner is a
sign that, contrary to Claudius's evaluation, Denmark is disjointed and out of frame. Unlike the other members of the
court, Hamlet probes beneath the appearance and unveils the
uncomfortable and horrible realities beneath. There is something going on at Elsinore that "passes show."

Hamlet's soliloquy (1.2.129-158) provides a direct
glimpse of his anguish. He is suffering from grief and depres-
sion, but not for the reasons that we might suspect. He has indeed been denied his hopes of succeeding his father, but
what makes the world "weary, stale, flat, and unprofitable"
(1.2.133) is not his thwarted ambition but rather the moral
outrage committed by his mother. At this point, he does not
know the entire story behind his father's death and his
mother's marriage to Claudius, but what he does know has
nearly crippled him emotionally. Gertrude married with
"most wicked speed" (1.2.156), only two months after her
husband's death, and she married her former brother-in-law,
a marriage that Shakespeare's audience, like Hamlet, would
understand as incestuous, forbidden by the Church.

His mother's actions have not only destroyed Hamlet's
confidence in love and in women, but they have left him

feeling defiled. He feels that somehow, as Gertrude's son, he participates in her sin. It seems too much to bear. But he will shortly find that he will have to bear much more before all is said and done. Significantly, he describes the world as an "unweeded garden" overtaken by weeds and thorns (1.2.135-37). Not only Hamlet, but the whole of Denmark is defiled by Gertrude's impatience, her wicked speed. Denmark is no longer an Eden of innocence and joy; it has become a fallen world full of disappointment, frustration, and pain—a world of thorns and thistles.

Horatio interrupts Hamlet with news of the ghost, the other sign that the "seeming" stability of the kingdom is not real. When he learns that his father's ghost has been haunting Elsinore, Hamlet states that "foul deeds will rise, though all the earth o'erwhelm them, to men's eyes" (1.2.256-257). This is the function of all ghosts in Shakespeare: they serve as reminders that crimes and sins cannot be kept hidden forever; at some point everything hidden will be revealed. More generally, ghosts reveal that all human actions, whether for good or ill, have an irreversible effect on the world. The effects of sin cannot be avoided forever, but will come back to "haunt" the sinner. Past sins may be forgiven, but they still place irreversible burdens on the present. Neither fathers nor their deeds are ever entirely dead.

One of the key questions for the interpretation of *Hamlet* is the nature of the ghost. The question of whether the ghost is real is secondary, and the answer fairly evident. A ghost witnessed by several members of the night watch, by the skeptical Horatio, and by Hamlet himself is as real as a ghost can be. The more important question is, where does the ghost come from (1.4.39-57; 1.5.3-5, 9-23, 58-59)? The late scholar Northrup Frye says, "if purgatory is a place of purification, why does a ghost come from it shrieking for vengeance? And why does purgatory, as the Ghost describes it, sound so much as though it were hell? The Ghost's credentials are very doubtful." Hamlet will later learn that the ghost was telling the truth about his father's death, but even this does not necessarily mean that the ghost is a messenger of heaven. Satan tempted by telling Eve some things that turned out to be true (Gen. 3:1-6), and Shakespeare has Banquo tell Macbeth that demons often tell us the truth in trifles only to betray us in more important matters. The evidence is weighted toward the view that the ghost is a tempter. This is made more certain by the whole structure of the play, which, as we have seen, condemns the revenge ethic in no uncertain terms, and in condemning revenge the play condemns the ghost.

If this is not King Hamlet's ghost, at least he has a lot of information about the King's death (1.5.25-39, 59-79). He describes it, to Hamlet's surprise, as "murder," and Shakespeare cleverly emphasizes the point by repeating the word "murder" three times in succession: "Murder"—"Murder"—"Murder" (1.5.25-27). The story had been published that the king was stung by a "serpent" while sleeping in an "orchard." In reality, the ghost tells Hamlet, he died when his brother poured poison in his ear, which curdled King Hamlet's blood and hardened his skin like a leper's. The serpent who killed King Hamlet now wears the crown.

The ghost's description echoes and reechoes with biblical allusions. Claudius is a Cain, who killed his brother Abel (Gen. 4:1-8). Being killed by a "serpent" in an orchard, moreover, is like falling to temptation in a garden. Claudius's murder of Hamlet is like another attack on Adam, the original human ruler of the world, with Claudius playing the role of Satan. Even Claudius's weapon—poison in the ear—reminds us of Satan, whose poisonous lie ("You shall be as gods") killed Adam and Eve. Ironically, at the very moment that the ghost is telling Hamlet how the King was killed, he is also giving Hamlet instructions to carry out revenge; even while the ghost tells how he died from poison in the ear, he is pouring poisonous temptation in Hamlet's ear. The ghost explains that Claudius was an adulterer who seduced Gertrude while King Hamlet was still living (1.5.42-57).

That Claudius seduced the king's bride adds to the satanic imagery that masses around Claudius like moss on a rotting tree, since Paul compares the serpent's temptation of Eve to seduction to adultery (2 Cor. 11:1-3).

Now Hamlet understands why Denmark has turned into an "unweeded garden." He knows why "time is out of joint." For Claudius is not only a serpent but an Adam. Like the sin of Adam, the sin of Claudius leaves Denmark under a curse. It is built upon a seething bed of quicksand because of the sin of its head. News of his mother's adultery and father's murder strikes like a thunderbolt over a Hamlet already suffering from excessive grief. On the surface, Hamlet seems eager to accept his task to set right the time that is out of joint. He says that he "with wings as swift as meditation or the thoughts of love may sweep to my revenge" (1.5.29-31). But the image hardly fits the task: what do meditation and thoughts of love have to do with revenge? His response to the ghost's instructions is less a matter of readiness to sweep to revenge than disorientation, confusion, and mental instability. After his encounter with the ghost, Hamlet speaks, as Horatio observes, with "wild and whirling words" (1.5.133). Hamlet tells Horatio and Marcellus that he is going to put on an "antic disposition" (1.5.172), that he is going to pretend to be mad. As the play proceeds, we will have occasion to wonder whether Hamlet is acting the part or if he has really lost mental balance. Is his "antic disposition" an action that a man might play, or is there something of madness in Hamlet that passes show?

Hamlet's dismay and confusion at the ghost's instructions are points in his favor. We certainly sympathize with his response more than if he had sped to his revenge with an energy that verges on glee, as Laertes later will do. We warm to Hamlet because he is a man divided. In his mind, he believes he ought to take vengeance, that he owes it to the memory of his father. Something within keeps stopping him. He has been tempted to set things right through violent revenge. Now, he must decide whether he will fall to temptation or resist it, whether he will rashly take things into his own hands or wait patiently on the Lord's vengeance, whether he will act as the First Adam or as the Last.

Review Questions.

1. What are some of the problems in *Hamlet*?

2. Discuss several ways in which Shakespeare unified the play.

3. What does Shakespeare think of revenge? How do you know?

4. What view of human nature does the play assume and depict?

5. Who is Fortinbras? How does he fit with the overall themes of the play? What is significant about the way Claudius links Fortinbras with Laertes and Hamlet?

6. What kind of character is Claudius? Claudius says that Fortinbras thinks "by our late dear brother's death our state to be disjoint and out of frame" (1.2.19-20). How is this ironic? What would Hamlet think of this statement?

7. Does Claudius perceive any threat to his kingdom? From whom?

8. What is Hamlet's state of mind at the beginning of the play? Why? How does he describe his feelings about the world?

9. Where did the ghost come from?

10. How was King Hamlet killed? What imagery does the ghost use to describe his death? Why is this significant?

Thought Questions.

1. How is the ghost dressed when Horatio sees him? (1.1.59-64). Why is this important?

2. Does Horatio expect to see a ghost? (1.1.23-29). What does this say about his view of the world? (see 1.5.166-167).

3. Claudius is constantly talking about drinking. What does this say about Claudius? Why is his drinking accompanied by cannon fire? (1.2.125-128).

4. How does Claudius compare to Hamlet's father? (1.2.139-156). Is Hamlet's description of his father accurate? Does it reflect his real feelings about his father?

5. Laertes warns Ophelia not to spend too much time with Hamlet. Why? (1.3.10-44).

6. What kind of character is Polonius? (1.3.54-81).

7. Explain the various uses of the word "tender" in Polonius's advice to Ophelia (1.3.99-109).

8. While Horatio and Hamlet wait for the appearance of the ghost, they observe and discuss the drinking customs of Denmark (1.4.13-38). What does this discussion have to do with the scene? How does it fit within the play in general?

9. What does Horatio fear will happen to Hamlet if he follows the ghost? (1.4.69-78). Why is this ironic?

10. Whom does Hamlet call "this fellow in the cellarage" and "old mole"? (1.5.144-162). Why do you think Hamlet speaks this way?

Lesson 2: Act 2

As Act 2 opens, Polonius is giving instructions to his servant Reynaldo before the latter leaves for France to deliver money and letters to Polonius's son, Laertes. Reynaldo's more important task, however, will be to spy on Laertes, and Polonius gives elaborate instructions about proper spying. He summarizes his advice in this way:

> Your bait of falsehood takes this carp of truth.
> And thus do we of wisdom and of reach,
> With windlasses and with assays of bias,
> By indirections find directions out. (2.1.63-66)

Instead of directly asking Laertes what he is doing, Polonius wants Reynaldo to discover by more round-about and indirect methods, by spying and strategic deceptions.

This opening scene thus introduces the theme of spying that will occupy much of this act and the next, as the main characters act on Polonius's advice. First Polonius and then Rosencrantz and Guildenstern pry into Hamlet; Claudius arranges for Ophelia to meet with Hamlet while the king and Polonius eavesdrop behind a curtain; finally, Gertrude invites Hamlet to her chamber while Polonius listens from behind the arras. For his part, Hamlet uses the players who visit Elsinore to set a trap to confirm that Claudius killed his father. Spying is related to acting and masks, which also form part of the imagery of this act. Claudius spies on Hamlet to penetrate behind the mask of madness to its cause, while Hamlet wants to tear away Claudius's mask of innocence and expose the villain behind the smile.

Constant spying has two results. First, those who are enlisted as spies, as tools, are crushed. Polonius, Rosencrantz, and Guildenstern are all killed as a direct result of their mediation between Hamlet and Claudius. Gertrude and Ophelia also die, as does Laertes, all indirectly because they agreed to spy on Claudius's behalf. Hamlet coldly comments on the deaths of Rosencrantz and Guildenstern, which he arranged:

> They are not near my conscience; their defeat
> Does by their own insinuation grow.
> 'Tis dangerous when the baser nature comes
> Between the pass and fell incensed points
> Of mighty opposites. (5.2.58-62)

Hamlet and Claudius are the two mighty opposites, and the references to "pass and fell" and "incensed points" are to the sport of fencing. The spying of Claudius on Hamlet and Hamlet on Claudius is an elaborate fencing match. After several scenes of give and take, of "fencing" between the mighty opposites, the play climaxes appropriately with a literal fencing match between Hamlet and Claudius's agent, Laertes. Just as it is dangerous to step between two skilled fencers, so those who interfere with the fencing of Claudius and Hamlet risk, and frequently lose, their lives.

Spies, secondly, become an extension of the one who enlists them. Claudius uses Polonius, Rosencrantz, and

Guildenstern as his eyes, and as they allow themselves to be used by Claudius, they become more and more like him. Hamlet calls Rosencrantz a "sponge" who "soaks up the king's countenance, his rewards, his authorities" (4.2.17-18). By their cooperation with the serpent who wears the crown, these agents become adders in their own right (3.4.201-202).

Act 2, scene 2 is extremely long. It may be outlined in a series of sub-scenes, as follows:

> · Claudius and Gertrude enlist Rosencrantz
>> and Guildenstern to spy on Hamlet.
>> · Polonius announces he will explain
>>> Hamlet's madness.
>>>> · The ambassadors return from Norway.
>>> · Polonius explains Hamlet's madness.
>> · Polonius, Rosencrantz and Guildenstern
>>> spy on Hamlet.
>
> · The Players arrive

This structure circles around the theme of Claudius's setting traps and spying on Hamlet, but ends with the arrival of a group of actors whom Hamlet will use to trap Claudius.

In the center of this structure, however, is news from the embassy to Norway. Voltimand tells Claudius that Fortinbras's uncle, the acting king of Norway, has suppressed

> His nephew's levies, which to him appear'd
> To be a preparation 'gainst the Polack,
> But better look'd into, he truly found
> It was against your highness; whereat griev'd,
> That so his sickness, age, and impotence
> Was falsely borne in hand, sends out arrests
> On Fortinbras, which he, in brief, obeys,
> Receives rebuke from Norway, and in fine
> Makes vow before his uncle never more
> To give th' assay of arms against your majesty. (2.2.62-71)

This is extremely significant: The first vengeful son to be introduced in the play has decided against vengeance. Given the link between Fortinbras and Hamlet established early in the play, Fortinbras's decision to forego revenge invites the question, Will Hamlet follow his lead?

The answer appears to be negative: Later, Hamlet, on his way to England under the guard of Rosencrantz and Guildenstern, meets Fortinbras's army as it marches through Denmark on its way to attack Poland. Hamlet ponders his own inaction in the light of Norway's willingness to expose "what is mortal and unsure to all that fortune, death, and danger dare, even for an eggshell" such as Poland (4.4.51-53). Hamlet concludes that his own "dull revenge" contrasts poorly with Fortinbras's "spirit with divine ambition puff'd" (4.4.33, 49). (Note in passing that Hamlet is chiding himself for lacking Fortinbras's ambition, another indication that his failure to receive his father's throne irritates him.) This seems precisely the wrong lesson to draw from Fortinbras's actions. Instead, Hamlet should have recognized that Fortinbras was breaking off plans to avenge his father's death and recover his father's lands, and Hamlet should have followed that example.

This is not to say that Fortinbras is a moral example in any general way. He does not renounce the violent life of an opportunistic soldier. When Hamlet runs across his army, Fortinbras is planning to risk the lives of thousands of his countrymen on a pointless invasion. Fortinbras does seem to act on the principle that Hamlet enunciates: To be great means to "find quarrel in a straw when honor's at the stake" (4.4.55-56). Fortinbras is, as Horatio puts it, a hot-headed and quarrelsome adventurer, just looking for a fight. Yet, in a specific way he challenges Hamlet's desire for revenge by bowing to his uncle's wishes and leaving off his plan to invade Denmark.

Voltimand's report on his mission to Norway interrupts a discussion concerning Hamlet's madness. Fortinbras presented an external threat to the safety and stability of Denmark, while Hamlet's madness presents an internal threat. As we have seen, the political dimensions of Claudius's concern for Hamlet should not be ignored; Claudius suffers the fear shared by all usurpers. But there is another political implication of Hamlet's madness. If a commoner goes mad, few people are hurt; if, on the other hand, a high official, such as the crown prince, is mad, the whole nation is threatened. Hamlet is such an interesting character that we often forget that he is a prince. But the characters in the play do not forget. Laertes reminds Ophelia that Hamlet cannot simply marry whomever he pleases, but rather his choice is "circumscrib'd unto the voice and yielding of that body whereof he is the head." Hamlet can never forget that "on his choice depends the safety and health of the whole state." Hamlet's will, by contrast with a commoner's, is "not his own" (1.3.17, 20-24). Rosencrantz puts the matter vividly:

> The cease of majesty
> Dies not alone, but like a gulf doth draw
> What's near it with it. It is a massy wheel,
> Fix'd on the summit of the highest mount,
> To whose huge spokes ten thousand lesser things
> Are mortis'd and adjoin'd; which, when it falls,
> Each small annexment, petty consequence,
> Attends the boist'rous ruin. Never alone
> Did the king sigh, but with a general groan. (3.3.15-23)

Princes never suffer but the nation suffers as well. Claudius's concern for Hamlet's madness recognizes Hamlet's station as prince: "Madness in great ones must not unwatch'd go" (3.1.197).

Every major character at court has a theory to explain Hamlet's madness, his sudden change in dress and behavior (see 2.1.77-100). Polonius is convinced that Hamlet is love-sick for Ophelia, who, following her father's instructions, has rejected Hamlet's advances. He proposes to test his theory by spying on a meeting between Hamlet and Ophelia. Polonius is so certain he is right that he says

Claudius can cut off his head if he is wrong (2.2.156). Polonius is wrong; and, though he does not lose his head, he loses his life. Gertrude believes that Hamlet is upset about his father's death and her hasty marriage. Claudius at this point does not suspect that Hamlet knows he murdered the king, but believes Hamlet is mad, or pretending to be, because he has been denied the crown, and thus Claudius fears Hamlet might try to overthrow him.

Hamlet's goal in the verbal fencing with Polonius, Rosencrantz, and Guildenstern is to distract and confuse everyone by confirming everyone's pet theory about the causes of his madness. In this way, Hamlet keeps anyone from suspecting the true cause of his madness—his knowledge of his father's murder and his struggle with the ghost's demand for revenge. Thus, he speaks to Polonius about his daughter, calling Polonius "Jephthah" (2.2.436-438), the Biblical Judge who took a vow to devote his only daughter to the Lord (Jud. 11). Polonius takes this as confirmation of his theory that Hamlet is still obsessed with Ophelia.

Rosencrantz and Guildenstern, Hamlet's schoolmates, share Claudius's theory that Hamlet suffers because of his thwarted ambition. Hamlet begins his conversation with them by calling Denmark a prison (2.2.250); indeed, Denmark is a prison to Hamlet, aware as he is of Claudius's surveillance of his every move. Rosencrantz assumes, however, that Hamlet thinks of Denmark as a prison because he has been blocked from inheriting his father's crown (2.2.259). Later, Hamlet adds fuel to the fire by saying that he grieves because he "lacks advancement," and quoting a proverb that hints vaguely at his frustration at not being able to feed on the grass that is due to him (3.2.356-361). No doubt, Polonius returned to Claudius to report that Hamlet's madness was certainly a result of his thwarted love for Ophelia, while Rosencrantz and Guildenstern reported that Hamlet's madness was certainly a result of his thwarted ambition for the crown. Hamlet acts his various parts skillfully, donning a variety of masks to keep everyone off balance, so that no one will be able to look carefully at his face.

While an overall purpose is discernible in Hamlet's actions, when we look in detail at his conversations with Polonius, Rosencrantz, and Guildenstern, his words seem designed to confuse readers as well as the characters in the play. A full examination of these exchanges would be far too long for this book. Instead, let us look closely at two sections of scene 2.

When Polonius first encounters Hamlet, they have the following odd conversation:

> *Polonius:* Do you know me, my lord?
> *Hamlet:* Excellent well; you are a fishmonger.
> *Polonius:* Not I, my lord.
> *Hamlet:* Then I would you were so honest a man.
> *Polonius:* Honest, my lord!
> *Hamlet:* Aye, sir. To be honest, as this world goes, is to be one man picked out of ten thousand.
> *Polonius:* That's very true, my lord.
> *Hamlet:* For if the sun breed maggots in a dead dog, being a god kissing carrion—Have you a daughter?
> *Polonius:* I have, my lord.
> *Hamlet:* Let her not walk i' the sun. Conception is a blessing, but as your daughter may conceive—friend, look to 't.
> *Polonius* (aside): How say you by that? Still harping on my daughter. Yet he knew me not at first; he said I was a fishmonger. He is far gone; and truly in my youth I suffered much extremity for love—very near this. (2.2.173-192)

Several things are going on here. First, Hamlet is playing with Polonius. It is clear here that Hamlet is putting on his "antic disposition" and not really suffering from delusions; he is acting a part. He calls Polonius a fishmonger, though he knows it is Polonius. When he goes on to speak in derogatory terms about the appearance of old men (2.2.199-207), he is directing his attack at Polonius himself. Polonius, however, seems completely taken in by Hamlet's act. He believes Hamlet really did mistake him for a fishmonger. Polonius, finally, is so convinced that Hamlet is lovesick that everything he sees confirms it. Hamlet gives him reason to believe he is distraught over Ophelia, and Polonius admits that he acted like Hamlet when he experienced youthful love—which makes me happy I wasn't around when Polonius was in love.

Even the dense Polonius, however, recognizes that "Though this be madness, yet there is method in 't" (2.2.208-209). Hamlet is pretending to speak nonsense but his whirling words reveal as well as conceal his meaning. He calls Polonius a "fishmonger," which in Shakespeare's day could refer to a man who manages a house of prostitutes, what in today's slang is called a "pimp." A fishmonger is someone who profits from the sexual infidelities of his girls. Hamlet evidently knows that Polonius plans to "loose" Ophelia on Hamlet, to use her to spy on her former lover. By calling Polonius a fishmonger, Hamlet implies that, like a "fishmonger," Polonius is profiting from his daughter's faithlessness.

Honesty is closely related to faithfulness, and Hamlet has learned from his mother's conduct and from Ophelia's rejection of him that honesty is a precious commodity among humans: less than one man (or woman) in ten thousand are honest. In line 181, Hamlet begins with "For if," which suggests that this statement is a continuation of his earlier statements about honesty. But what does the sun breeding maggots from carrion have to do with honesty? The image is made more difficult by the fact that Hamlet never finishes the sentence he begins in line 181, but breaks off to ask Polonius about his daughter. The meaning seems to be this: "Carrion" refers to what the Bible calls "flesh" or "sinful nature." There is a play on the word "sun," which already in 1.2.67 Hamlet linked with "son." Thus, if the sun, which is (in Hamlet's image) a god, breeds maggots from dead dogs, what will a "son" breed from sinful flesh? Certainly not honest men! The point is brought back to Ophelia in lines 182-183 and 185-187. Hamlet is warning Polonius that it is dangerous for him to play the fishmonger with Ophelia. If Ophelia is used to spy on Hamlet, the "son" of Denmark, what will the product be? If Polonius prostitutes his daughter by "loosing" her on Hamlet, the results may be disastrous. The result may be the breeding of something worse than maggots.

Our second example comes from the obscure comment with which Hamlet closes his conversation with Rosencrantz and Guildenstern:

> *Hamlet:* But my uncle-father and aunt-mother are deceived.
> *Guildenstern:* In what, my dear lord?
> *Hamlet:* I am but mad north-northwest. When the wind is southerly, I know a hawk from a handsaw. (2.2.400-405)

Students of the play have suggested that "handsaw" may be a corruption of "hearnshaw," a kind of heron. This may be part of Hamlet's meaning: he knows the difference between a bird of prey (hawk) and a harmless heron. In effect, he is saying that he knows that Rosencrantz and Guildenstern, far from being the supportive friends they pretend to be, are really preying on him; they are hawks, not hearnshaws. It is possible, however, that Shakespeare deliberately compared two incompatible things: a bird and a tool. In that case, Hamlet's point is that he knows not only that they are preying on him, but also discerns that they are tools, and he knows which carpenter is wielding them.

In the course of Hamlet's conversation with Rosencrantz and Guildenstern, Rosencrantz announces the arrival of a troupe of traveling actors. When the players arrive at Elsinore, Hamlet requests the first player to recite a favorite speech about Pyrrhus, the son of Achilles. Pyrrhus fits perfectly in *Hamlet*; like Fortinbras and Hamlet, Pyrrhus sought to avenge the death of his father. The First Player's speech details Pyrrhus's gory killing of King Priam of Troy. Deeply engrossed with the sins of his mother, Hamlet particularly asks the player to recite the description of the grief of Hecuba, queen of Troy, after seeing her husband hacked to death by the vengeful Pyrrhus (2.2.462-548). Not only does

Pyrrhus take vengeance for Achilles's death, but the First Player's speech emphasizes his hesitation before delivering the fatal blow (2.2.507-512). It will become apparent especially in the next act that Hamlet too hesitates to avenge his father, though much longer than Pyrrhus. Hamlet takes the speech as a rebuke, considering the monstrous fact that the Player feels more strongly about Hecuba than Hamlet feels about his own father.

The appearance of the actors, and Hamlet's soliloquy, neatly close out an act concerned with playing roles, spying, and traps. Not only do the actors reinforce the themes of appearance and reality, acting, and role-playing, but Hamlet closes Act 2 by speaking of his conclusion that "the play's the thing wherein I'll catch the conscience of the king" (2.2.639-640). He plans to shape the play, "The Murder of Gonzago," so that it will be understood as "The Murder of Hamlet by Claudius." By watching Claudius's reaction, Hamlet will be able to confirm the ghost's report. Using the play, he will determine if in fact it is a serpent that wears the crown.

Review Questions.

1. Why does Act 2 open with Polonius's instructions to Reynaldo?

2. Discuss how the theme of spying and setting traps develops in the play. What are the results of spying?

3. What does Voltimand report about his trip to Norway? What has young Fortinbras decided to do? Why is this important?

4. What does Polonius think is the cause of Hamlet's madness?

5. What does Claudius think about Hamlet's madness?

6. How does Hamlet confirm everyone's suspicions at once? Why does he do this?

7. Explain one of the exchanges between Hamlet and Polonius or Hamlet and Rosencrantz and Guildenstern.

8. What does Hamlet ask the First Player to recite? Why?

9. How does Hamlet react to the First Player's recitation?

10. How does Hamlet hope to "catch the conscience of the king"?

Thought Questions.

1. How does Polonius suggest that Reynaldo learn about Laertes? (2.1.1-73).

2. How did Hamlet look when he visited Ophelia? (2.1.77-83). Why does he appear this way? How is the imagery of clothing used in this scene?

3. What reaction does Hamlet have to Ophelia? (2.1.87-100). Why does he act this way?

4. How are the beginnings of scenes 1 and 2 similar to each other?

5. Explain the conversation between Hamlet and Rosencrantz and Guildenstern about Fortune (2.2.234-241). How does this conversation fit with other themes of the play— e.g., fortune, faithfulness, prostitution?

6. Hamlet says that he is plagued by bad dreams (2.2.263). What do Rosencrantz and Guildenstern make of this comment? How is Hamlet's comment related to Claudius's statement in 2.2.9-10?

7. How does Hamlet describe man in 2.2.321-329? Why does neither man nor woman bring him delight? Is his view of man a Christian one?

8. How does Hamlet act when the Players arrive? Does he seem grieved? Mad? Why does he act this way?

9. Hamlet says that the players are "the abstract and brief chronicles of the time" (2.2.554-555). In the context of Hamlet's plan to trap Claudius, what does this imply?

10. Hamlet castigates himself for not acting but instead "unpacking my heart with words" (2.2.620). To what does he compare himself in this regard? How is this significant in the light of the imagery of the rest of the act?

Lesson 3: Act 3

Act 3, like the previous act, begins with talk of spying. First, Claudius interrogates Rosencrantz and Guildenstern about their efforts to "pluck out the heart" of Hamlet's mystery, and then Claudius and Polonius arrange to spy on Hamlet as he speaks with Ophelia. Hamlet has been fencing skillfully, giving everyone reason to believe his interpretation of Hamlet's madness is correct. Confused, his opponents are forced to put out more bait and set more traps.

Ophelia is Polonius's preferred bait, and he prepares her for her encounter with Hamlet by instructing her to pretend to read a prayer book in order "color your loneliness," adding that "with devotion's visage and pious action we do sugar o'er the devil himself" (3.1.45-49). It is common, in other words, to cover over evil with pretended devotion and piety. Claudius overhears Polonius's instructions and is deeply stricken in conscience. Claudius recognizes himself in this description. He compares himself to a aging prostitute; just as she puts on make-up to cover her wrinkled face, so Claudius covers up the ugliness of his crimes with a "painted word" (3.1.53). This brief comment reveals a new side of Claudius. For the first time, it appears that Claudius is sensitive to his spiritual and moral condition. He recognizes that he has sinned and that he continues to sin by using painted words to hide the crime of murder. Just as Hamlet sees in every event a rebuke of his laxity in taking revenge, so everything around Claudius reminds him of his guilt. There is a profound point about in this. The Reformer John Calvin claimed that a guilty man is frightened by a falling leaf; he is so full of guilt and fear of God's wrath that the whole world seems to him an enemy. This fear also has its positive side; if Claudius is conscious of his crime, perhaps he will repent.

When Hamlet appears, he is in the midst of the soliloquy that begins with the most famous lines of Shakespeare: "To be or not to be: that is the question" (3.1.56-89). This is a very difficult speech to interpret. On the one hand, it seems odd that Hamlet would be contemplating suicide after he has finally hit upon a plan to "catch the conscience of the king." On the other hand, it is hard to understand the speech as anything but a consideration of suicide. Generally, it reveals that Hamlet continues to be a deeply divided man, one who wishes for death to relieve him of the burden he carries, but who at the same time fears that death, being an undiscovered country, contains ills that we know not of.

Ophelia interrupts Hamlet's meditations. Hamlet's treatment of Ophelia is harsh and cruel. There are no excuses, but several explanations for this. First, Ophelia has rejected Hamlet, following her father's instructions, and has apparently given Hamlet no explanation of her conduct. In this scene, she appears to blame Hamlet for breaking off their relationship (3.1.90-94). Hamlet resents her for following her father's instructions. After all, Hamlet's dilemma is precisely a question of whether or not he should obey his father. Because he has deep but unstated resistance to committing an act of revenge, he resents the ghost's demand, and also therefore resents everyone who simply "follows orders," especially the orders of a father.

On the other hand, Hamlet has already recognized that Ophelia is a tool of Claudius and Polonius. This explains his questions about her honesty. Honesty, as we have seen, is related to faithfulness, and by questioning Ophelia's honesty he is implicitly calling her a prostitute. She has prostituted herself by becoming a tool of the serpent who wears the crown. She has allowed beauty to transform honesty into its image by using her beauty as bait in Claudius's trap. This is why Hamlet tells Ophelia to get to a nunnery (3.1.124); becoming a nun would be an appropriate penance for her unfaithfulness to him, and would ensure that she would not conceive sinners—sinners like Hamlet. There is another edge to the exhortation, "Get thee to a nunnery." In Elizabethan England, "nunnery" was sometimes a polite word for a house of prostitution. Ophelia belongs in a "nunnery" because she allows herself to be controlled by her father, the "fishmonger."

In his relationship with Ophelia, moreover, Hamlet

always has Gertrude close to the front of his mind. He is already hostile to his mother for her rapid marriage to Claudius, and from the ghost he has learned about her prior adultery. He generalizes from his mother's actions to draw conclusions about women, and his attitude has been confirmed by Ophelia's abrupt rejection of his affections. Hamlet concludes that all women are unfaithful, all are whores who put on a face other than the one God gave them, who jig and amble and lisp, who put on painted words to cover their dishonesty (3.1.151-153). Marriage should be abolished, he concludes, because it inevitably leads to betrayal (3.1.155-158).

Much of what Hamlet says to Ophelia may be intended for Polonius and Claudius, for Hamlet may know they are eavesdropping on his encounter with Ophelia. And he is still giving support to everyone's pet theory. He lends support to the theory of Polonius when he tells Ophelia, "I did love you once." His words for Claudius are threatening: he raves about being "very proud, revengeful, ambitious, with more offenses at my beck that I have thoughts to put them in, imagination to give them shape, or time to act them in" (3.1.128-131), and says that "those who are married already, all but one, shall live" (3.1.156-157)—a chilling reference to the royal couple. Though he seems to be talking to Ophelia, he is still fencing with his mighty opposite. Ophelia just happens to get caught in the cross fire.

In interpreting Hamlet's actions this way, however, we may be giving him too much credit for sanity, for it appears that he is getting quite out of control. It may be best to say that Hamlet is not entirely aware what he is saying to Ophelia. His boiling anger toward Claudius, Gertrude, the meddlesome Polonius, Rosencrantz, and Guildenstern, all explodes at Ophelia because she happens to be close at hand. Hamlet twice says "Farewell" and then returns to Ophelia to explode again (3.1.139, 148). The scene leaves the impression that Hamlet has become a tornado, his unstable emotions driving him frantically from here to there.

Throughout Act 2 and 3.1, Hamlet has been the object of traps, spying, and interrogation. In 3.2, Hamlet turns the tables and takes the initiative. The play is Hamlet's most direct thrust in his struggle with Claudius. The play scene opens with Hamlet directing the players. Many have suggested that Shakespeare here puts in the mouth of one of his characters a set of instructions he endorsed in his own theater. That may be. In the context of the play, however, the more important issue is the way Hamlet intends to use the drama. The key portion of his opening speech is this:

> Suit the action to the word, the word to the action, with this special observance, that you o'erstep not the modesty of nature; for anything so overdone is from the purpose of playing, whose end, both at the first and now, was and is to hold as 'twere, the mirror up to nature—to show virtue her own feature, scorn her own image, and the very age and body of the time his form and pressure. (3.2.19-27)

Drama holds up a "mirror" to nature, to man and the world, and shows the world what kind of world it is. This is precisely what Hamlet intends to do in the play: He wants to show that Denmark is disjointed and out of frame, that something is rotten in the state of Denmark. The play will enact, in a thinly veiled way, the murder of Hamlet by Claudius and thus will hold up a mirror to Claudius. Hamlet will later do the same to his mother, trying to force her to look at herself through his eyes (3.4.19-20). By holding a mirror before Claudius and Gertrude, Hamlet hopes to expose their sin and prick their consciences. In itself, it is a worthy enterprise. But it will not, of course, satisfy the ghost. And by this point Hamlet lacks the self-control to limit himself to pricking consciences.

Hamlet has deliberately behaved in ways that each of his opponents will interpret in their own way, and he continues this at the play. When Claudius asks him how he "fares," Hamlet pretends that Claudius asked him about his diet ("fare" can mean what we eat), and says that he lives on a chameleon's diet. Chameleons were reputed to live on air, and Hamlet says that he is living on the "promise-cramm'd" air (3.2.99-101), that is, he is living on promises—in context, promises from Claudius that he is heir to the throne. The tone of Hamlet's reply suggests that he is looking for a more substantial diet, having grown thin by living on promises. Claudius may miss Hamlet's subtle wit, but he could hardly miss Hamlet's exchange with Polonius about the latter's university acting career. Polonius once played Julius Caesar, who was killed by Brutus. On one level, this foreshadows Polonius's fate; he will soon suffer Caesar's fate at the hands of another Brutus. Mention of Caesar and Brutus also serves as a warning to Claudius about the fate of tyrants and usurpers (3.2.104-111). Hamlet not only feeds Claudius's fears by his words and conduct, but he plays to Polonius's and Gertrude's theories as well. He refuses to sit with Gertrude, instead lying down at Ophelia's feet, which Polonius takes as evidence that he is right after all. Then Hamlet reminds his mother that her marriage to Claudius followed shortly after her husband's death (3.2.133-141).

Hamlet has brilliantly arranged the play so that it, like his own behavior, will be read differently by the various people in the audience. The discussion between the Player King and Queen catches Claudius's and Gertrude's attention with talk of a second marriage. Up to this point, Claudius has been distracted, but now the bait is set and Hamlet's trap is ready to be sprung. Everyone in the court now knows that the play is intended as a "mirror" of recent events in Denmark. When the murderer, Lucianus, appears, Hamlet cannot control himself and identifies the murderer as the king's "nephew" (3.2.254). Unlike King Hamlet, who was killed by his brother, Gonzago, the king of the play, is killed by a nephew. At this point, Hamlet's play has ceased to be a mirror and has become a threat. For who is nephew to King Claudius? Why, of course—Hamlet!

Everyone in the audience understands that Hamlet has deeply insulted and threatened the king. Claudius, however, sees much more than the others. As he watches, his suspicion that Hamlet might seize the throne seems confirmed. At the same time, he sees before his eyes a re-enactment of his murder of his brother. Until this moment, he had not the least suspicion that anyone knew how King Hamlet had died. Now, Claudius knows that Hamlet knows. Indeed the play is the thing to catch the conscience of the king. Though Hamlet dismisses the play as "false fire," it burns like a brand in Claudius's conscience (3.2.278). He calls, desperately, for light (3.2.281-282).

For Shakespeare, to give yourself over to violence and revenge is to give yourself over to madness and damnation. There is no single point at which Hamlet explicitly submits to the ghost's temptation. His descent into hell is gradual, as is the transformation of an antic disposition into real insanity. But if we were looking for a single moment when Hamlet allies himself with hell, it would be immediately after the play scene. When he is finally alone, he says:

> 'Tis now the very witching time of night,
> When churchyards yawn, and hell itself breathes out
> Contagion to this world. Now could I drink hot blood,
> And do such bitter business as the day
> Would quake to look on. (3.2.408-412)

Soon he will do bitter business indeed.

Hamlet almost immediately has the opportunity to carry out his vengeance but he hesitates. He catches Claudius in the midst of a prayer of contrition. Claudius recognizes that his sin is of a basic character, in that he sees that "it hath the primal eldest curse upon it" (3.3.37). The allusion is to the Cain's murder of his brother Abel; Claudius is another Cain, and just as Abel's blood cried out to heaven against Cain, so Claudius realizes that "my offense is rank, it smells to heaven" (3.3.36). He wonders how he can make true repentance. It would not be enough to say "I repent," because he would still possess the rewards of his crime—the crown and the queen. Claudius knows there is a difference between the earthly and heavenly treatment of sin. On earth, it is possible to use money to buy a favorable judgment: "Offense's gilded hand may shove by justice, and oft 'tis seen the wicked prize itself buys out the law" (3.3.57-60). In heaven, however, there is no "shuffling," no way to disguise one's sin or to buy off the Judge. Before the heavenly court, painted words cannot plaster over the ugliness of sin. Claudius is very close to true repentance here. He confesses the seriousness of his sin, acknowledges that he cannot disguise his sin in the sight of God, and has some inkling of what repentance would cost him. But this is as close as Claudius gets. In the end he is unwilling to pay the price. And so, his "words fly up, my thoughts remain below. Words without thoughts never to heaven go" (3.3.97-98).

When he first discovers Claudius praying, Hamlet is inclined to kill him immediately. As Hamlet noted in his soliloquy earlier in the act, however, the "pale cast of thought," the endless weighing of consequences, causes enterprises to lose the name of action. Hamlet believes that killing Claudius in the midst of a prayer of confession would send Claudius to heaven; to kill Claudius now would be "hire and salary, not revenge" (3.4.79). He chooses to wait for a opportunity to kill Claudius while Claudius is in his sins, and so ensure that he sends him to hell. Hamlet's descent is almost complete; he is acting not only for revenge but to ensure that his victim spends eternity in hell. He not only wishes to take into his hands that vengeance that belongs to the Lord, but also wants to rule in the court of the eternal Judge (see 5.2.46-47).

Instead of carrying out the ghost's instructions by killing Claudius at prayer, Hamlet takes out his rage on Gertrude. He plans to be "cruel, not unnatural," and says he "will speak daggers to her, but use none" (3.2.415-417). His speech follows two tacks: first, he holds up a "glass" or mirror to Gertrude, trying to expose her condition (3.4.18-20), and second, he compares his father the king to Claudius (3.4.52-87). He even vaguely informs Gertrude of Claudius's murder (3.4.27-28). Gertrude feels the stab of his words, and asks him not to speak any more: "These words like daggers enter in my ears" (3.4.94). By all the evidence from this scene, Gertrude was unaware of the murder. She is deeply distressed by Hamlet's revelations; the mirror he holds to her turns her "eyes into my very soul, and there I see such black and grained spots as will not leave their tinct" (3.4.88-90). She asks Hamlet how she can repent, and he instructs her not to go again to Claudius's bed.

Hamlet has held up a mirror to both Claudius and Gertrude, and we have seen some glimmers of repentance in both. This the ghost will not tolerate. He appears to Hamlet in Gertrude's chambers to remind him of his "almost blunted purpose" and to urge him to kill Claudius (3.4.109-110). The ghost's appearance also short circuits any effect Hamlet was having on Gertrude. She becomes convinced that her son is mad, and she does not come to a full repentance. In 4.1, she shows no evidence that she has altered her relationship with Claudius, a sign that she does not take Hamlet's accusations very seriously.

Given Hamlet's erratic behavior, and the fact that he has implicitly threatened the king, it is not surprising that Gertrude should fear for her life (3.4.21). When she cries out, Polonius, who also believes Hamlet to be dangerous, cries out as well. Thinking it is the king spying on him, Hamlet rashly thrusts his sword through the curtain and kills Polonius. This is a key turning point in the play in several respects. Hamlet's uncontrolled anger, his lust for revenge, his madness lead, as they inevitably must, to outright murder. The fencing match of words and spying between the mighty opposites has turned bloody, and the first of the intermediaries is crushed between them. Not only is it the beginning of actual bloodshed, but it also marks a major transition in Hamlet's situation. He is now legally and morally guilty. His willingness to ally with the ghost has led him to kill an innocent man. Hamlet shows no remorse for the crime, an indication that he is morally declining. Before he kills Polonius,

Hamlet has been a hunter, looking for the right opportunity to kill Claudius; from this point on, Hamlet is not only hunter but prey. Violent revenge begets further violence. The blood of another dead father calls up another offended and vengeful son.

Hamlet's failure to bring Gertrude to a full repentance is part and parcel of his failure to take a good look at himself in the mirror he held up to Claudius and Gertrude. Through most of 3.4, the body of Polonius is lying in plain view. Hamlet rants and rages at his mother for her shameful conduct, while ignoring the blood that now stains his own hands. Hamlet has become as guilty as Claudius and Gertrude. Before, the dramatic question was whether they would be brought to repentance; now we are forced to ask the same question about Hamlet himself.

Review Questions.

1. How is the beginning of Act 3 similar to the beginning of Act 2?

2. How does Claudius react when he overhears Polonius's instructions to Ophelia? Why?

3. Why, according to Hamlet's soliloquy, do men accept the pains of this life rather than end life with suicide?

4. How does Hamlet treat Ophelia? Why? How is Hamlet's conversation with Ophelia similar to his conversation with Polonius in Act 2?

5. What is the purpose of the performance of a play? How does Hamlet intend to use the play?

6. Explain how the play is understood differently by different members of the audience.

7. Summarize Claudius's prayer. Is he genuinely repentant?

8. Why does Hamlet choose not to kill Claudius while he is praying? How does this relate to other parts of the play? What does this say about Hamlet's spiritual condition?

9. How does Hamlet speak to Gertrude? Why? What effect do Hamlet's words have on his mother?

10. Why does the ghost appear during Hamlet's conversation with Gertrude?

Thought Questions.

1. How does Ophelia describe Hamlet's condition? (3.1.159-170). In the light of what happens in Act 4, why is this significant?

2. What kind of direction does Hamlet give the actors? What is the best kind of acting, according to Hamlet? Does Hamlet follow his own instructions in his behavior? Do the Players?

3. Hamlet tells Horatio that he prefers a man who is "not a pipe for fortune's finger to sound what stop she please" (3.2.76-77). Looking at the context of this remark, what does Hamlet mean by this? Is Hamlet such a man? Is Horatio?

4. For those who have studied *Julius Caesar*, how is Hamlet similar to and different from Brutus?

5. How does Hamlet treat Ophelia during the play scene? How does this compare with his treatment of her in the previous scene?

6. What does Hamlet mean when he says, "The players cannot keep counsel—they'll tell all"? (3.2.151-152).

7. What kind of mood is Hamlet in after the success of his "Mouse-trap"? What kind of mood is Horatio in? Why?

8. What is Claudius planning at the beginning of 3.3? What does this indicate about the sincerity of his prayer?

9. In what way is Claudius like a man "to double business bound"? (3.3.41). Does this description apply to anyone else in the play?

10. Hamlet says he will wring Gertrude's heart "if damned custom have not brass'd it so that it be proof and bulwark against sense" (3.4.36-37). What does this mean? How does this fit with other passages in the play that speak of "custom"?

Lesson 4: Acts 4-5

Polonius, like other dead fathers, haunts the living. Act 4 draws out the consequences of Hamlet's murder of Polonius: for Hamlet, for Laertes, and for Ophelia. Blood has been shed; Hamlet has committed an act of rash violence. Polonius's blood does not, however, cleanse King Hamlet's; on the contrary, in consequence of Hamlet's murderous act, things spin out of control. Even the structure of Act 4 underlines the chaos that comes in the wake of Hamlet's murder of Polonius: the opening scenes are brief and flit from one place to another like Hamlet darting through Elsinore hiding Polonius's body. Hamlet fell into temptation and acted as the ghost instructed, and the result is devastation on every side—all of it Hamlet's responsibility.

Throughout the play, Claudius has considered Hamlet a danger to the security of his throne, but now that Hamlet has acted violently, he is justified in taking firmer action. In his conversation with Gertrude, several concerns emerge. First, he realizes that he could have been in Polonius's place. Hamlet has become a threat to the whole state not only because he is potentially violent but also because rumors about Hamlet's behavior and Claudius's failure to control him might circulate through the royal courts of Europe. Claudius wants to make sure to protect the good name of Denmark (4.1.38-44). For the audience, it is clear that the trail of blood began with Claudius's murder of King Hamlet. His question, "How shall this bloody deed be answer'd?" (4.1.16) applies as much to his own crime as to Hamlet's. Claudius seems to forget he shares responsibility for the rottenness that is now spreading through the state of Denmark.

The immediate consequence for Hamlet himself is exile to England. Claudius, we later find, did not intend for Hamlet to return. Hamlet explains to Horatio that Rosencrantz and Guildenstern were carrying orders to the king of England to execute Hamlet upon arrival. When Hamlet discovered this, he changed the orders so that Rosencrantz and Guildenstern would be killed instead. As Hamlet says with chilling indifference, they simply got caught between mighty opposites and paid the consequences (5.2.1-79).

Ophelia too has been caught between the adversaries in their increasingly violent thrust and parry. When Hamlet learned of his father's murder he went mad, and Polonius's death has the same effect on Ophelia. Her madness is, of course, less dangerous and violent than Hamlet's; she roams aimlessly about the castle, singing. For the most part, her songs are about her dead father, but some are songs about a lover who refuses to marry a girl after she sleeps with him (4.5.49-68), clearly alluding to her frustrated love for Hamlet. The confusion of Polonius and Hamlet in Ophelia's songs is significant in two ways. First, as far as Ophelia knows, her rejection of Hamlet was the catalyst for the chain of events that led to her father's death. She has no way of knowing the real reasons behind the intrigues of the Danish court. From her perspective, what happened was this: she rejected Hamlet, he went mad as a result, and he eventually killed her father. Second, Ophelia's confused mixing of Hamlet and Polonius foreshadows Hamlet's future.

By his father's death, Laertes has been transformed into a ferocious avenger. Well might Hamlet say, as he does to Horatio: "by the image of my cause I see the portraiture of his [Laertes's]" (5.2.77-78). He becomes in an instant everything Hamlet took several acts to become; the moment he hears about his father's death, he is ready to drink hot blood and do bitter business. While something in Hamlet resisted revenge, everything in Laertes drives him ahead for instant satisfaction. As Laertes approaches Elsinore, the people proclaim him king (4.5.100-110); Laertes, not Hamlet, makes a bid for the throne. When he confronts Claudius about Polonius's death, he says he would risk damnation, so long as he can get his revenge (4.5.132-138). He pointedly says he dares do to Hamlet what Hamlet did not dare do to Claudius: "cut his throat i' the church" (4.7.127). Claudius approves of Laertes: "No place indeed should murder sanctuarize; revenge should have no bounds" (4.7.128-129).

How perfectly stated! If one operates, as Laertes and Claudius do, on the principle that revenge has no bounds, then the result will be that revenge will go on without limit, everywhere, forever; if one acts on the principle that revenge should know no bounds, then in fact revenge will know no bounds. Hamlet, though he does, as we have seen, fall to the ghost's temptation, does so with resistance, only after a terrific struggle of conscience. He knows, for reasons that he never fathoms, that revenge should be kept within very strict bounds.

As Hamlet's father's ghost tempted him to revenge, so Claudius—the serpent who wears the crown—plays tempter to Laertes. Claudius appeals, like the ghost, to Laertes's love for his father: "was your father dear to you? Or are you like the painting of a sorrow, a face without a heart?" (4.7.108-109). Claudius knows that the passion for revenge comes and goes, as it has for Hamlet, and he advises Laertes, "That we would do we should do when we would" (5.7.119-120); in other words, we should act while we have the will to do so, and not let thought make us lose the name of action. Claudius wants Laertes to take revenge before he has time to reconsider, or even consider, what he is doing.

Claudius proposes that Laertes kill Hamlet during a fencing match, with an "unbated" or unblunted sword. The pass and fell, the fencing of words, spies, and traps, that has dominated the play from Act 2, is going to come to a climax in a literal fencing match. Laertes, for his part, is a good student. He suggests that, to ensure that Hamlet is killed, he could "anoint" his sword with poison (4.7.141). The serpent king has a convert, who kills with "venom" (4.7.162). Claudius, to make extra sure that Hamlet gets killed, suggests in turn that a cup of poisoned wine be offered to him between passes (4.7.157-163). The Danish king, famous for his ability to drink, kills with a poisoned chalice. The serpent plans to poison the son as he poisoned his father.

The opening scene of Act 5, which begins with a conversation between two "clowns" as they dig Ophelia's grave, establishes the theme of death as the focus of the final act. This is where the revenge ethic leads. Hamlet's discourse to Yorick's skull deepens the theme. What brings horror is not death *per se*, but the vanity of a life that ends in death. The skulls thrown up by the grave diggers could be from a politician, a courtier, a lawyer; whatever their station in life, their end is the same—the grave, decay, return to the dust and clay. Even Caesar and Alexander turn to clay and might be used to close up a chink in a peasant's hut so that the wind cannot get through (5.1.221-237).

Hamlet's meditations on death are sometimes witty, sometimes serious, but in general he seems altogether a different man at the beginning of Act 5. His volcanic rage seems calmed. He refers to the "divinity that shapes our ends, rough-hew them how we will" (5.2.10-11). He rants at Laertes during Ophelia's funeral, but later tells Horatio that he is sorry for his conduct. He seems to have no plan to take revenge on Claudius. He is ready to die if it is his time:

> . . . we defy augury. There's a special providence in the fall of a sparrow. If it be now, 'tis not to come; if it be not to come, it will be now; if it be not now, yet it will come: the readiness is all.(5.2.227-231)

Yet we must not make too much of the contrast between the earlier and later Hamlet. He may be calmed but he still makes a scene at Ophelia's funeral. He may be calmed, but he still speaks with terrifying indifference about arranging the deaths of his former friends, Rosencrantz and Guildenstern (5.2.38-62). Indeed, when he speaks of the divinity that shapes our ends, he is telling Horatio about how he disposed of them, almost as if to say that God not Hamlet was responsible for their deaths.

The conflicting picture of Hamlet at the beginning of Act 5 may have been forced on Shakespeare by dramatic necessity. On the one hand, Hamlet is a sympathetic and heroic character; we like him for his energy, his wit, even his weaknesses.

If he goes about ranting and raving like a lunatic, as he did through much of Acts 3-4, the audience will feel that he deserves precisely what he gets in the end. To make him a sympathetic hero, Shakespeare must make him likeable again and this means Hamlet must calm down. On the other hand, if Hamlet is killed even though he has repented of his crime, then his death will seem an enormous injustice. Shakespeare needs for the final scene a Hamlet who is both likeable and guilty.

Shakespeare makes the audience cheer and weep for Hamlet largely by painting Claudius as a villain and a cheat. For Claudius and Laertes, all notions of fair play and honor have gone out the window because, of course, revenge should have no bounds. Yet, Claudius's plan backfires. He falls into the very trap that he laid for Hamlet. The serpent who wore the crown dies by his own poison; the king famed for drinking Rhine wine himself empties a poisoned chalice. And not only Claudius, but everyone falls into the traps that the avengers have set. The point is clearly that once a quarrel or vengeance breaks out, there is no stopping it. It becomes impossible to control it, to keep it within bounds. Everyone gets caught in the vortex, and many innocent people get hurt and, in the play, killed.

Fortinbras appears again at the very end of the play. Denmark's king, queen, and crown prince lying dead on the floor, Fortinbras takes charge of the situation, ordering the removal of the bodies and making appropriate funeral arrangements. More than that, Fortinbras claims "some rights of memory in this kingdom, which now to claim my vantage doth invite me" (5.2.398-99). He ends the play with more than he bargained for: he not only receives the lands lost by his father but also the crown and kingdom of Denmark. Among the vengeful sons, Fortinbras is the only one alive and prosperous when the curtain closes.

The final ends of the vengeful sons dramatically challenges the revenge ethic: Laertes, the hot-blooded avenger, falls into the trap he made for Hamlet; Claudius, the serpent, is killed by both the venomed blade and the poisoned chalice; Hamlet, the reluctant avenger, has fallen victim to Laertes's revenge. Fortinbras, who has disavowed vengeance, inherits the kingdom. He may be no angel but at least he did not pursue revenge. In the context of this bloody tragedy, Fortinbras's history alone has a comic trajectory.

Hamlet thus presents a negative view of redemption. Denmark is a fallen world, needing to be set right. Instead of showing us the Redeemer, however, Shakespeare shows us the folly and danger of man's efforts at self-redemption and especially redemption through violence. Time out of joint is not set right by the wrath of men. It is not the grasping of the first Adam who secures redemption but the patient suffering of the Last Adam. Those who seek vengeance do not prosper. The crown usurped by the serpent is finally worn by one who rejected revenge. And the meek inherit the land.

Review Questions.

1. What does Claudius do to Hamlet after he kills Polonius? Why?

2. What effect does Polonius's death have on Ophelia?

3. Explain the significance of Ophelia's songs.

4. What effect does Polonius's death have on Laertes? How does Laertes become like Hamlet? How is he different?

5. How does Claudius encourage Laertes to take revenge? How does Claudius's role compare with that of the ghost in Act 1?

6. How does Claudius plan for Laertes to take revenge on Hamlet? What is significant about this method?

7. Why does Act 5 open with the grave-digging scene?

8. Why is it fitting for this play to end with a fencing match?

9. What is significant about how the major characters die in the final scene?

10. What is Fortinbras's situation at the end of the play? Why is this important?

Thought Questions.

1. As Claudius sends men throughout the castle to search for Polonius's body, Hamlet says that Polonius is at dinner (4.3.18-33). What does he mean? How does what he says here fit with other passages in the play about death?

2. Hamlet says that the "body is with the king, but the king is not with the body" (4.2.29-30). What does this mean?

3. Claudius tells Laertes that he could not prosecute Hamlet because he feared that his "arrows . . . would have reverted to my bow again" (4.7.21-24). What does he mean? Why is his image of arrows returning to the bow significant?

4. At the opening of Act 5, the grave diggers are discussing the circumstances of Ophelia's death (5.1.1-66). What is their conclusion? How does this fit with the circumstances of King Hamlet's death? Rosencrantz and Guildenstern's?

5. Horatio says of the singing grave digger that "Custom hath made it in him a property of easiness" (5.1.74). What does this mean? Does Hamlet agree that one can become accustomed to death? Did he believe this in Act 1?

6. Hamlet says that no amount of "paint" or makeup could prevent anyone from dying and ending up a skull (5.1.210-214). Compare this statement to others about "paint" and makeup.

7. What does Gertrude say as she places flowers on Ophelia's grave? (5.1.264-267). What contrasting uses of flowers does she mention? Compare this to Ophelia's use of flowers in her death (4.7.168-185).

8. Why do Laertes and Hamlet fight at Ophelia's funeral? What is significant about this?

9. Is Hamlet's apology to Laertes satisfying? (5.2.239-248).

10. Before the fencing match begins, Claudius promises to drink to Hamlet's health (5.2.276-288). Why is this ironic?

Video Versions of Hamlet

I viewed three versions of *Hamlet*: Lawrence Olivier's classic 1948 film; a production from the 1960s starring Ian Richardson in the title role; and the 1990 Franco Zeffirelli film starring Mel Gibson.

For students, the Zeffirelli *Hamlet* is by far the most watchable. It looks like a movie, not a stage play, and helps the students sense that *Hamlet* is not a stuffy drama but an exciting story. The fencing scenes are good, and the settings are realistic. In Olivier's film, Elsinore is almost deserted, while in the Zeffirelli film it is a constant bustle, as certainly a medieval castle would have been. The acting is quite good. Gibson is competent, playing a Hamlet of explosive power. Sometimes, Gibson's energy gets the best of him and his "antic disposition" consists mainly of popping his eyes open really, really wide. The main drawback is that the film does not follow the play at all closely. Gibson says his "to be or not to be" speech while alone in a crypt, instead of while walking in the castle; this is not a bad touch, but it makes a different impression than the play. Other speeches and scenes are changed and edited. The film does tell the story effectively, and for that reason it is useful. The only questionable scene for students is Hamlet's meeting with his mother in her bed chamber, which plays up the Freudian dimensions of their relationship by suggesting an incestuous relationship between Hamlet and Gertrude.

The Olivier *Hamlet*, which earned Academy Awards for both Best Actor and Best Picture, is still excellent, but will probably hold interest of young viewers only if they are already Shakespeare fans. It has the feel of a filmed stage play. The acting is uniformly good; Olivier's soliloquies are quite moving. Olivier, of course, imposed his own interpretation on the play, which unfortunately tends to answer questions that the play leaves unanswered. Moreover, some important portions are simply cut: There is no mention of Fortinbras, and no Rosencrantz and Guildenstern.

The 1960s version starring Ian Richardson follows the

text more closely than the other two. It is obvious from costumes, sets, and acting that the film was produced in the '60s but if you get past the quasi-hippy elements, it is a decent film. Richardson plays Hamlet as a languid, sensitive aesthete; that may appeal to some, but Mel Gibson's volcanic, energetic portrayal is closer to the Hamlet I find in the text.

Suggested Paper Topics

1. Discuss the theme of revenge in *Hamlet*. Does the play promote revenge? Why or why not?

2. Is Hamlet's madness genuine?

3. Discuss in detail one of Hamlet's great soliloquies (1.2.129-158; 1.5.92-109; 3.1.56-89; 4.5.31-66). Pay attention to the context of these soliloquies, what happens immediately before and after, and to the imagery that Hamlet uses.

4. Take a position for or against this statement: The ghost is a messenger from hell, who tempts Hamlet to commit a great evil. Defend your conclusion.

5. Discuss the role of Horatio in the play: Hamlet's friend, commentator on the action, moral standard by which Hamlet and other characters are to be judged.

6. Examine "acting" as a theme in the play: Hamlet's acting of various parts, his use of the actors in the play scene, comments that the play makes on acting.

7. Discuss the character and function of one of the lesser characters: Polonius, Ophelia, Rosencrantz and Guildenstern.

8. Compare Hamlet to other Shakespearean characters: e.g., Brutus, Macbeth. Write a play in which Macbeth is placed in Hamlet's position. Does he hesitate to take revenge?

9. Examine the theme of death in *Hamlet*: Hamlet's reaction to the death of his father, his comments on death in Acts 4-5, etc.

10. Trace the use of a particular image through the play: mirrors, weeds, poison and venom, corruption and decay.

If It Were Done When 'Tis Done:
Macbeth

Though his plays were frequently based in fact, Shakespeare took liberties with chronology and historical detail in order to highlight certain moral and dramatic issues. This is true of *Macbeth*, which, though based on the life of the Macbeth who ruled Scotland during the eleventh century, differs from Shakespeare's principal source, Raphael Holinshed's *Chronicle of Scottish History*, in several respects. In Shakespeare's play, King Duncan is not the incompetent tyrant depicted by Holinshed but a model Christian king. He is said to be "gracious" and without fault (1.7.16-20). Moreover, in the play, Banquo is not part of the conspiracy against Duncan. Shakespeare's Macbeth acts without aid from the other thanes of Scotland, but with the knowledge and encouragement only of his wife. Finally, in the play Macduff kills Macbeth at the battle of Dunsinane, and Malcolm immediately takes the throne, while in actual fact neither of these events followed so closely after Dunsinane.

Especially the first two changes are important to Shakespeare's purposes. His Macbeth is no Brutus, who joined the plot to kill Caesar because he hoped to save Rome from tyranny. Far from seeking the good of his nation, Macbeth himself admits that "I have no spur to prick the sides of my intent, but only vaulting ambition, which o'erleaps itself and falls on the other" (1.7.25-28). The play directs its primary attention to the consequences of vaulting ambition and the deeds it inspires. There are, of course, times and places where the existing order of things has become so unjust and evil that it must be resisted to the point of over-throwing it. This was the situation in the Soviet Union and Eastern Europe until the rapid collapse of communism after 1989. Even in extremely unjust societies, one should act cautiously; as John Calvin said, the order of tyranny is often preferable to the chaos of revolution. But Scotland under Duncan is not a totalitarian state, and Macbeth is not resisting injustice. Assaulting the proper order of things, attacking due authority, has disastrous consequences—personal, social, and political.

Whether or not Macbeth will act on his ambition depends on his answer to the question, What does it mean to be a man? Two answers to this question are presented by the play, and Macbeth is forced to choose between them. When Lady Macbeth urges him to kill Duncan, he protests, "I dare do all that may become a man; who dares do more is none" (1.7.46-47). On this view, one cannot be a man without placing limitations on desires and actions. Whoever tries to do more than "becomes a man" becomes less than a man. Lady Macbeth, by contrast, operates on the view that you are not a man unless you act on every single desire. She asks her hesitating husband,

> wouldst thou have that
> Which thou esteem'st the ornament of life,
> And live a coward in thine own esteem,
> Letting "I dare not" wait upon "I would". (1.7.41-44)

and adds, "When you durst do it, then you were a man" (1.7.49). Any effort to control desire, to deny and suppress evil, or to place any limits whatever on action—all these for Lady Macbeth amount to nothing but cowardice. To be a man is to ignore all moral constraints. In the final analysis, for Lady Macbeth to be a true man is to be a murderer. Only the bloody man is truly a man.

After hesitations and doubts, Macbeth acts on the latter

view, a choice that is personally devastating. On this level, the play is about the collapse of a man's soul, about a man sliding, due to his own unrepented sins, into hell. Macbeth is a man who gains the whole world but loses his soul. Sliding is not quite right, though. It is more that Macbeth, once having decided which direction to go, rushes, dashes, leaps into and embraces hell. Macbeth begins as a hero of Scotland and a somewhat admirable character. He seems loyal to his king, and his wife's description suggests that he has moral scruples as well. His assault on the order of the world turns him into a beast. Having tried to lift himself above his place, he ends up falling into an abyss (see Ezek. 28:1-10). As a consequence of his ambition to be more than human, he becomes less than human (see Dan. 4:1-37). By the end of play, Macbeth is being seen, and even sees himself, as a subhuman creature: a baited bear, a hell-hound, a devil. He has dared do more than becomes a man, and at the last he is none.

Shakespeare shares the opinion, reflected in different ways in both ancient paganism and in Christianity, that one can lead a good life only in a community, only as he shares that life with others. Christianity teaches that God is One and Three, both a Person and a society of Persons. Man, made in God's image, reflects that image fully only when he lives in close communion with his fellows, for it is not good for man to be alone. Because of sin, men and women are not only separated from God but from each other. One of the first effects of sin was a rupture in Adam's relationship with Eve, as he changed from her protector to her accuser (Gen. 3:12). Persistence in sin breaks the bonds that hold people together as families, neighborhoods, Churches, nations.

Macbeth powerfully depicts this process. As Macbeth pursues his ambitions, he becomes increasingly isolated. This is why Shakespeare did not include Banquo in Macbeth's original conspiracy: In order to murder Duncan, Macbeth removes himself from the company of the other thanes of Scotland, lest they discover his plans. Though Lady Macbeth encourages his plot to murder Duncan, even his bond with her is eventually broken as she follows her own pathetic pathway to hell and insanity, finally committing suicide. The people of Scotland turn against their king; though their curses are not "loud," they are "deep" (5.3.27). In a despairing mood, Macbeth reflects that old age should be accompanied by "honor, love, obedience, troops of friends," but as he grows older he is more and more alone (5.3.24-26). Deprived of fellowship, and with his own reason dethroned, Macbeth's life becomes meaningless. Informed of Lady Macbeth's death, he muses on the uselessness and vanity of it all. Unrepented evil can only lead to despair and nothingness: no friends, no companions, no love, no sleep.

The political consequences of Macbeth's ambition are equally profound. Overthrowing the established order turns the world to chaos. "Boundless intemperance," Macduff observes, "is a tyranny" (4.3.67-68). Driven by the logic of his ambition and his view of manhood, Macbeth becomes willing to do whatever it takes to maintain his power. Power is not evil; Jesus has all power in heaven and earth, and exercises it with perfect justice. Sinful human beings are capable of using power for good ends. Even the aspiration to have and use power is not evil; Paul says it is a good thing for a man to aspire to the office of overseer in the Church (1 Tim. 3:1), and no doubt the same thing could be said of those who aspire to political office (Rom. 13:1-7). The important point is that power is not an end in itself. If you seek power in order to do something good, then your use of power will be guided by your larger goals. If you run for Congress because you want to "clean up Washington," then you will try to avoid doing anything that would add to the dirt. If, however, you want power only for itself, if power is an end and not a means to other ends, then you will be willing to do anything to maintain power. When power is the only good, anything that secures power is, by definition, good. This is Macbeth's situation after he kills Duncan. As one crime leads to another, Macbeth comes to see the blood of his victims as a river, into which he has "stepp'd so far" that he thinks he cannot turn back (3.4.136-138). Ruled by Macbeth, Scotland plunges into a dark age.

The social and political chaos of Scotland is highlighted especially by the use of "equivocal" language, words with deceptively double meanings. We have all been reminded to "Say what you mean and mean what you say." No one follows this advice in *Macbeth*, where communication is cloaked under ambiguous and misleading words. Macbeth trusts the witches, but their words prove unreliable. Macbeth, having entrusted himself to the "juggling fiends" (5.8.19), becomes like them, using words to hide his real intentions and feelings. One of Satan's main lines of attack is the corruption of language (Gen. 3:1-6), for he knows as well as anyone that "in the beginning was the Word" (Jn. 1:1). Again, this is part of the breakdown of Scottish society that results from Macbeth's ambition, as well as a cause of further unraveling of social ties. There is no possibility for orderly communal life if we cannot trust that people mean what they say. If no wife can trust her husband's "I do", if no buyer can trust the merchant's sale's pitch, or if rulers cannot trust their advisors to speak honestly, society collapses. Jesus' command, "Let your Yea be Yea, and your Nay, Nay" (Mt. 5:37), is not only a demand for individual honesty, but a basic requirement for civilized human life.

Macbeth is the shortest of Shakespeare's great tragedies. It relentlessly follows the story of Macbeth's and Scotland's decline, with no digressions, no subplots, no comic relief. This tragic story, however, is framed by a story of Scotland's salvation. *Macbeth* begins with witches, rebellion, and murder, with war, the hurlyburly and the bloody man, but it ends with Malcolm talking about the triumph of Grace. Speaking of the many things that must be done to restore Scotland, Malcolm concludes:

> this, and what needful else
> That calls upon us, by the grace of Grace
> We will perform in measure, time, and place. (5.8.71-73)

The movement of the play is through darkness and hell and night back into daylight and Paradise. The play is tragic as far as Macbeth is concerned; for Scotland and Malcolm, the plot line is redemptive, as they pass through winter to spring, from the dominance of demons to the triumph of grace, through the cross to the resurrection.

Lesson One: Act 1.1-4

Macbeth begins with witches, instruments of hell. And throughout the play, they are never far from the action or from Macbeth's mind. By opening the play with witches, Shakespeare points to the ultimate origins of Macbeth's actions, the sparks of whose ambition are brought to full flame by the temptations of the witches. This is not to say that Macbeth is doomed to do what he does. This is not a Greek tragedy on the order of Oedipus. As Harold Goddard puts it, "Fire is hot. And fire is fascinating to a child. If the child goes too near the fire, he will be burned. We may call it fate if we will. It is in that conditional sense only that there is any fatalism in *Macbeth*." Macbeth is conscious of and responsible for what he does, but what he does is to accept an alliance with hell, doing the devil's business in exchange for crown and scepter. By so doing, Macbeth himself repeats Satan's original sin, for in Shakespeare's day, it was common belief that Satan had fallen from heaven because he exalted himself above his station.

The witch scene not only highlights the demonic influence behind Macbeth's sins, but also introduces another important theme of the play, the equivocation of the devil's tongue (1.1.4, 9-10). The witches use words demonically, changing and shifting meanings, saying one thing but meaning another, reversing, twisting, and tangling the meanings of words. The devil is a liar, Jesus said; more than that, the devil lies by saying things that sound true. Satan twists words to make them sound good, but what he says is a lie. The meaning of the witches' haunting chant, "fair is foul and foul is

fair," is difficult to explain, but at least it signals the over-
turning of all values. Witches are agents of chaos, intent on
creating a world in which good will be called evil and evil good.
They find in Macbeth an all too willing accomplice.

The witches exit saying, "Hover through the fog and
filthy air" (1.1.10). It is partly through the imagery of air that
Shakespeare creates the impression of pervasive evil in this
play. The witches themselves materialize out of the air, and
vanish again into it (1.3.81-82). Elsewhere in the play we
read that the air is foul, heavy, dark, thick. By contrast,
Duncan and Banquo comment on the sweetness of the air as
he approaches Macbeth's castle at Inverness (1.6.1-9). They
can no more read the true atmospheric conditions than they
can read a man's mind from his face (1.4.11-14). Far from
being filled with sweet and delicate air, the atmosphere is
filled with poison. Witches surround and hover in the very
air Macbeth breathes.

As the first scene sets out the spiritual context of the
play, the second scene describes the political context.
Duncan has been putting down the rebellion of one of his
thanes, Macdonwald, who has received help from Norway
(1.2.9-15, 28-33). Just as the sergeant who has reported to
Duncan is being led away for medical attention, Ross comes
with a report that Norway has been attacking Fife, assisted by
the thane of Cawdor (1.2.50-59). Initially, Macbeth is altogether Duncan's man. He is credited for the victory over
Macdonwald (1.2.16-43), and Duncan confers Cawdor's title
on him (1.2.65-67). It is noteworthy the play begins with rebellion and war. A new and more serious threat to Duncan
will later appear, and it will come from the very man that
Duncan invests with the position of the traitor Cawdor.
Moreover, the witches decide to tempt Macbeth precisely at
the moment "When the hurlyburly's done, when the batt'
lost and won" (1.1.3-4). As Goddard says, war plows tʰ
into which the witches will sow seeds of murder ʳ'
bear the fruit of chaos.

As the sergeant approaches King Duncan

the battle, the king asks, "What bloody man is that?" (1.2.1). "Bloody man" is also, we quickly learn, a good description of Macbeth. As he often does, Shakespeare introduces a character through third parties before bringing him on stage. As described by the sergeant, Macbeth is clearly a bloody man. Here, he sheds the blood of Duncan's enemies and proves himself a loyal thane, but he will be a bloody man in different ways as the play progresses. The bloody Macbeth beheads Macdonwald, a rebel, and sets his head on the battlements (1.2.15-23), which foreshadows the later fate of another rebel—Macbeth himself.

Macbeth's enters saying, "So foul and fair a day I have not seen" (1.3.38). Macbeth has already been associated with the "bloody man" of scene 1, as well as with the rebel Cawdor. With his first appearance, a more significant connection is made, since his words recall those of the witches in 1.1.9 ("Fair is foul and foul is fair"). Even before he sees the witches, Macbeth is not only breathing a demonic atmosphere, but already speaking their language. Like the witches, and under their inspiration, he will prove an expert in deception and equivocation.

As Banquo and Macbeth ride from the battle, they are met by the witches, who predict that Macbeth will become thane of Cawdor and king, and that Banquo's children will be crowned (1.3.48-69). When the witches' first prediction comes true, Macbeth halts between two courses of action (1.3.130-144). On the one hand, he reasons, "I became Cawdor without doing anything, so maybe I can just wait and become king in the same way." But his soliloquy shows that he is already contemplating a more active course. His mind is full of a "horrid image"; his imaginings frighten him and dominate him so much that he cannot perform his immediate duties. He is "smother'd in surmise," in hopes and plans and calculations. The only thing that really *is* for Macbeth is what has not yet happened: his promised rise to the throne. His ambition has become more real to him than anything else.

Banquo's reaction to the announcement that Macbeth is

thane of Cawdor is more fundamental: "What, can the devil speak true?" (1.3.107). Banquo does not think in political terms, as Macbeth does; he gets to the heart of the question: can the devil (the witches) be trusted? The fulfillment of the witches' prophecy to Macbeth seems to provide evidence that they can. Banquo, however, does not believe witches can be trusted, and his skepticism becomes even clearer when, after a few moments of silence, he warns,

> But 'tis strange,
> And oftentimes, to win us to our harm
> The instruments of darkness tell us truths,
> Win us with honest trifles, to betray's
> In deepest consequence. (1.3.122-126)

Satan does not come initially with an outright lie. That would be too obvious. Instead, he tells us trivial truths so that, when we see his words confirmed, we begin to place our confidence in him. Once we are hooked, he betrays us in matters that are far from trivial. Banquo's words precisely predict Macbeth's future, but Macbeth ignores the warning.

Scene 4 is the execution of Cawdor, and is important for a number of reasons. First, Malcolm reports that Cawdor died penitently, sorry for his treason. As Malcolm puts it, "Nothing in his life became him like the leaving it" (1.4.7-8). Though a rebel in life, he confessed and made amends in death, and so died better than he had lived. The scene raises the question, How will the new Cawdor conduct himself in life and death? He is already contemplating murder and treason. Will he repent? In this context, Duncan comments on his absolute trust in the former Cawdor and the impossibility of judging what a man is thinking from looking at his face (1.4.11-14). Duncan has no sooner finished commenting on his surprise at Cawdor's treachery when Macbeth enters— the new Cawdor!—in whom Duncan again places his absolute confidence. Macbeth's face, however, is as impossible to read as anyone's.

In reaction to the rebellions he has been facing, Duncan

takes the wise step of naming as successor his son Malcolm. In this way Duncan makes sure that, should he die, the throne is secure and power can transfer in an orderly way to a new king. This forces Macbeth to choose between the two courses of action. When Malcolm is named as heir to the throne, Macbeth loses hope that he can wait patiently for the crown. If the title of king is to be his, he is going to have to act; the forbidden fruit is not going to drop into his lap, so he will have to seize it. He realizes that the elevation of Malcolm to Prince of Cumberland is a "step on which I must fall down, or else o'erleap" (1.4.48-49), something that will frustrate his ambitions if he does not find a way around it. In the end, he just can't wait to be king.

In the following lines, Macbeth calls on the stars to go out, so that no light will shine on the dark desires of his heart. Darkness here is not just a symbol of evil, but a covering for evil. He wants to be clothed by dark night, to take on a new set of clothes, not as a new honor and identity, but to disguise and hide his plans. Macbeth invokes darkness as a cover not only to hide his intentions from others, but to hide them from himself:

> The eye wink at the hand; yet let that be
> Which the eye fears, when it is done, to see. (1.4.52-53)

There is a deep ambivalence here. He wants to become king, and he is ready to kill Duncan to achieve his ambition, but already he is horrified by the prospect of the crime that he must commit. He lusts for the crown, but wants it without having his conscience bother him. Darkness, however, will not clothe him forever. Nor will he always be able to hide behind words. Crimes will come to light—not only to Scotland, but before Macbeth's own eyes.

Review Questions.

1. In what ways did Shakespeare modify the story of Macbeth that he found in Holinshed? Why are these changes important for Shakespeare's play?

2. What is the essential moral issue of the play? Explain how sheer ambition for power turns a man into a murderer.

3. What happens to Macbeth when he assaults the proper order of Scotland? What happens to Scotland?

4. What two views of manhood are presented in the play?

5. Why is it important that the play begins with the witches? How is this beginning related to the end?

6. What is the political situation in Scotland when the play opens?

7. How is Macbeth described in scene 2, before he appears? With whom is Macbeth associated? How does scene 2 foreshadow events in the rest of the play?

8. Why are Macbeth's first words important?

9. What is Banquo's reaction when the witches' first prediction comes true? Why does the devil speak truth?

10. What effect does Duncan's announcement that Malcolm is his heir have on Macbeth's plans?

Thought Questions.

1. When we first see the witches, they are planning to meet Macbeth on the heath (1.1.1-10). Why do they want to meet Macbeth? What does this tell you about the witches' role in Macbeth's later actions?

2. Why do the witches say they will meet "when the battle's lost *and* won"? (1.1.4). Wouldn't it be more proper to say "lost *or* won"?

3. According to the sergeant, what is Macdonwald's relation to fortune? (1.2.10-15). What is Macbeth's relationship to fortune? (1.2.17). How does this fit with the later events of the play?

4. The sergeant suggests that Macbeth and Banquo meant to "memorize another Golgotha" during their battle with the king of Norway (1.2.40-41). What does this mean?

5. What are the witches talking about at the beginning of scene 3? (1.3.1-29). How does this conversation relate to the main action of the play? How is Macbeth like the man mentioned by the first witch? (1.3.15-26).

6. How does Banquo describe the witches' appearance? (1.3.45-47). How does this fit with larger themes of the play?

7. What is Macbeth's immediate reaction to the witches' prediction that he will be king? (1.3.51-52). What does this tell us about Macbeth's ambitions prior to meeting the witches? (see 1.3.130-142).

8. How does Banquo explain Macbeth's distraction at the witches' prediction? (1.3.144-146). Is Macbeth distracted because he has been dressed in Cawdor's garments? Or does he have other garments in mind?

9. Is Duncan a discerning man? Is he a good judge of character?

10. How does Duncan's use of "star" imagery (1.4.39-42) contrast with Macbeth's? (1.4.50-53).

Lesson Two: Acts 1.5-2.4

When Lady Macbeth appears, she is fearful that Macbeth lacks the courage to take the "nearest way" to the throne. She recognizes his ambition, but also knows that he does not like to get his hands dirty. He is too full of "the milk of human kindness" (1.5.18), which suggests that in her opinion Macbeth is rather feminine. This is not a description we would expect from our initial introduction to Macbeth, the hero of Duncan's victory over Macdonwald, who "unseam'd him from the nave to the chaps and fix'd his head upon our battlements" (1.2.22-23). Lady Macbeth's evaluation of her husband is based on her view of manhood. She is contemptuous of Macbeth's wish to achieve his ambitions "without the illness should attend it"; she thinks him womanish for wanting to act "holily" (1.5.20-22). To spur his ambition, she will have to "pour my spirits in thine ear" and "chastise with the valor of my tongue" (1.5.27-28). In *Hamlet*, temptation is linked to pouring poison in the ear, and this is precisely what Lady Macbeth plans. She is a temptress, an aggressive Eve to Macbeth's reluctant Adam. (In Genesis, it should be noted,

Adam is primarily responsible for the sin, since he was present with Eve when she was tempted—Gen. 3:6.)

In fulfilling her role as temptress, Lady Macbeth appeals for help to the "spirits that tend on mortal thoughts" whom she calls "murdering ministers" (1.5.41-42, 49). From this point on, Lady Macbeth becomes a demonic instrument who browbeats Macbeth into taking Duncan's life. She asks the instruments of evil to

> Unsex me here,
> And fill me, from the crown to the toe, top-full
> Of direst cruelty! Make thick my blood,
> Stop up th' access and passage to remorse,
> That no compunctious visitings of nature
> Shake my fell purpose, nor keep peace between
> Th'effect and it! Come to my woman's breasts,
> And take my milk for gall, you murd'ring ministers.
> (1.5.42-49)

"Unsex me here" means "Make me a man," and for Lady Macbeth, as we saw above, being manly means putting aside all moral restrictions, all boundaries and limits on desire and action, all natural feelings of sympathy and tenderness. Specifically, being manly means being willing to kill to achieve one's desires. Macbeth is too full of the milk of kindness, but Lady Macbeth asks that her milk be exchanged for gall, a bitter liquid that does not nourish, the very opposite of milk. Gall is also daring ("he had the gall to . . ."); Lady Macbeth wants to replace the milk of kindness and moral restraint with the gall to dare to do all that she can imagine doing. All of this associates her with the witches. Banquo notices that, though the witches look like women, they have beards. Bearded witches cross over and blur the fundamental categories of male and female (1.3.45-47). They are sexually chaotic, agents of disorder. Lady Macbeth now will fulfill the same role. It is no accident that her greeting to Macbeth echoes the greeting of the witches (1.5.55; see 1.3.48-50).

From the moment of Macbeth's appearance, his wife

takes control of their plans, and she has just relinquished control to the murdering ministers. She is both Eve and the serpent. As an instrument of the witches, she gives Macbeth a lesson in deception. Duncan had put his trust completely in the former Cawdor, and commented to Malcolm that it is impossible to "find the mind's construction in his face." Lady Macbeth, however, fears that Macbeth's face is too transparent. To protect their plans, Macbeth needs to "look the time," welcoming Duncan as if everything were normal. Macbeth is to dress as the flower, but be a serpent (1.5.64-67). She wants Macbeth to clothe himself in innocence, to put on a show of truth, in short, to be like the witches, who win with honest trifles but betray in deepest consequence. Macbeth is to be a Satanic serpent disguised as an angel of light.

Scene 7 is a key to understanding the themes and action of the play as a whole. This scene takes place while Duncan and the rest of the people are feasting. Macbeth withdraws from the feast to consider what he should do. Even before the decisive act, his isolation is beginning. The feast is a symbol of social harmony, peace, fellowship, but Macbeth is not at the feast. Instead, he removes himself to contemplate an act that will destroy all feasting, fellowship, and order in Scotland. Macbeth's soliloquy begins with these lines:

> If it were done when 'tis done, then 'twere well
> It were done quickly. If th' assassination
> Could trammel up the consequence, and catch,
> With its surcease, success; that but this blow
> Might be the be-all and the end-all here,
> But here, upon this bank and shoal of time,
> We'd jump the life to come. (1.7.1-7)

Throughout the play, "done," "do," and "act" are key words. *Macbeth* is about the risks that attend all human action. By tracing the consequences of Macbeth's act, the play shows insistently that human doing always has results. Macbeth, however, wishes for a world where this is not true.

In the opening lines of his speech, Macbeth is using "done" in two senses. In the first use ("If it were done"), the word means "finished" or "completed." The second use ("when 'tis done") refers to doing the act of murder. Thus, we could paraphrase Macbeth this way: "If all my ambitions could be completely satisfied by this one act of murder, then I should act quickly to kill Duncan." He wants, as he says, his one act to be the "be-all and end-all" and to "jump the life to come." In short, he wants his killing of Duncan to stop the historical process of cause and effect, of sin and judgment, and bring an end to time. This throws some light on Lady Macbeth's instructions about how to "beguile the time" (1.5.64). Both Macbeth and his wife want to fool time, to act murderously without suffering the temporal effects of the action. They hope that darkness will not only hide them from light's exposure but from time itself.

As Macbeth's soliloquy moves on, however, it is clear that he knows he cannot beguile time or escape the temporal results of what he does. He knows that there is a justice operating in the world, and that this justice "commends th' ingredients of our poison'd chalice to our own lips" (1.7.11-12). God punishes by causing the wicked to fall into their own traps, to drink the poison they intend for others. By the end of the soliloquy, he has concluded, "We will proceed no further in this business" (1.7.31). He is operating on an understanding of manhood that is completely different from his wife's; his soliloquy is based on the principle that he "dare do all that may become a man; who dares do more is none" (1.7.46-47). Being a man as opposed to a beast means accepting limitations and acting according to moral laws. Macbeth's hesitations are based not only on fear but on a sense of the moral obligations that go along with his roles as Duncan's subject, host, and kinsman. He is still, like the former Cawdor at his death, open to repentance.

If Macbeth's soliloquy shows that he is open to grace, Lady Macbeth, the tempting instrument of hell, works to close it off, with ultimate success. The fact that Macbeth follows his wife into what he knows to be sin is a sign of the disorder that is already beginning. She shames Macbeth by saying, in effect, that she is more daring than he, and her violent language employs again the imagery of mother's milk:

> I have given suck, and know
> How tender 'tis to love the babe that milks me.
> I would, while it was smiling in my face,
> Have pluck'd my nipple from his boneless gums
> And dash'd the brains out, had I so sworn as you
> Have done to this. (1.7.54-59)

Lady Macbeth's milk of human kindness has been turned, as she hoped, to gall. By her own definition, she has become more the man than her husband. We feel that she has not only been "unsexed," but that she has entirely left off her humanity. And we know that Macbeth has been won over by her demonic will when, instead of being horrified by his wife's willingness to kill her own children, he says admiringly, "bring forth men-children only" (1.7.72). At this very moment Macbeth exchanges his view of manhood for his wife's. Henceforth, morality no longer makes the man; murder does.

The imagery of the exchange between Macbeth and Lady Macbeth is worth noting. Macbeth protests that he cannot kill Duncan after Duncan has honored him; he should enjoy wearing the golden opinions that have been put on him, rather than throwing away everything so soon (1.7.31-34). Macbeth is picking up on the clothing imagery used earlier when he was invested with the "borrowed robes" of the thane of Cawdor (1.3.108-109; 1.3.144-146). Lady Macbeth turns the clothing imagery against her husband. She charges that Macbeth was like a drunkard who did not know what he was doing when he imaginatively "dressed" himself in royal garments. People speak boldly when they are drunk, but in the morning, with a hangover, they feel less confident. So also, Macbeth's hope that was drunk and bold now wakes pale and green (1.7.35-38). Lady Macbeth says that her husband seems willing to trade appearance for self-esteem; he is satisfied to wear the garments of a good reputation, even though he knows himself a coward beneath the robes (1.7.39-44).

Macbeth is finally won over by his wife. He knows that things cannot be done when one deed is done, that justice will bring his crimes upon his head, but he ends the scene by speaking of his plan to "mock the time with fairest show: False face must hide what the false heart doth know" (1.7.81-82). Lady Macbeth has deceived her husband into believing they deceive time, enjoying the benefits of killing Duncan without suffering the evil consequences. He has been convinced that the deed can be done when 'tis done. Lady Macbeth is not the only force that prompts Macbeth to murderous action. He is guided to Duncan's room by a floating dagger (2.1.33-49), a dagger that hovers in the same filthy air into the witches melted.

When he returns from murdering the king, Macbeth explains to his wife what happened in Duncan's chambers (2.2.22-43). He heard the guards awaken crying "Murder," but they put themselves back to sleep by saying prayers, God bless you, and Amen. Macbeth tried to repeat the Amen, but it got stuck in his throat. Though he needs blessing, he knows that he cannot ask for God's blessing on this deed. Macbeth is moving beyond the reach of grace, separating himself from God. Crossing the threshold into Duncan's room was a crossing into a new world, a world where prayers get stuck in the throat. And a world without sleep. While in Duncan's chambers, he heard a voice announce that sleep had died, murdered by the thane of Glamis (2.2.36-40). Like Duncan, sleep is innocent; like Duncan, sleep is dead. And with it dies all that makes life bearable:

> Macbeth does murder sleep—th' innocent sleep,
> Sleep that knits up the ravel'd sleave of care,
> The death of each day's life, sore labor's bath,
> Balm of hurt minds, great nature's second course,
> Chief nourisher in life's feast. (2.2.36-39)

There is no rest for the wicked. In killing sleep Macbeth has condemned himself to a life without comforts. Because Macbeth has murdered sleep, his cares will unravel him, his mind will become filled with scorpions (3.2.36), he will enjoy no feast. Afraid even to think of what he has done, Macbeth dares not return to Duncan's chamber (2.2.51-52). The combination of "done" and "dare" reminds us of Macbeth's earlier line, "I dare do all that becomes a man." Now he realizes that he has dared to go beyond the deeds of a man, and that he therefore is no man.

Macbeth notices the blood on his hands, and in the exchange that follows we see how Macbeth's view of the murder differs (at this point) from his wife's. Macbeth is again the bloody man. Earlier, he was stained with the blood of Duncan's enemies, now with Duncan's own; before, he was bloody in king's service, now in treason. His hands are so bloody, so defiled by his murder of an innocent and helpless king, that if he tried to wash them, they would defile the seas and yet not be cleansed. Nature itself, far from removing his defilement, is itself defiled by his crime (2.2.60-63). When Macduff later discovers Duncan's body, Macbeth makes a speech in which it is evident that he already feels the weight of his act (2.3.96-101). From now on, life seems pointless: "all is but toys" (2.3.99). These words have a triple meaning: to the audience in the theater, Macbeth is putting on a show, play-acting his grief, and his equivocal words hide his meaning rather than revealing it; to the thanes, his words indicate the depth of Macbeth's grief and his love for the dead king; at the deepest level, he is revealing his own sense of the meaninglessness and futility of life. It is important to realize that "all is but toys" are the words of a murderer; they do not represent Shakespeare's own view of life.

Lady Macbeth does not believe in guilt. She wants to return to Duncan's room and "gild" the faces of the guards so that it seems their "guilt" (2.2.55-57). By putting a "gilt" of blood on them, she will clothe them with "guilt." This clothing of guilt does not identify and reveal, but disguises and misleads. For Lady Macbeth, guilt is nothing more than gilt. Guilt is for her purely an external, public matter; so long as no one knows we are guilty, she says, we are fine. Where Macbeth believes that even the ocean could not cleanse his hands, Lady Macbeth believes that the job can be done with "a little water" (2.2.67). Her hands, she says, are bloody too: but her heart is not lily white (milky) like her husband's (2.2.64-65). Lady Macbeth is still playing the man, or, perhaps we should say, the beast.

It is brilliant dramatic touch that knocking begins while Macbeth and Lady Macbeth are still discussing the murder. Horrified as he is by what he has done, Macbeth understands the knocking as the approach of judgment. This becomes more significant when we consider that it is Macduff who is knocking outside, the first appearance in the play of the man who will eventually avenge Duncan's murder. No sooner has Macbeth crossed the threshold into Duncan's room than Macduff crosses the threshold into Inverness to discover the murder. No sooner has Macbeth seen the blood on his hands than the avenger of blood appears.

Lennox, who accompanies Macduff, reports on the strange occurrences of the preceding night (2.3.58-65; 2.4.4-20). Winds blew so hard that a chimney was toppled, and the air—the filthy, demon-filled air—was filled with strange noises. As in _Julius Caesar,_ the death of a ruler is reflected in natural omens; the disorder of nature reflects the disorder of the nation. Later, an anonymous old man tells Ross of a similar omen: a falcon towering in the sky was attacked and killed by a "mousing hawk" (2.4.10-13). This is even more pointedly a natural sign of the murder of Duncan; a low bird (the mousing hawk; Macbeth) killed a higher (the falcon; Duncan). As the old man comments, "'tis unnatural"—as unnatural as a thane killing his king (2.4.10). The blood on Macbeth's hands has, as he realized it would, defiled the world. The darkness that Macbeth called upon has not covered his deed, but it has enveloped the nation (2.4.6-9).

When Macduff discovers that Duncan is dead, an alarm

goes through the castle. Macbeth rushes to Duncan's room and kills the guards who had been charged with watching the king. The real reason, we know, is to protect himself by keeping the guards from testifying against him. He cannot know whether they will remember anything. To the thanes, however, Macbeth offers another reason. His loyalty to and love for Duncan was so great that he could not refrain from vengeance; when he saw their "gilt," his "violent love" outran the "pauser reason" (2.3.112-124). Macbeth disguises himself in garments of loyalty, covering up an act of treason and regicide; as Lady Macbeth had urged him, he puts on the innocent flower, but is the lying and murderous serpent underneath. In this second murder, Macbeth is again acting on the witches' inspiration. Lady Macbeth had said the wine would put Duncan's guards into a "swinish sleep" (1.7.67). Macbeth, like the Second Witch in 1.3.2, has been busy "killing swine."

Malcolm and Donalbain sense something rotten in the state of Scotland. There are, Donalbain says, "daggers in men's smiles" (2.3.146). The thanes of Scotland hide their hatred and plots of murder behind flattery and good cheer; everyone breathes the same air. And the nearer they are related to the king, the nearer they are to being killed. As Donalbain puts it, "The near in blood, the nearer bloody" (2.3.146-147). They know they are innocent, and they know that whoever killed Duncan will likely go after them next, since Malcolm has been announced as heir. To protect themselves from becoming bloody, they flee to England. But of course, their flight gilds them with the blood of their father, and everyone in Scotland believes them guilty (2.4.24-27). Their escape from becoming bloody, moreover, leaves the throne open to the ranking thane, Macbeth, the bloody man.

Macbeth has followed his wife's example by putting aside the milk of human kindness and replacing it with gall and thick blood. He has overleaped Malcolm and seized the throne. He has done the deed. The remainder of the play will show, however, that things are not done when the deed is done, that the deed does not trammel up the consequence nor catch with its surcease, success.

Review Questions.

1. How does Lady Macbeth describe her husband? What imagery does she use?

2. On whom does Lady Macbeth call for help as she encourages Macbeth to act?

3. Explain the opening lines of Macbeth's soliloquy in scene 7.

4. Why does Macbeth hesitate to kill Duncan? What does this say about his spiritual condition? What does it say about his view of manhood?

5. How does Lady Macbeth persuade her husband to kill the king?

6. What guides Macbeth to Duncan's chambers? What is significant about this?

7. How does Macbeth's decline begin from the moment of killing Duncan? What did he kill when he killed Duncan?

8. Contrast Macbeth's view of guilt with that of his wife.

9. Who knocks at the door early in the morning? Why is this important?

10. What are the natural signs that Macbeth's crime brings chaos and disorder? How are these signs connected to Macbeth's belief that the ocean cannot wash away his guilt?

Thought Questions.

1. How does Duncan describe Inverness castle? (1.6.1-3). What does this say about Duncan's judgment? Does Banquo agree with Duncan? (1.6.3-9). What does this imply about Banquo?

2. What has Banquo been thinking and dreaming about? (2.1.4-21). How does his attitude to the witches compare to Macbeth's?

3. How has Lady Macbeth made herself bold? (2.2.1-4).

Has it worked? How does this relate to Macbeth's statement that God's justice brings the poisoned chalice to our own lips?

4. Macbeth says that he would turn the green ocean red if he were to wash his hands (2.2.61-63). What is the significance of the colors he mentions?

5. What does the Porter call himself as he answers Macduff's knocking? (2.3.1-3). How is this significant?

6. According to the porter, how is drink an equivocator? (2.3.30-39). How does his description relate to Macbeth's situation?

7. Macduff calls the murder of Duncan "sacrilegious" (2.3.70-73). What is sacrilege? How is killing a king sacrilege? How does this highlight the parallel between Macbeth's crime and Adam's sin?

8. What does Macduff say to Lady Macbeth when she asks what the alarm is about? (2.3.88-91). How is this ironic?

9. How does Macbeth describe Duncan's wounds? (2.3.117-119). What is the significance of this description?

10. To what does Macbeth compare the daggers of Duncan's two guards? (2.3.120-122). What does he mean by this comparison? Why is it fitting?

Lesson Three: Acts 3-4

Once you have acted on the principle that power is the only good, one murder will not be enough. There will always be people who threaten your power—because they have too much power, or because they know how you got power—, and you will have to find ways to get rid of them. You will begin to see daggers in every smile. In *Hamlet*, Shakespeare shows how the violence of revenge spreads out and out until it engulfs everyone; in *Macbeth*, Shakespeare shows that unchecked lust for power has a similar effect. An ambitious murder is like a pebble dropped into a pool, which produces ripples of violence that spread to the furthest edges.

Macbeth wants to drop the pebble without making ripples. In one sense, obviously, his wish does not and cannot come to pass. Murder has effects, some of them immediate. In another, more subtle sense, Macbeth gets precisely what he wished for. He wants his act to bring an end to time, with its ceaseless flow of actions and consequences, of sins and judgments, and for Macbeth, time does end. Macbeth no longer marks his life by a rhythm of waking and sleeping; instead, he exists in a sleepless present. Time does not have meaning and direction; it becomes a tale told by an idiot, meandering here and there with no pattern. Life does not move, as it should, toward an old age surrounded by troops of friends but toward utter isolation. Sleep is not Macbeth's only unintended victim. Glamis has also murdered time.

Primarily, however, time ends because, though Macbeth has become king, he has no future, and he has no future because Banquo has an assured future (3.1.47-71; 3.2.13-26). The weird sisters told Banquo that his children would be kings. Since the prophecies of the sisters have come true for Macbeth, he concludes they will come true for Banquo as well. Macbeth, moreover, killed to make the prophecies come true, and perhaps he fears Banquo will also kill. Banquo, after all, admitted that he has been thinking about the weird sisters (2.1.20-21), and he suspects Macbeth's "play'dst most foully" for his new position (3.1.3). Though Macbeth is now king, so long as Banquo and his sons live, Macbeth knows that his is a "fruitless crown" and a "barren scepter"(3.1.60-61), since his children will not succeed him. He realizes bitterly that he has given his "eternal jewel" to the "common enemy of man"—he has sold his soul to the devil—to make the seed of Banquo kings (3.1.67-69). Macbeth concludes that being king is not enough: "To be thus is nothing, but to be safely thus" (3.1.47-48). To be safely thus, Macbeth hires three murderers to kill Banquo and Fleance, Banquo's son. He wants to make sure that no seed of Banquo lives to see the last prophecy fulfilled.

Just as killing Duncan was not the "be-all and the end-all," so things are not done when Banquo is killed, as Macbeth discovers in the banquet scene (3.4). In the Bible, the feast portrays the ideal world. According to Jesus' teaching, the kingdom of heaven is a place of feasting (Mt. 8:11-12), and the book of Revelation speaks of the "marriage feast of the Lamb" that will be celebrated at the end of history (Rev. 19:9). Feasts are occasions that enact the proper harmony of man and man, man and creation, and in Scripture, man with God. Feasts involve fellowship and friendship, enjoying and sharing in the fruits of the earth, joy and peace and good will. The feast embodies the way things really ought to be.

Macbeth's banquet is not only a picture of an ideal world in general, but a picture of the harmony that should exist in Scotland. What makes a feast different from a common meal is ceremony, and ceremony is in part a way of highlighting order, status, and hierarchy. Calling the Queen of England by the proper title, waiting to eat until the hostess is seated, bowing in the presence of a king—all these ceremonies manifest people's positions and relations to one another. At Peterhouse, the Cambridge college of which I am a member, no one addresses the head of the college as "Mr." or "Dr." or even "Sir," but as "Master," a verbal token of his status. Similarly, though Macbeth's royal feast is a time of fellowship, it is a ceremonial and therefore an ordered fellowship.

Lady Macbeth is especially careful to make sure that the feast displays the orderly hierarchy of Scottish society. She instructs the guests to sit in their proper places at the table, which is of course presided over by the king. Lady Macbeth encourages her distracted husband to be a more cordial host. She chides him for not offering the customary welcomes and toasts. Such ceremonies turn the feast into something more than an occasion for eating. Ceremony is to a gathering, she says, as "sauce to meat" (3.4.36-37). There is a pun on "meet" and "meat": Without ceremony, "meeting" would be a bare as "meat" without sauce. Under Lady Macbeth's direction, the feast thus begins as a small-scale model of what

Scotland should be: a place where people live in peace and harmony with one another, ordered under the wise and benevolent rule of the king.

In *Much Ado About Nothing*, Benedick comments at the first, disastrous wedding of Claudio and Hero, "This looks not like a nuptial." Had Benedick been present at Macbeth's feast, he would have said much the same: "This looks not like a feast." The feast is supposed to portray an orderly and harmonious Scotland, the way Scotland ought to be, but ends revealing what Scotland in fact is. At the earlier feast, Macbeth withdrew to contemplate murder. Here he is present at the feast, but disrupts the whole affair by his reaction to the appearance of Banquo's ghost. As he repeatedly promised, Banquo attends the feast (3.1.14-18, 27-28), not letting a little thing like death keep him away. Banquo's ghost not only appears but usurps Macbeth's place at the table, a sign of Macbeth's future. Though he murdered Duncan and had Banquo killed, Macbeth is still not safely thus. He will lose his seat of honor—to the descendants of the dead Banquo.

People are very hard to kill in Shakespeare. Well might Macbeth long for the good old days

> when the brains were out the man would die,
> And there an end; but now they rise again,
> With twenty mortal murders on their crowns,
> And push us from our stools. (3.4.79-82)

Caesar, Hamlet's father, Banquo—all return from the dead to haunt the living. The point is not that Shakespeare was superstitious. The point is that crimes will not go away. Sinners cannot avoid judgment for our actions. The blood of innocent Abel will cry out from the ground against Cain. Nothing is ever entirely done when 'tis done.

Lady Macbeth tries to cover for him by explaining that "My lord is often thus, and hath been from his youth" (3.4.53-54), but it can hardly be comforting for the nobles of Scotland to learn that their king has frequent hallucinations and fits of madness. Finally, Lady Macbeth concedes the feast is over, accusing Macbeth of "displacing the mirth" and breaking "the good meeting" with "most admir'd disorder" (3.4.108-109). As the guests leave, Lady Macbeth urges them to go quickly, without worrying about exiting in the proper ceremonial order: "stand not upon the order of your going, but go at once" (3.4.119-120). The joy, the fellowship, the decorum and order of the feast have been disrupted because the king is haunted by ghosts of his victims, just as the land is robbed of joy, fellowship, and order because of Macbeth's crimes. What began as a sign of the way Scotland ought to be ends with a shocking reminder of the way Scotland actually is. For the ghosts of Duncan and Banquo haunt not only Macbeth but the whole land.

Macbeth knows precisely what is happening. As he predicted in his soliloquy, God is putting the poisoned chalice to his own lips; as he says here, "blood will have blood" (3.4.122). Macbeth speaks as if the whole creation acts in concert to expose bloody crimes:

> Stones have been known to move and trees to speak;
> Augures and understood relations have
> By maggot pies and choughs and rooks brought forth
> The secret'st man of blood (3.4.123-126).

These are not, as some scholars have suggested, nonsense lines. Blood guilt, Macbeth realizes, will not go unavenged. There is a moral order in the universe, deeds have consequences, and bloody deeds will end in blood. Even the trees and rocks cry out as witnesses against the bloody man. Darkness has not after all been able to cloak Macbeth's crimes.

Though Macbeth knows all this, still he does not act on it. He defies the whole creation's unanimous testimony against him. He knows that he is wading in a river of blood, one that will only get deeper and harder to cross, but he concludes it is easier to keep on going in the same direction than to turn back (3.4.136-140). He rejects repentance, which literally means "turning around," as an option. Looking ahead, he sees only greater crimes, and concludes "we are yet but young in deed" (3.4.144). The First Murderer had it right. As the three murderers lay in ambush for Banquo and Fleance, the First Murderer observed, "The west yet glimmers with some streaks of day" (3.3.5). Prior to the murder of Banquo, the sun—the sun of Macbeth's sanity and of Scotland's prosperity—was setting but had not quite disappeared over the horizon. With the murder of Banquo, Macbeth and Scotland enter a perpetual and thickening darkness. The answer to the third murderer's question, "Who did strike out the light?" (3.3.18) is—Macbeth.

To embolden and strengthen himself to finish crossing the river of blood, Macbeth returns to the witches (4.1). In his first meeting, the witches sought out Macbeth. Now he seeks them, an indication that he is actively pursuing a Satanic course. They show him three apparitions, each of which is accompanied by a prophecy. But there is a dissonance, a contradiction or at least a tension, between the words and the pictures. The visions tell one story, the words another, and this makes the words equivocal. Macbeth hears the words of encouragement, but does not examine what messages are being communicated by the images. He believes he has good reason to conclude that the answer to Banquo's question, "Can the devil speak true?" is "Yes." Macbeth has himself become a master of equivocation, but he cannot discern equivocation in others. He, like his predecessor, is unable to read the mind's construction in the face.

First, there is an apparition of an armed head, and the first witch says, "He knows thy thought" (4.1.69). Who knows Macbeth's thoughts but Macbeth himself? The armed head is Macbeth's own, but it is a head severed from its body. Had Macbeth stopped to think about it, it may have occurred to him that this is a prophecy of his own future; as Macbeth severed the rebel Macdonwald's head from his shoulders, so will Macduff do to the rebel Macbeth. Thus, the first apparition says, "Beware Macduff" (4.1.71). This is the only lesson that Macbeth learns from the first apparition: Macduff is dangerous. Macbeth is ready to act on this warning: In the next scene, soldiers, under orders from Macbeth, kill Macduff's wife and child in cold blood (4.2). The river of blood gets deeper, and it becomes even harder to return.

The second apparition is a bloody child. Macbeth has been a bloody man from the beginning: bloody in fighting for Duncan; bloody with Duncan's blood; bloody with Banquo's blood; wading and splashing and swimming in blood. As Macbeth himself recognizes, blood will have blood. A bloody man will be avenged by a bloody man. During this second apparition, the witches assure Macbeth that no man of woman born shall harm him, but Macbeth never stops to think what the apparition has to do with the words. A bloody child is perhaps a child that is not of woman born. If such children exist, Macbeth had best not become overly confident.

Third, Macbeth sees a crowned child with tree in hand. The words announce that Macbeth will not be vanquished until Birnam wood comes to Dunsinane. Macbeth takes this as a good omen; he believes he is secure since no one can press a forest into military service. Again, the apparition tells a different story. It shows a child-king who has marshaled an army of trees. Macbeth has forgotten what he has been told by Banquo: the powers of darkness often "tell us truths, win us with honest trifles, to betray us in deepest consequence." Macbeth believes the witches' prophecies have come to pass, and has placed his full confidence in them. Now, when Macbeth is desperate for direction, when everything is at stake, they are betraying him.

Macbeth has gone from arranging the murder of Banquo, to seeing Banquo's ghost at the feast, and immediately to visit the witches. The intense sequence of events has left us breathless, and Shakespeare provides 4.3 partly to give us a chance to catch our breath before the final scenes. While this scene provides an emotional contrast to the preceding scenes, it is not a pointless digression. Often in comparatively restful scenes such as this Shakespeare explicitly highlights themes of his plays. Here, Malcolm and Macduff, exiled in England, engage in a discussion of Scotland's condition under Macbeth and the virtues of a good king.

Throughout the scene, Malcolm is testing Macduff's loyalty. He realizes that Macbeth would reward Macduff handsomely if he betrayed Malcolm and offered up the young prince as "a weak, poor, innocent lamb t'appease an angry god" (4.3.16-17). To determine if Macduff will be loyal to him, Malcolm tells him that, should he become king, he would make Macbeth's tyranny look like the pranks of a schoolboy. Malcolm claims that his sexual lust is such that no wife or daughter in Scotland would be safe; that his greed would endanger every noble's lands and goods; that he possesses none of the virtues of kingship but would create chaos and havoc, and "pour the sweet milk of concord into hell" (4.3.98; note another use of "milk" as an image). He is the opposite of everything that makes a king good. Macduff is horrified that Scotland might go from the tyranny of Macbeth to the worse tyranny of Malcolm. Malcolm's confession of his evil nature, he says, has "banish'd me from Scotland" and driven away all hope for his country (4.3.113). Malcolm then tells him that it was only a test to determine if Macduff was loyal to Macbeth. It has revealed that Macduff loves his nation and is not a tool of Macbeth. Malcolm's test leaves Macduff confused: "Such welcome and unwelcome things at once, 'tis hard to reconcile" (4.3.138-139).

In the course of this discussion, Macduff comments:

> Boundless intemperance
> In nature is a tyranny; it hath been
> Th' untimely emptying of the happy throne
> And fall of many kings. (4.3.66-69)

Macduff may be confused by Malcolm but he has a solid sense that good and enduring government requires "bounds" and limits. The source of tyranny, he says, is unlimited ambition, lust, and greed. Unlike Lady Macbeth, he knows that a man cannot be a king, unless he lives within boundaries. Like Macbeth at his better moments, he knows that whoever dares do more than becomes a man is none.

Macbeth's evil is highlighted not only by the conversation of Malcolm and Macduff, but also by the appearance of England's King Edward the Confessor, whose miraculous powers Malcolm describes:

> strangely visited people,
> All swoln and ulcerous, pitiful to the eye,
> The mere despair of surgery, he cures ...
> With this strange virtue
> He hath a heavenly gift of prophecy,
> And sundry blessings hang about his throne
> That speak him full of grace. (4.3.150-152, 156-159)

In *Macbeth*, there are always spiritual forces operating behind and within the human decisions and actions. Macbeth has become a scourge to his land by allying with hell, and he uses his power only to secure and maintain and add to his power. Good King Edward, inspired by heavenly spirits, uses his power to heal his land. Edward, full of grace, has promised to supply troops to Malcolm for the recovery of the throne of Scotland. Malcolm thus becomes an instrument of the triumph of grace.

Review Questions.

1. What does Macbeth mean by his "fruitless crown" and "barren scepter"?

2. Why does Macbeth want to kill Banquo?

3. What does the play show about the consequences of limitless ambition?

4. What does the feast symbolize? What makes a feast different from a common dinner? How?

5. How does Macbeth behave at the feast? Why?

6. What effect does Macbeth's behavior have on the feast? How does this reflect the situation in Scotland?

7. What does Macbeth mean by "blood will have blood"?

8. Does Macbeth intend to turn away from his bloody course? Why not?

9. What are the three apparitions that the witches show Macbeth? Explain how the apparitions are equivocal and misleading.

10. Why does Malcolm tell Macduff how evil he is? How does scene 3 highlight Macbeth's tyranny?

Thought Questions.

1. Is Banquo contemplating overthrowing Macbeth? (3.1.1-10).

2. What does Macbeth call Banquo? (3.2.13). Is this an accurate description? Why does Macbeth think of Banquo this way? Compare this description to Macbeth's description of himself in 3.2.36.

3. Who is the mysterious "third murderer" in 3.3? Is it Macbeth himself? Why or why not?

4. Who is blamed for Banquo's death? (3.6.16-20). How is Banquo's death like Duncan's?

5. What are the witches preparing in 4.1.1-21? What are the ingredients? How does this concoction reflect the disorder and chaos that Macbeth's crimes have caused?

6. What is the fourth vision that the witches show Macbeth? (4.1.101-124). How does this confirm Macbeth's worst fears? Who are the kings who bear "twofold balls and treble scepters"? (4.1.121). Whom is Shakespeare referring to?

7. After Macbeth meets with the witches, he says, "From this moment the very firstlings of my heart shall be the firstlings of my hand" (4.1.146-148). What does this mean? What does this say about the changes in Macbeth's view of manhood?

8. According to Malcolm, what are the "graces" of a king? (4.3.91-94). Does he possess them? (see 4.3.123-137).

9. What effect has Macbeth's tyranny had on the people of Scotland? (4.3.165-173, 181-189).

10. How does Macduff react to the news of his family's death? (4.3.201-240). Did he really love his family? (see 4.2.6-14). Why is Malcolm encouraged by Macduff's reaction?

Lesson Four: Act 5

Act 5 begins with the words of a Doctor who is observing Lady Macbeth's sleepwalking. His vocation and words foreshadow the whole of the final act, which is about the restoration of the rightful king, the return of order and normalcy, the healing of the land of Scotland. The Doctor is asked to treat Lady Macbeth, but what he says has implications for the healing of the land. This connection of Lady Macbeth's sickness with the sickness of the land is explicit in the Doctor's conversation with Macbeth in 5.3. Lady Macbeth, the Doctor says, is not sick, but troubled with "thick-coming fancies" (5.3.38). Macbeth wonders that the Doctor cannot help her, and the Doctor says in such cases the patient must help herself. Macbeth immediately launches into a speech about sick Scotland:

> If thou couldst, doctor, cast
> The water of my land, find her disease,
> And purge it to a sound and pristine health,
> I would applaud thee to the very echo,
> That should applaud again. (5.3.50-54)

Lady Macbeth's disordered soul is a symptom of the larger disorder of Scotland; the king's land and the king's bride are parallel realities. Like Scotland, Lady Macbeth suffers "a great perturbation in nature" (5.1.10), mixing sleep and waking as Scotland suffers a confusion of night and day (2.4.6-9).

The Doctor's words are also significant because he realizes that Lady Macbeth's problems are outside his capacity to heal. What she needs is God's forgiveness: "More needs she the divine than the physician. God, God forgive us all"

(5.1.82-83). No medical technique can heal a wounded conscience; only Divine mercy is sufficient medicine for such an illness. The Doctor's diagnosis is taken up by Malcolm at the very end of the play. Malcolm proves himself an ideal king when, after his victory over Macbeth, he shares his plans to return exiles to Scotland, to purge out whoever remains of Macbeth's supporters (which cannot be very numerous), all with reliance on the "grace of Grace" (5.8.72). Like the Doctor, Malcolm recognizes that healing and redemption from sin and its effects comes only from God. From the Doctor's opening words to Malcolm's last speech, the whole point of Act 5 is to emphasize that Scotland can only be healed and restored with God's intervention.

Lady Macbeth has changed immensely during the course of the play. After Macbeth had killed Duncan, she spoke of "guilt" as if it were nothing but "gilt." She believed that a little water could wash away the bloody evidence. She urged Macbeth not to worry, and to get some sleep. Now, everything has changed. Now she cannot sleep, for Macbeth has murdered sleep for her as well as for himself. She had told Macbeth to forget his crimes, but now she cannot clear her conscience of her share in Duncan's murder, or the killing of Banquo and the family of Macduff, the "thane of Fife" (5.1.47). She has learned that guilt is not "gilt." She no longer believes a little water can remove the stain from her hands; in fact, even all the perfume of Arabia cannot sweeten the smell of her defiled hand, no more than Neptune's ocean could cleanse Macbeth's (5.1.56-58). Before, she had said, "What's done is done" (3.2.12). Now, she says, "what's done cannot be undone" (5.1.75). These may sound the same, but they are exactly opposite. The first statement means, "Duncan is dead, and we cannot bring him back to life. There is no reason to make a fuss. So let's just forget about it and get on." The second statement is despairing: Now she wishes she could undo what has been done, and lives in anguish because she cannot. Before, she had wanted to be cloaked in the "dunnest smoke of hell"(1.5.52); now she finds herself in "murky" hell (5.1.40-41), and is horrified.

Macbeth meanwhile has become isolated not only from his increasingly insane queen, but also from his subjects. Even his servant Seyton does not respond to Macbeth's calls to him (5.2.19-20, 29). It is at this point that Angus comments that Macbeth's title hangs loose like a giant's robe upon a dwarfish thief (5.1.20-22). The robe is symbol of office, authority, and rule. Angus's comment means that Macbeth's title as king does not fit his character. He may be king externally, but the royal robe was not made for him. He has stolen a robe that is not his size. Contrary to Banquo's initial expectations, these are not robes that will "cleave to their mould . . . with the aid of use" (1.3.144-146), but ones that become more ill-fitting with each day.

What is lacking that makes Macbeth's robe so unfit for him? Angus says, "Those he commands move only in command, nothing in love" (5.2.19-20). Macbeth also recognizes that what he really lacks is love, loyalty, obedience from heart. Instead, he has only "curses, not loud but deep, mouth-honor, breath, which the poor heart would fain deny, and dare not" (5.2.27-28). Genuine authority is a two-way street; it involves not only the exercise of power by a ruler but also love and loyalty from his subjects. Now, the thanes and people are abandoning Macbeth. They bear him no love, loyalty, or respect. Without these, a king (or pastor, or father, or husband) cannot have true authority. Unless the people love the king, the robe does not fit.

In the absence of love and loyalty, a ruler only has power, the ability to force obedience to his will. The people Macbeth commands "move only in command," obeying not because they want to please their king but only because they fear punishment for disobedience. Without authority and its corollary of love and loyalty, a king can rule only through the barrel of a gun. Macbeth's ambition has reached its logical conclusion: Ambition has made him tyrannical, and his tyranny has further isolated him from his subjects, thus destroying his authority. Macbeth wanted nothing but power, and now he is left with nothing but power. There is yet a further ironic twist. As Malcolm's army advances, he discovers that "we have met with foes that strike beside us" (5.7.28-29). Even those who had remained outwardly loyal to Macbeth turn against him and fight beside Malcolm's troops. The wheel of political fortune has turned completely round: Ambitious only for power, Macbeth ultimately finds himself completely powerless.

Macbeth loses the one dearest to him: Lady Macbeth. He reacts to the news of her suicide with one of the most famous speeches in Shakespeare (5.5.17-28). Though these lines powerfully express the emptiness that many people sometimes experience, they should not be taken as Shakespeare's last word on the meaning of life. They are the words of a man steeped in blood, a man who commits unspeakable crimes and refuses to repent, a man who has been robbed by his own sins of all joy, friends, love and loyalty. In this sense again, Macbeth's hope that his deed could be done when it was done is ironically fulfilled. Once he carried out his fateful decision to kill Duncan, life was emptied of meaning and in that sense life did come to an end. For Macbeth, each day is just one more weary step toward death. There is no hope, no future, no real tomorrow. Because he could not escape the consequences of his act, Macbeth's life has become aimless and meaningless. His is a deeply paradoxical condition: Precisely because he could not escape the meaningfulness of time, time has become meaningless; precisely because things were not done when the deed was done, things were done when the deed was done.

Ultimately, the last thing Macbeth trusts—the witches' prophecy—also betrays him. Birnam wood does come to Dunsinane; when Macbeth learns of Malcolm's advance, he realizes the sisters have equivocated (5.5.40-45). Strangely, he is still confident he is invincible, a sign that he still trusts their prophecy. Too late, when Macduff reveals that he was not of woman born, Macbeth realizes that "these juggling fiends" use a double sense and "keep the word of promise to our ear, and break it to our hope" (5.8.19-22). At this point, he fights on merely to save a bit of dignity, to avoid being ridiculed.

Malcolm's time in England has been well spent, for he returns to Scotland performing the same miracles of healing as the saintly Edward. Scotland's healing is symbolized by the coming of Birnam wood to Dunsinane. The moving wood is an encroaching spring after the winter of Macbeth's tyranny. Lennox, one of the lords fighting with Malcolm, says that the task of the thanes is to pour themselves out so much as is needed to dew the flower (Malcolm) and drown the weeds (Macbeth) (5.2.29-31). Macbeth himself says he is like a yellow autumn leaf (5.3.22-23). Macbeth's regime is fading and dying, but Malcolm's regime of spring is advancing. Significantly, the army is made up of young men in the first blush of manhood, a fact that underscores the springtime imagery. The coming of the rightful king transforms the world, so that the desert begins to bloom like the rose.

Allied with Malcolm, who is in turn allied with Edward, full of grace, Macduff is triumphant. The "bloody child" of the second apparition takes vengeance against the bloody man. The new Cawdor, like the old, is put to the sword; like the rebel Macdonwald, the rebel Macbeth is beheaded. The product of a miracle birth, Macduff slays the "serpent" who under the cover of the "innocent flower" has poisoned Scotland. Like another great Hero, Macduff crushes this serpent's head, and Malcolm proceeds to take the throne and begins the restoration of Scotland relying on the "grace of Grace."

Review Questions.

1. Why does Act 5 begin with a doctor?

2. How is Lady Macbeth's illness similar to her husband's? How is it similar to Scotland's?

3. What causes Lady Macbeth's distress? How has she changed through the course of the play?

4. What is Lady Macbeth doing as she sleepwalks? Why?

5. Why is it fitting that Malcolm's army marches to Dunsinane carrying branches from trees?

6. Explain how Macbeth has become isolated from his subjects. What does this say about the true nature of authority?

7. How does Macbeth react to the news of Lady Macbeth's death?

8. When does Macbeth conclude that the witches cannot be trusted?

9. How does Macduff fulfill the witches' prediction?

10. What is significant about Macbeth's being beheaded?

Thought Questions.

1. Lady Macbeth sleepwalks carrying a light (5.1.25-27). How does this compare with her earlier desire to be covered with darkness? Has she really allowed herself to be exposed to the light?

2. How does Caithness describe what Malcolm's army intends to do? (5.2.27-29). How does this fit with the rest of Act 5? What is the medicine that will purge the land?

3. How does Macbeth treat his servants? (5.3.11-17). How does this fit with Agnus's comment about Macbeth's ill-fitting robes?

4. Why is Macbeth not horrified by the shrieks of women within the castle? (5.5.9-15). What does this tell you about the state of Macbeth's soul? What is the image of "supping full" with horrors? How does this connect to the feast scene in 3.4?

5. What does Macbeth mean by saying that Lady Macbeth "should have died hereafter"? (5.5.17).

6. To what does Macbeth compare himself as Malcolm's army approaches? (5.7.1-2; see 5.8.29). How does this relate to Macduff's name for Macbeth? (5.8.3).

7. Macduff mentions an "angel" whom Macbeth has served (5.8.14). To whom he is referring?

8. How does Siward react to the death of his son? (5.8.35-53).

9. What does Malcolm promise to the thanes who fought with him? (5.8.60-64).

10. Malcolm describes his restoration of Scotland as a new planting (5.8.65). Why does he use this image? How does this relate to the fact that Malcolm defeated Macbeth by enlisting Birnam wood?

Video Productions of Macbeth

I have viewed all or part of four different video versions of *Macbeth*. Orson Welles's 1948 film is, in my view, the best of the lot. Marked by quirky visual effects and odd cave-like sets (which reminded me of a big-city sewer system), it captures something of the eery atmosphere of the play, but is not too intense. There is nothing objectionable in this film. Welles did not follow the play exactly; for example, he moved the famous witches' lines, "double, double, toil and trouble" from the fourth to the first Act. There are a couple of other drawbacks: it was filmed in black and white and the scenes are sometimes shadowy and hazy (though this is probably at least partly deliberate); the dialogue is sometimes difficult to follow; and some of the effects seem quaint today. Overall, it lives up to its reputation as a classic.

My second choice would be the Century Home Video production. Jeremy Brett, who plays Sherlock Holmes on the PBS Mystery series, has the lead role. Brett makes a decent Macbeth, but he is infinitely better as the annoying, know-it-all detective. This version follows the text of the play to the T, including even the longest scenes and speeches, which may detract from its interest for students. It is a film of a stage play, and for that reason is visually less interesting than a film version; it is difficult, for example, effectively to stage an army marching toward a castle. Dramatic techniques (gestures, voice range) that are necessary on stage sometimes look like over-acting on film. There are a couple of problems beyond this. When Macbeth returns to his wife after battle, their embrace is realistically passionate; it would probably pass for PG if rated. The witches are a big problem. First, they are way too young and pretty; when Banquo mentions the witches' "beards" and their "withered fingers," you wonder what he has been drinking. Second, the witches are followed everywhere by slithering, crouching, crawling, froglike demons; this would not be too distracting except that the demons and the witches frequently stop to embrace and fondle each other sensually. I suppose this might have some dramatic purpose, but it makes the video somewhat less suitable for children.

Roman Polanski's *Macbeth* follows the text of the play very closely and is the most technically contemporary version I've seen. Polanski effectively recreates the atmosphere of the play. He made a few irritating changes. Polanski's most blatant error of artistic judgment is to show Macbeth's assassination of King Duncan, which in the play is "ob-scene" (off-scene). Showing the murder adds blood and violence while detracting from the dramatic effect—not a good trade-off. (Welles follows Shakespeare by not showing the murder, but only its effect on Macbeth and his wife.) Apart from artistic issues, however, Polanski's film is not at all suitable for young students. It is much too violent. Lady Macbeth is completely nude during her sleep-walking scene, and the witches are all nude when Macbeth visits their "den" in Act 4. Polanski's *Macbeth* certainly earned its "R" rating. *Playboy* publisher Hugh Hefner was the executive producer of this film, and this was before his recent, belated decision to stop acting like a middle-aged adolescent. Enough said.

Bob Jones University has produced a video of their stage production of *Macbeth* that follows the play quite closely. This is a very competent college production. Like the Century Home Video, it is a filmed stage play and is not as visually interesting as a film. Moreover, it is clear that most of the actors are students, not professional actors.

Suggested Paper Topics

1. Discuss the function of the witches in *Macbeth*. What is their relation with Lady Macbeth and Macbeth himself? What

does the play suggest about Macbeth's responsibility for his actions.

2. Trace the imagery of blood, bloody men, bloody children through the play.

3. Examine the character of Banquo. Describe how he functions as a contrast to Macbeth. Or, examine the character of Malcolm or Macduff in the same light.

4. Discuss the character of Lady Macbeth, her views on manhood, her relationship to the witches, and the way she changes through the play.

5. Examine the imagery of darkness in *Macbeth*: darkness as a symbol of evil, as a covering for evil, and the reversal of day and night as a consequence of evil. Examine the contrasting imagery of light.

6. Write a revision of *Macbeth* using contemporary political figures for the characters. Whom would you cast as Macbeth? Lady Macbeth? Banquo?

7. Write a revision of *Macbeth* in which your favorite fictional detective comes to Inverness to investigate the murder of Duncan. Would Sherlock Holmes, Brother Cadfael or Father Brown have been suspicious of Macbeth?

8. Discuss the different portrayals of kingship and authority: Macbeth versus Edward the Confessor and Malcolm. Focus especially on the lengthy discussion of the virtues of kings in 4.3.

9. Examine the seasonal imagery in the play: e.g., winter, Macbeth's statement that he is like a yellow autumn leaf, the triumph of Birnam wood.

10. Research the life of the real Macbeth. How does Shakespeare's portrayal compare to what actually occurred?

Section III:

Comedy

Introduction: Comedy

Comedy is a particular literary "genre." The word "genre" refers to a group of literary works with certain characteristics in common. Tragedy, comedy, and epic are classical "genres," but we are perhaps more familiar with dividing literature into categories such as novel, short story, poetry, and drama, and it is possible to call these "genres" as well. We even speak of "sub-genres" like fantasy, science fiction, or magical realism.

What is it that all works in the genre "comedy" share? Today, we think of a comedy as a funny play or show, with lots of jokes and ridiculous situations. Comedies are not serious but have a light and cheerful tone. Our definition of comedy shares something with ancient drama. Classical Greek comedy was originally highly satirical. These plays made fun of the philosophers and of serious tragedy. Roman comedies concentrated on romances, the efforts of young lovers to overcome the obstacles put in their way by a father or another authority figure. In Roman comedy, the lover is generally aided by a wily and cunning slave and has to outwit others who vie for the beloved's affections. Lucentio in *The Taming of the Shrew* is a classical Roman comic lover.

Shakespeare includes a lot of jokes in his comedies, though they were funnier for his original audiences than they are for us today. There are also funny characters, such as Benedick, Dogberry, Katherina, Petruchio, Grumio. And there are ridiculous situations, such as the unmasking scene in *Taming of the Shrew* 5.1. Like tragedy, however, comedy is defined by the structure of its plot. Tragedy depicts a movement from prosperity to affliction, and comedy portrays the opposite movement from affliction to prosperity. While tragedy can be diagramed as an upside-down U, comedy is a right side-up U. Comedy does not ignore the reality of evil and the possibility of tragedy. Shakespeare's comedies have a dark side. As we shall see in *Much Ado About Nothing*, there are threats to happiness, and the comic world of Messina is constantly on the verge of turning tragic. But in the end tragedy is avoided. To put it simply but fairly accurately: At the end of a tragedy, all the main characters are dead and at the end of a comedy, all the main characters get married.

In Christian terms, tragedy depicts the fall of man while comedy depicts his salvation. Comedies are "redemption stories," and thus it can be fruitful to study comic plays in terms of the various ways in which the Bible describes the story of salvation in Christ. We need to be careful here. I will suggest some analogies between Christ and Petruchio, but I certainly would not want to press those analogies too far. Still, just as every drama that shows the consequences of sin bears some resemblance to story of the fall of Adam, so every drama that involves a rescue from tragedy and ends with reconciliation and happiness reflects, if only vaguely, the reality of redemption, and every comic hero who wins his bride bears some likeness to the Divine Bridegroom.

Till She Stoop She Must Not Be Full-Gorged:
The Taming of the Shrew

The Taming of the Shrew begins with two "Induction" scenes about one Christopher Sly. Sly is a tinker of Warwickshire whom a lord, returning from a hunt, finds in a gutter sleeping off his drunkenness. The lord decides to play a trick on the slumbering tinker, so he orders his servants to take Sly into his house, put him in his bed, and treat Sly as the lord. When he wakes, Sly is understandably confused; he protests that he is not a lord, but finally is convinced. Upon hearing about his wife, Sly asks, "Am I a lord, and have I such a lady? Or do I dream? Or have I dreamed till now?" (Induction, 2.66-67). A young boy page dresses up to play the part of Sly's wife, players are called in, and a play begins. The play Sly watches from his bed is what we know as *The Taming of the Shrew*. In short, *The Taming of the Shrew* is a play within a play.

Sly appears again only at the end of the first act to put in his evaluation of the play: "'Tis a very excellent piece of work, madam lady: would 'twere done!" (1.1.251-252). Some productions have left Sly on stage through the whole play, and in a parallel play, *The Taming of a Shrew*, which may be an earlier version of Shakespeare's play, Sly appears again at the end, when he wakes up in a gutter and decides to go home to tame *his* wife. In the play as we have it, however, Sly disappears after the first scene.

The Induction scene is a remarkable piece of dramatic writing in itself, and shows Shakespeare's astonishing ability to set out believable scenes and characters, like a sketch artist, with a few strokes of the pen. Sly bursts onto stage in the midst of an argument with the Hostess of his favorite tavern about repayment for the glasses he has broken (Induction, 1.1-10). Sly's moral character is immediately revealed by his refusal to make restitution for the damage he has caused, and his intellectual capacity is as quickly manifested by his misquotations of history and literature. He says "Richard Conqueror" when he means "William the Conqueror," not only mistaking William's first name but apparently taking "Conqueror" as a surname. He swears by "Saint Jeronimy," confusing St. Jerome the Church Father with Hieronymus, a character from Kyd's *Spanish Tragedy*. It is only ten brief lines, but it is enough for Shakespeare to give a vivid characterization and let us know more about Sly than we probably wanted to know.

Though the Induction scenes are skillfully written and paced, at first glance they seem to have little to do with *The Taming of the Shrew* itself. Shakespeare, however, rarely if ever includes such scenes without purpose. First, the Induction scenes set the tone of the entire play. When the play explodes before us with a shatter of glass and a raucous argument, we know immediately what kind of play we are watching. We know it is not going to be a tear-jerker or a quiet, meditative play. It is going to be fun, and rather boisterous fun at that. As the Induction proceeds, Shakespeare skillfully fills in the setting. Huntsman appear, comparing notes on their hunting dogs. Their leisurely discussion, full of technical hunting terms, stands in sharp contrast to Sly's oaths and contentiousness, and gives us a sense of a real country setting.

Moreover, these scenes introduce some of the important themes that are developed in the course of the play. The Induction scenes are concerned with mistaken and confused identity. Sly is not who people say he is. He has not been dreaming; he has been tricked into believing he is someone other than Christopher Sly, "old Sly's son of Burton-heath,

by birth a pedlar, by education a cardmaker, by transmuta-
tion a bear-herd, and now by present profession a tinker"
(Induction, 2.16-19). He takes on a new identity because he
relies on the servants' testimony, because he trusts the names
they give him and the way they describe the world. The notion that one's character and personality can be shaped by
submission to the word of another will, we see, be central to
the relationship of Petruchio and Katherina. But the Induction scene shows that the influence of a new name may be no
more than skin deep. We know that eventually Sly's dream
will come to an end, the lord will kick him out the door, and
he will find himself back in the gutter. The servants will stop
calling him "master" and "lord" and again call him "monstrous beast," "swine," "foul and loathsome," a "drunken man"
(Induction, 1.31-33). Names can identify; but people can also
assume false names, titles, and identities. Calling a Christopher Sly a lord does not make him one.

A name or title is like an article of clothing, and like a
name clothing is a double-sided image. On the one hand, there
is a truth in the saying, "The clothes make the man." We recognize doctors and nurses, judges and policemen by their
uniforms. But we know, on the other hand, that uniforms can
be counterfeited. We have all heard stories about people who
sneak into hospitals and impersonate doctors, sometimes even
performing surgery for years before their fraud is uncovered. People put on the uniforms of clergymen, policemen,
or judges without really holding those positions; they put on
the clothing that identifies, without really having the identity.
Clothing does not identify who they really are; clothing becomes a mask and a disguise to hide their real identity from
others. Sometimes the clothes do not make the man.

Clothing's potential as a disguise is highlighted in *The
Taming of the Shrew*. Sly is dressed in "sweet clothes," has
rings on his fingers, and is surrounded by the "garments" of
noble life—a soft bed, paintings, attending servants, music
and drama. In Sly's case, the clothing is designed to hide Sly's

true identity from himself. In this way, the Induction scenes fit perfectly into a play dominated by clothing imagery, where disguises abound and where nearly every character puts on someone else's clothes at some point in the play. As we read this play, we should keep in mind that disguises can be more subtle as well. Putting on an act can be as much a disguise as putting on a false beard and sunglasses.

The theme of identity, and the related imagery of clothing, are closely intertwined in the play with issues of change and transformation. Transformations of name, identity, position—changes of "clothing"—fill the play to overflowing: Lucentio and Tranio trade places, and then Lucentio takes on another name; Hortensio disguises himself to gain access to Bianca; Tranio convinces an anonymous traveler to impersonate Lucentio's father Vincentio. Nearly the only relationship that does not involve disguise and deception is that between Petruchio and Katherina. Petruchio arrives at his wedding wearing mad attire, and later offers Katherina a new gown, but neither uses clothing as a disguise. Ironically, it is this relationship, from which superficial transformations and masks are absent, that produces the most lasting and profound transformation of all. In the end, Baptista, whose relationship with Katherina has been, to put it mildly, cool, says, with accuracy and admiration: "For she is changed, as she had never been" (5.2.115).

Transformation comes through education, and two models of education are suggested by the play, embodied in Lucentio and Tranio on the one hand and Petruchio on the other. Both views of education have a practical goal; Lucentio wants to study philosophy so as to acquire virtue, and Petruchio's training of Katherina has the practical goal of taming her wildness. Their methods, however, are very different. In the opening scene, Tranio tells Lucentio that learning best takes place in an atmosphere of leisure and ease:

> The mathematics and the metaphysics,
> Fall to them as you find your stomach serves you.

No profit grows where is no pleasure ta'en.
In brief, sir, study what you most effect. (1.1.37-40)

Lucentio agrees. Petruchio, by contrast, operates on the assumption that education in virtue, true practical transformation, requires imposition of strict boundaries, rigorous discipline, and a kind of coercion. Petruchio believes that a successful teacher demands that his pupils fall to their studies even when their stomachs do not affect it, even when they do not want to study. A successful teacher requires his students to accept his answers as the right answers, to accept his labels and names for the world. For Petruchio, as Gunnar Sorelius has put it, acquiring true wisdom requires a "discipline of pain as well as ease." This notion of education is taken to a comic and even farcical extreme in the play but the educational method behind it is quite serious.

It does not goes too far to suggest that, making allowances for the comic setting, Petruchio's training of Katherina is similar to Christ's training and discipline of His unruly Bride, the Church (see, for example, Ezek. 16; 23; Rev. 2-3). If a comparison of Petruchio and Christ seems far-fetched, it is well to recall that the Jesus of the gospels is not all "sweet Jesus, meek and mild." He also is the One who sharply denounces the hypocrisy of the Pharisees (Mt. 23) and drives merchants from the temple with a whip (Jn. 2:13-21). As is said of Aslan in the Narnia Chronicles, Jesus is good but He is "not tame." Sorelius points out that Petruchio takes on divine attributes and powers in the play. He is able to command time, the sun and moon, and to turn an old man into a fresh young maid with nothing more than a word. For Katherina at least, Petruchio's word is reality, and molds reality in its image.

J. Dennis Huston has helpfully pointed to parallels between *The Taming of the Shrew* and fairy tales. Petruchio is a fairy tale hero, who rescues the other characters, and the action of the play has a dreamlike quality that one finds in folk stories. Instead of killing the monster and marrying the princess,

Huston points out, Petruchio must marry the monster and turn her into a princess. This is not a tale of beauty and the beast; it is a tale where beauty is the beast. In this context, we can understand the significance of the pervasive animal imagery of the play. Katherina is the "shrew" of the title. A shrew is a small, mole-like rodent that has long been considered mean and ferocious. Kate is also called a "fiend of hell" (1.1.88) and a "devil's dam" (1.1.104), and Petruchio compares his taming of Kate to training a falcon for hunting (4.1.175-183). Kate's progress is from bestial savagery and ferocity to tame and gentle womanhood. Petruchio represents the power of civilization and religion, which employs authority and even force to shape a depraved humanity. Petruchio, like Christ, is preparing a savage child of hell to become Queen at his right hand.

Important as Petruchio's education and discipline is to Katherina's "conversion," it is not enough in itself. Sorelius's insightful essay on this play bears the sub-title, "Metamorphosis as Divine Gift." Petruchio's efforts play their part, but in the final scene, the characters recognize they have witnessed a miracle. Lucentio sits open-mouthed, and cannot use the word "wonder" (which in Shakespeare's day had the same meaning as "miracle") often enough: "Here is a wonder, if you talk of wonder" (5.2.106), and he pronounces the final words of the play: "'Tis a wonder, by your leave, she will be tamed so" (5.2.189). *The Taming of the Shrew* does not present a picture of redemption by education alone, for it ends with a recognition that, without the intervention of God's grace and power, even the most consistent discipline and training has no deeper or more lasting effect than dressing a tinker in a lord's bedclothes.

Lesson One: Act 1

Act I contains two parallel scenes:

	Scene 1	Scene 2
Arrival	Lucentio	Petruchio
Plan to Court	Bianca	Katherina
Disguise	Lucentio	Hortensio

The act opens with the arrival of the two major male characters in Padua. Both announce their reasons for coming to Padua in opening speeches. Each makes plans to court one of the two main women characters. Baptista's refusal to allow Bianca to marry before Katherina brings the two characters and their plans together. Petruchio answers the prayers of Bianca's suitors, for by courting Katherina, he cuts through the Gordian knot that prevents Bianca from marrying. These scenes set up an immediate parallel and connection between Lucentio and Petruchio, between Bianca and Katherina, and between the two courtships, and thus we are invited to compare their intentions, their methods, their results. The whole play is structured by the progress of these contrasting courtships.

Lucentio arrives in Padua as a student. Initially Padua is above all the "nursery of the arts" a place to "institute a course of learning and ingenious studies." His interests are especially in the branch of philosophy that "treats of happiness by virtue specially to be achieved" (1.1.8-9, 18-20). He makes a point of saying that he comes with authorization from his father. The authority of fathers is an important issue in the play, though not one that we will take time to develop. Lucentio announces that he comes to Padua to fulfill the hopes that all have for Vincentio's son (1.1.14-16); Petruchio's move to Padua is occasioned by the death of his father (1.2.49-55); the crux of the problem in the play is Baptista's exercise of paternal authority, since he refuses to marry Bianca before Katherina is married; later, Tranio will find an old man to play Lucentio's father, Vincentio; at the beginning of Act 5, the real Vincentio appears and the confused relations of fathers and sons must be unraveled. In addition to the contest between the sexes the play also depicts a contest between generations.

For Tranio, Padua holds attractions that cannot be called philosophic. He makes a passing gesture of respect for his mater's scholarly pursuits, but then he gets to his real message:

> Only, good master, while we do admire
> This virtue and this moral discipline,
> Let's be no stoics, nor no stocks, I pray,
> Or so devote to Aristotle's checks
> As Ovid be an outcast quite abjured.
> (1.1.29-33)

Aristotle, the Greek philosopher who represents serious study, philosophy, logic, and moderation in all things, should be balanced with Ovid, the great Roman poet of love. All philosophy and no play, Tranio says, makes Lucentio a dull boy. As we saw above, Tranio is also suggesting a view of education that minimizes discomfort and authority in favor of ease and free choice.

That reference to Ovid has additional importance. Ovid was not only the author of the *Art of Love* but also a compiler of myths. One of his works, *Metamorphosis*, is a collection of myths that all have in common some kind of transformation—from animal to man, from man to animal, from man into plant, etc. Lucentio will shortly be transformed into Tranio and Tranio into Lucentio, and all around them the characters will trade their identities. At the heart of the play is the transformation of a shrew into a woman. In such surroundings, Ovid is indeed worth Lucentio's attention.

Moments after Tranio has given his advice, Baptista, Katherina, and Bianca appear, trailing a little cloud of Bianca's admirers. The moment Lucentio sees Bianca and hears her speak, arts, philosophy, virtue, logic are out the window. Goodbye, Aristotle; Hello, Ovid! Lucentio and Tranio trade places. Tranio, who had been urging the study of Ovid, becomes realistic and logical, calling Lucentio's attention to the storm and din raised by Katherina and explaining the obstacles that lie between Lucentio and Bianca (1.1.168-181). Tranio sets himself to determine how the obstacles can be overcome: Goodbye, Ovid; Hello, Aristotle. Fittingly, since Lucentio and Tranio have already exchanged viewpoints, their plan involves an exchange of clothing and identity (1.1.185-214). Lucentio will disguise himself as a teacher in order to get close to Bianca, while Tranio pretends to be Lucentio and woos Bianca.

When he first hears Bianca, Lucentio compares her to Minerva (1.1.84). This is a significant insight, one that Lucentio himself does not fully comprehend. On the one hand, the comparison fits in the context. Minerva or Athena was the goddess of all technical arts. Above all goddesses in ancient mythology she was believed to be equipped with practical intelligence and skill. Like Minerva, Bianca has just mentioned her devotion to books and music: "My books and instruments shall be my company, on them to look and practise by myself" (1.1.82-83). There is an additional level to the comparison, however. Minerva was not only the goddess of technical arts but also a goddess of war. (Athena is called Pallas Athene throughout Homer because she had killed Pallas in her youth.) While Lucentio believes he has found a goddess of skill and beauty, his words hint that he may also have found a woman devoted to conflict. The silent, mild, sober Bianca may prove more a Minerva than her shrewish sister.

Later in the play, it will be said of Petruchio that "he hath some meaning in his mad attire." If Katherina clothes herself in madness and shrewishness, her attire is not without meaning either. Her first words are directed to her father: "I pray you, sir, is it your will to make a stale of me among these mates?" (1.1.57-58). There is a multi-leveled pun in this question. First, Katherina is referring to the game of chess with her play on the word "stalemate." A stalemate is a final position in which the king can no longer move without being placed in check though he is not in check. There is no real winner in a game that ends in stalemate; the game simply ends because the king is trapped and cannot make another move. Katherina asks whether her father has deliberately put her in a similar position.

What has trapped Katherina is her father's policy with respect to his daughters. He obviously favors Bianca and wants her to be happy. At the same time, he refuses to permit Bianca's marriage until Katherina is married. Katherina believes that in her father's eyes, and surely in Bianca's, she is little more than an obstacle to her sister's happiness. No one is interested in Katherina for herself, not even her father, who seeks husbands for Katherina less for her sake than for Bianca's. Katherina's sense of being "stalemated" by her father and sister offers a partial explanation of her shrewish behavior. Some have suggested that her conduct is something like a "self-fulfilling prophecy." Unloved by her father, she concludes she is unlovable, so she behaves in a way that ensures no one will love her. The more she makes herself unlovable, the more she proves she is unlovable. Others have suggested that Katherina is fearful of intimacy: To prevent anyone from getting near, she makes herself into someone that no one wants to be near. More simply, her behavior is a way of avenging herself on Bianca. By making sure no one wants to marry her, Katherina is also making sure that Bianca will not get married.

"Stale" has some other important connotations as well. In Shakespeare's day, a "stale" was a laughing stock, someone who was the object of mockery and joking. Katherina has to endure abuse from her sister's suitors, who talk about her as if she were not there, as well as from the whole city of Padua, where no doubt she is well known as the shrewish sister of sweet Bianca and the daughter who stands in the way of her sister's marriage. Finally, a "stale" is a prostitute. Katherina is saying that Baptista is willing to accept any husband, no matter how unsuitable, to take Katherina off his hands. He is willing to sell her to the highest bidder, which reduces her to a whore. It may be possible to understand and even sympathize with Katherina, but her conduct is inexcusable. She lives up completely to her reputation. Though she may be old enough to marry, she still acts like a child, with her violent tantrums, her envy of her sister, her self-centeredness. Bianca, on the other hand, clearly knows she is her father's favorite and makes the most of the situation. She is a little "goody-two-shoes," the Pharisaical daughter who always says the right thing and does the right thing not because she really is good but because she wants everyone to think she's good. Her first words are as revealing as Katherina's (1.1.80-83). When Lucentio hears her speak, he thinks he is listening to Minerva. We hear her say, essentially, "I'll do whatever you say, daddy dear. And now may I please go do my homework? Please?"— and we know that she is simultaneously building herself up in daddy's eyes and making sure daddy knows how different she is from mean, old Katherina. Her words are so sweetly manipulative they make you vomit.

Gremio has said that it would be better to look for a devil rather than a man to marry Katherina (1.1.120-123). Enter Petruchio, who seems to fit the bill. Petruchio, like Katherina and Sly, bursts onto the scene like a storm cloud, almost immediately beginning to beat his servant Grumio for not knocking on Hortensio's door. Grumio testifies that this master is mad (1.2.18), and he may even be a bit drunk. Like Lucentio, Petruchio comes to Padua seeking happiness, but the happiness he seeks is not that which is achieved by virtue. For Petruchio, happiness means finding a wealthy wife (1.2.74-75). As he tells his old friend Hortensio, he is not choosy:

> if thou know
> One rich enough to be Petruchio's wife—
> As wealth is burden of my wooing dance—
> Be she as foul as was Florentius' love,
> As old as Sibyl, and as curst and shrewd
> As Socrates' Xanthippe, or a worse,

She moves me not—or not removes at least
Affection's edge in me, were she as rough
As are the swelling Adriatic seas. (1.2.64-73)

With his few half-hearted attempts to dissuade Petruchio, Hortensio may in fact intend to encourage him. Petruchio is a man who enjoys a challenge, and Hortensio's descriptions of Katherina's sharpness only whet his appetite for the courtship. He insists on seeing Katherina immediately. This of course suits Hortensio, who now has hope that Bianca will be freed for marriage. The parallel with the first scene is completed when Hortensio disguises himself as a musician and asks Petruchio to present him to Baptista.

Whatever else we might say about Petruchio, our first impression is one of unpredictability, even danger. No doubt, even his best friends and servants never know what is going to come next. We don't yet know whether he is good but we are quite sure that this tamer is himself untamed. Perhaps this is precisely what is required if a shrew and fiend of hell is to be subdued to teachableness.

Review Questions.

1. Describe the overall structure of *Taming of the Shrew.*

2. What is the point of the two "Induction" scenes with Christopher Sly? How do these scenes relate to the action of the main play?

3. What is the structure of Act 1? Why did Shakespeare arrange the scenes in this way?

4. Why has Lucentio come to come to Padua?

5. What is Tranio's advice? How does it fit with the two models of education discussed above?

6. What does Lucentio call Bianca when he first sees her? Why is this significant?

7. What kind of character is Bianca?

8. What does Katherina mean by saying that her father has made her a "stale"? How does this help to explain her shrewish behavior?

9. Why is Petruchio in Padua? How do his reasons for coming to Padua differ from Lucentio's? How are his reasons similar?

10. What kind of man is Petruchio?

Thought Questions.

1. What are the huntsmen debating when they find Christopher Sly? (Induction, 1.13-28). Why is this significant? How does it fit with other imagery and themes of the play?

2. Whom does the lord meet on his way back from the hunt? (Induction, 1.74-101). How does "acting" fit with the themes of the Induction scenes?

3. The pictures that the lord puts on the walls of Sly's bedroom are mainly scenes of stories from Ovid (Induction, 2.47-65). What stories do the pictures illustrate? How do these pictures reinforce the theme of transformation?

4. What is Baptista's theory of education? (1.1.90-99). Is it closer to Lucentio's or Petruchio's? What kind of character is Baptista?

5. Why do the rivals Gremio and Hortensio make an alliance? (1.1.105-142). What kind of characters are they?

6. Lucentio compares Bianca's beauty to that of the "daughter of Agenor," Europa, whom the god Jupiter wooed in the disguise of a white bull (1.1.164-167). How does this reference fit with the larger themes of the play? How does it foreshadow what Lucentio himself is about to do?

7. Still looking at the reference to Jupiter and Europa (1.1.164-167), Lucentio says that Europa's beauty made "great Jove humble him to her hand." How does this foreshadow Lucentio's future?

8. Why is Tranio content to become Lucentio? (1.1.213-214). Why does Lucentio become Tranio? (1.1.215). How does this fit with the larger themes of the play?

9. Hortensio tells Petruchio that Katherina was "brought up as best becomes a gentlewoman" (1.2.86). Compare this to the following lines; how is Hortensio's statement ironic?

Does the traditional training of a "gentlewoman" produce gentle women?

10. Petruchio assures Bianca's suitors that he is prepared to tame Katherina by recounting his experience with lions, the sea, and war (1.2.197-206). Some of his experiences bring out parallels with Hercules (1.2.254-255). How is Petruchio like Hercules? Why is it significant that Hercules' ninth labor was to subdue the Amazon Queen Hippolyte?

Lesson Two: Act 2

Act 2 contains one long scene, divided into four sub-scenes:

Main Characters	Main Action
Katherine and Bianca	Katherine has Bianca's hands tied
Petruchio and Baptista	Bargaining for Katherine
Petruchio and Katherine	Petruchio "courts" Katherine
Baptista, Gremio, Tranio	Bargaining for Bianca

The act opens with a fight between Baptista's daughters. Katherina has tied Bianca's hands, which pointedly symbolizes their relationship. Katherina feels stalemated but she has also effectively stalemated Bianca. Bianca cannot marry without Kate marrying, and since Katherina is so shrewish she has figuratively tied Bianca's hands. She has indeed made Bianca a "bondmaid and a slave" (2.1.2). The opening scene also symbolizes the situation because Katherina is directing her attack against Bianca. Though in most scenes Katherina is attacking someone else, in a real sense all of her anger is against Bianca and her father. This becomes clear in the bitter words she speaks to Baptista when he comes to break up their fight:

> now I see
> She is your treasure, she must have a husband,
> I must dance bare-foot on her wedding-day,
> And for your love to her lead apes in hell.

Talk not to me, I will go sit and weep,
Till I can find occasion of revenge. (2.1.31-36)

The images are allusions to proverbial wisdom about unmarried women: An unmarried older sister danced barefoot at her younger sister's wedding; old maids do not, like married women, lead children to heaven but apes into hell. It is significant that the act ends with the suitors' making arrangements with Baptista for Bianca's marriage. During the course of the act, Katherina's marriage is arranged, and therefore Bianca's hands are untied. Petruchio the tamer is indirectly Bianca's liberator. The fairy tale hero delivers everyone who has lived in bondage to the monster.

Poor Baptista. He has brought much of his grief upon himself, but one cannot help feeling some pity for him. He has no sooner broken up a fight between his daughters when suddenly his house is full of uninvited and mostly unfamiliar guests. Of the suitors that crowd through his door, only Gremio and Petruchio are not disguised, and Baptista has never before seen Petruchio. Petruchio, moreover, does not waste time with formalities; he is, as Gremio says, "marvellous forward" (2.1.72) and gets right to the point, before he has even introduced himself: "Pray have you not a daughter called Katherina, fair and virtuous" (2.1.41-42). He is, at this point, most interested in the financial arrangements, asking Baptista directly about the dowry. Baptista is also a practical man, and his requirement that Petruchio must obtain Katherina's love (2.1.128) is an afterthought.

Petruchio's courtship of Katherina bears out his own description: "I am rough and woo not like a babe" (2.1.136). Wasting no more time with Katherina than he did with her father, the tamer leaps immediately into his program:

> *Petruchio:* Good morrow, Kate—for that's your name, I hear.
> *Katherina:* Well have you heard, but something hard of hearing: They call me Katherine that do talk of me.
> *Petruchio:* You lie, in faith, for you are called plain Kate,
> And bonny Kate, and sometimes Kate the curst,

> But Kate, the prettiest Kate in Christendom,
> Kate of Kate Hall, my super-dainty Kate,
> For dainties are all Kates, and therefore, Kate,
> Take this of me, Kate of my consolation:
> Hearing thy mildness praised in every town,
> Thy virtues spoke of, and thy beauty sounded,
> Yet not so deeply as to thee belongs,
> Myself am moved to woo thee for my wife. (2.1.181-193)

Several things are going on here. First, Petruchio insists on re-naming Katherina as Kate. Naming is an assertion of authority. Parents name their children, not vice versa, and it is a reflection of the Christian notion of male headship that wives take the names of their husbands. In the Bible, God named Adam, but Adam named the animals and his bride (Gen. 2). God names man, but man does not name God; God must reveal His name (Exod. 3:13-14). By giving her a new name, Petruchio is asserting his authority over Kate, something that no doubt surprises a young woman who is used to bullying others. Petruchio know that coaxing will not work with an unruly person; if you want to get anywhere, you have to seize control.

A name is also an identity. This also is very clear in the Bible, where people's names tell something about their place in God's plans: Melchizedek: "King of righteousness"; Abraham: "Exalted Father"; Jesus: "Savior." Re-naming Katherina as "Kate" is Petruchio's invitation to Kate to take on a new identity, his call to Katherina to put on new "clothes." This invitation lies behind much of what Petruchio says in this scene. Up to this point in the play, Kate has consistently been referred to as a devil, a fiend from hell, a beast. Petruchio, however, plans to describe her in terms precisely the opposite of what she really is:

> Say that she rail, why then I'll tell her plain
> She sings as sweetly as a nightingale.
> Say that she frown, I'll say she looks as clear
> As morning roses newly washed with dew.
> Say she be mute and will not speak a word,

> Then I'll commend her volubility
> And say she uttereth piercing eloquence.
> If she do bid me pack, I'll give her thanks,
> As though she bid me stay by her a week.
> If she deny to wed, I'll crave the day
> When I shall ask the bands, and when be married.
> (2.1.169-84)

Speaking directly to Kate, he says:

> I find you passing gentle,
> 'Twas told me you were rough, and coy, and sullen,
> And now I find report a very liar,
> For thou art pleasant, gamesome, passing courteous,
> But slow in speech, yet sweet as spring-time flowers;
> Thou canst not frown, thou canst not look askance,
> Nor bite the lip, as angry wenches will,
> Nor hast thou pleasure to be cross in talk;
> But thou with mildness entertain'st thy wooers,
> With gentle conference, soft and affable. (2.1.241-250)

It has been suggested that Petruchio is trying to confuse and disorient her, and this is true enough. Petruchio is naturally an unpredictable personality, one who keeps everyone off balance all the time. But this is more than just a matter of confusing Katherina and giving Petruchio the upper hand in a battle of wills and wit. Nor is it merely that Petruchio's compliments are, as Harold Goddard puts it, "manna" to a woman starved for love.

Petruchio's re-naming and his reversal of all the normal descriptions of Kate is an essential part of his educational program. Part of Petruchio's purpose is to put up to Kate an image of what kind of woman she can and ought to be. He paints a Kate with his words that is, at this point, only imaginary. Petruchio is playing a game of make-believe, and he invites Kate to take part. By reversing Kate's every expectation—by commenting on her gentleness not her violence, by praising her beauty, by demanding to marry her when no other man dare—Petruchio is trying to convince Kate of her

worth. To stop here, however, would be to stop short. For
the world he speaks is not, strictly speaking, in his "imagination." Something is "imaginary" when it exists only in the mind.
The world Petruchio creates is not "imaginary" but "verbal,"
made of words, and something that exists in words is very
different from something that exists only in the mind.

It is true that Petruchio recognizes Katherina's shrewishness is a matter of "policy" (2.1.292), that is, he sees that she
is deliberately acting a part in order to avenge herself on her
father and sister. It is not quite true, however, to say that
Petruchio looks past Katherina's rough and shrewish exterior,
discovers that the "real" Kate underneath is gentle and mild,
and pulls the real Kate to the surface. Petruchio is not like a
miner who digs up treasure that already exists under the surface of the ground. It is rather the case that by acting the part
of the shrew, Katherine has actually *become* a shrew. The power
to become a new person does not lie sleeping inside her,
waiting to be awakened by a kiss from Prince Charming; that
power comes from outside. It comes as an invitation to accept a new reality; it comes from the word. By offering a
new reality with his words, Petruchio offers Katherina hope
that she and her circumstances can be changed, hope that she
can escape becoming a stale among these mates.

Illustrated here is a profound point about the power of
language. It is clear that God's word has power to create:
God made the world by His Word (Gen. 1; Jn. 1). But it is
also true that human words have a creative power. We do not
create out of nothing, as God did; but our words can shape
and mold the world. On a small scale, we can see in our own
lives how the words of parents, pastors, or teachers have
deeply influenced our lives. This is why I said that there is a
difference between something existing in "imagination" and
something existing in "words." You have all heard the childish saying, "Sticks and stones may break my bones, but
words will never hurt me." Forget it. It's not true. The Bible,
especially the Proverbs, make it clear that words *do* things to

other people: they can give life (Prov. 10:11) and feed (10:21), or destroy (11:9) and tear down (11:11). Thoughts and imaginations lead to actions that affect other people. But thoughts and imaginations are not in themselves actions that directly affect other people or the world around us. Words are.

We can see this distinction in our everyday lives. Suppose you want to start a school newspaper. You imagine what kinds of articles you would publish, how much it would cost, what the name should be. You can go on imagining and imagining for years and nothing will happen. But put your ideas on paper in words, or talk to your friends about it, and things happen. What you have imagined goes out into the world, out in the open, in public. Your proposal may not lead to a real newspaper; words are not magic formulas. You may not be able to find other people who are interested, and your friends may even laugh at the idea. Putting your idea out in words is far riskier than merely thinking about it. That's because putting an imagined project into words affects the world in ways that imagination alone does not. Or, to take another example, think of the difference between thinking about being in love with someone and actually saying, "I love you." Different, isn't it?

We can especially see the power of human words in the influence that certain books have had on the course of history. It is no exaggeration to say that St. Augustine created the medieval Christian world by writing his masterpiece, *The City of God*. The Reformers, through their preaching and writing, as well as through their other activities, changed the face of Europe during the sixteenth century. Both Augustine and the Reformers said "This is the way things ought to be," and eventually their preaching and writing "created" a new church and a new world. Think, for a negative example, of how radically the world was affected by Charles Darwin's *Origin of Species* or Karl Marx's *Communist Manifesto*. We find in Scripture and history the same principle at work: First there is a reality, whether for good or ill, that exists only in word, and then the word remakes the world. First God justifies—pronounces righteous—the ungodly; then the ungodly are sanctified—made righteous. In the beginning, always, is the word; then the word becomes flesh and dwells among us.

Petruchio paints a word-picture of Kate as she might be, and he invites her to live up to it. He creates a world by his words and invites her to make it her real world. At this point, it is words. That is something; but it could remain words. Katherina could reject the new identity and the new world that Petruchio offers her. She could decide to remain the shrew, the fiend of hell. For every *City of God* or *Communist Manifesto* that decisively shapes history, there are a thousand books gathering dust in the basements of university libraries that have had virtually no effect on the world. Creatures cannot remake the world merely by speaking or writing words. What exists in words becomes flesh and remakes the world only when people accept the invitation to live in the reality that the words describe. Luther's sermons and tracts changed the face of Europe because thousands of spiritually starved people believed the biblical gospel of justification by grace through faith, rejected the myriad idolatries of late medieval Christianity, and began to live according to the truth. They accepted Luther's word-world as the real world, and the real world was changed accordingly. In the play, the issue is whether Kate will submit to the way Petruchio names the world, whether she will submit to his words, whether she will submit to becoming "Kate." Only when she has accepted the world that Petruchio describes, only when she lives in that world, only when she embraces the hope he offers, will she be turned "from a wild Kate to a Kate conformable as other household Kates" (2.1.276-277).

Kate's first and for a long time her only reaction is to resist Petruchio's world, holding hope at a distance. She rejects his invitation to enter a new reality by combating him with wit. Their first conversation proceeds by puns. Throughout, Petruchio is consistent with his initial policy: He continues to assert his authority by giving new meanings to

Kate's words and he continually returns to his alternative world. He continues to use his words to remake the world. Kate tries to insult Petruchio, but Petruchio turns all of Kate's insults into images of marriage.

Their courtship begins with a series of puns on "move." Petruchio says he is "moved" to woo Kate. Kate picks up on "move" and says that she knew he was "movable," meaning fickle and easily changeable. Petruchio asks what a movable is, and Kate answers that a "stool" is movable. Here, she is using "movable" in a legal sense; "movable" property like chairs and tables contrasts to "immovable" property like land and buildings. Petruchio picks up on "stool" and says, in effect, "If I'm a stool, come sit on me," turning Kate's scorning words into an image of sex and marriage. Kate answers that asses were made to bear; by this she means that asses are made to be sat upon, and the implication, of course, is that if Petruchio wants to be sat upon, he is an ass. Petruchio picks up on "bear," which Kate had used in the sense of "bear a burden" and changes it to "bear children." Women, not asses, are made to bear. Again, he has turned her insult into an image of marriage. Similarly, when Kate compares him to a cock, he says, be my hen.

In the play, unlike the movie version with Richard Burton and Elizabeth Taylor, the courting proceeds purely by words. This is a verbal not a physical wrestling match. Only once does Katherina strike physically, when Petruchio makes one particularly vulgar pun (2.1.219-221). Petruchio threatens to hit her back if she strikes him again. This exchange sets limits to the battle of courtship they are engaged in. Petruchio the tamer uses authority and a kind of force but it is not the force of physical strength. Their conflict is not about physical strength; it is a conflict about whose word will gain supremacy.

In the midst of the puns and the insults and the wildness of their courtship, we are left with the distinct impression that Petruchio and Kate are attracted to one another. On reflection, the reasons are not hard to find. Petruchio expressed a willingness to marry the first wealthy woman he could find in Padua, even if she had not a tooth in her head. From that starting point, he certainly must feel very lucky indeed to end up with a chance to court and marry Katherina, whose beauty no one has denied. And, from his viewpoint, her violence and sharp wit are no obstacle, for he considers himself and is as "peremptory as she proud-minded" (2.1.130), a strong man who wants a strong woman. Katherina protests, but how can she not find Petruchio refreshing? After all, she has been surrounded by Gremio's and Hortensio's for who knows how long! Finally, she must be thinking, a man who does not run and hide when I sharpen my tongue and make a thrust, a man who does not back down when I rant and rave. For she is a strong woman who has nothing but contempt for a man weaker than she.

Throughout the taming process, this mutual attraction must be kept in mind. We will misunderstand Kate completely if we do not see that she is falling in love with Petruchio. We will misunderstand Petruchio completely if we do not see a progression in his feelings toward Katherina: from seeing her as a means to wealth, to seeing her as a challenge to his masculine powers, to seeing her through eyes of admiration and love.

Review Questions.

1. Explain the structure of Act 2. Why is it significant that Katherina has tied Bianca's hands? What happens to Bianca's "hands" by the end of Act 2?

2. Explain Katherina's speech about "dancing barefoot" and "leading apes to hell." What does this speech tell us about the motives behind her behavior?

3. How does Petruchio approach Baptista? What does Baptista seem most interested in?

4. Why does Petruchio insist on calling Katherina "Kate"?

5. Give some biblical examples of the importance of names.

6. What is Petruchio's method for courting and taming

Kate? Why does he approach her this way?

7. What does the relationship of Petruchio and Kate suggest about the importance and power of words?

8. Explain or illustrate the difference between "imagining" and "saying" something. What does it have to do with the play?

9. How does Petruchio constantly change Kate's meaning? How does this fit with his plan to tame her?

10. Are Petruchio and Kate in love? How do you know?

Thought Questions.

1. Whose side does Baptista take in the fight between Katherina and Bianca? (2.1.25-28). Does he have good reason for this? What does this scene tell you about his relations with his daughters?

2. How does Petruchio describe Katherina's reputation? (2.1.46-53). Why? How does this fit with his plans?

3. What does Petruchio call Baptista? (2.1.129). How does this fit with Petruchio's character? How does it fit with his "educational program"?

4. To what does Petruchio compare his style of courtship? (2.1.129-136).

5. What happens to Hortensio when he tries to teach Katherina music? (2.1.141-158). What does this say about Baptista's method of education? Are they effective in civilizing a shrew?

6. List some of the animal names that Petruchio and Kate call each other. Why is there so much animal imagery in their conversation? How does it fit with the other themes of the play?

7. What is Kate's description of Petruchio? (2.1.285-289). Who else in the play is described like this? What is significant about Kate's description?

8. What does Kate say when Petruchio announces their wedding on Sunday? (2.1.299). After this, Kate does not speak again in Act 2. Why has she fallen silent?

9. Petruchio says, "Kiss me, Kate" three times in the play (2.1.326; 5.1.131-140; 5.2.180). Do you think Kate kisses Petruchio at 2.1.326? Why or why not? What is similar about the three times Petruchio asks her to kiss him?

10. How does Baptista decide who shall marry Bianca? (2.1.334-400). What does this suggest about Baptista? What problem does this make for Tranio? How does he intend to solve it? (2.1.406-413).

Lesson Three: Acts 3-4

These Acts have a structure similar to that of Acts 1 and 2. In general, scenes again alternate between the two courtships:

Lucentio and Hortensio court Bianca, 3.1
        Petruchio's wedding to Katherina, 3.2
        Petruchio's taming (food and sleep), 4.1
Tranio, Hortensio, and Bianca, 4.2
        Petruchio's taming (food and clothing), 4.3
Tranio presents false Vincentio to Baptista, 4.4.
        Katherina tamed, 4.5

3.2 is the wedding scene. As we see in our discussions of *Much Ado About Nothing* and *Henry V*, weddings are important settings in Shakespeare and other literature. We come to the wedding scene in *The Taming of the Shrew* with certain expectations about what will happen. We expect the husband and wife to exchange vows, and we expect an atmosphere of joy and festivity, but also of seriousness and decorum. Petruchio, however, almost never conforms to expectation. He makes a farce of the whole wedding by coming late and by being dressed in wild clothing (3.2.42-61), something like a jester. During the wedding he swears loudly and knocks the priest over. At the end of the ceremony, he kisses Kate so loudly that the church echoes with the sound (3.2.156-182). Then he leaves before the reception is over, acting as if the wedding guests were trying to kidnap Kate (3.2.237-241).

Tranio says, "He hath some meaning in his mad attire" (3.2.123). What does Petruchio mean? Possibly, he is trying to confuse Kate, to keep her bewildered and off-balance in order to make her easier to handle. Perhaps, too, Petruchio wants to force a public confrontation with Kate. When she refuses to leave with him before the wedding party is done, Petruchio has an opportunity to state publicly that she belongs to him, lumping her together with his other property:

> I will be master of what is mine own.
> She is my goods, my chattels, she is my house,
> My household stuff, my field, my barn,
> My horse, my ox, my ass, my any thing,
> And here she stands, touch her whoever dare! (3.2.231-235)

We saw in the courtship scene that Petruchio's method is to create a world of words, verbally to remake Katherina into Kate, and to invite Kate to accept this new identity. Here we see another level of his program. With his wild clothing and behavior, Petruchio is holding up a mirror to Kate. From the beginning, the other characters have commented on the similarity between Petruchio and his bride, usually to say that Petruchio is as wild and rough as Katherina. At the wedding and in the following scenes, Petruchio is the one who acts the shrew, and his purpose is to manifest to Kate how she behaves toward others. With Petruchio held up before her as a mirror, Kate comes to know herself as she never has and to see how destructive she has been. Seeing the truth is a first step toward repentance. Petruchio's attire, moreover, fits with the rest of the wedding, which is really a parody of a wedding. Not only does Petruchio act outrageously during the ceremony, but when he finally gets home with his new bride, they fast on their wedding night and abstain from marital relations. A mock wedding is followed by a mock wedding night. Petruchio behaves madly on his wedding day as an object lesson demonstrating Kate's unpreparedness for civilized marriage.

Petruchio explicitly states another "meaning in his mad attire." When Baptista expresses surprise that Petruchio would be married in such clothing, Petruchio responds:

> To me she's married, not unto my clothes.
> Could I repair what she will wear in me
> As I can change these poor accoutrements,
> 'Twere well for Kate and better for myself. (3.2.116-119)

We have already seen how a change of clothing can signify a change of position and identity. Here, however, Petruchio distinguishes between himself and his clothes, and points out that it is far more difficult to change one's character than to change one's clothes. This insight undergirds Petruchio's entire plan to transform Kate. He knows that an external change of status does not automatically produce a change of character. As we see below, even words, basic as they are, cannot of themselves turn the beast into beauty. Real transformation demands sterner stuff.

Bianca's education proceeds in a much more superficial way. We know from Act 1 that she is devoted to books and music; like Lucentio, her education is a discipline of ease and leisure not of pain. This becomes even clearer in 3.1. Lucentio and Hortensio are fighting with each other about what Bianca will study next, but she rejects both their proposals:

> Why, gentlemen, you do me double wrong
> To strive for that which resteth in my choice.
> I am no breeching scholar in the schools,
> I'll not be tied to hours nor 'pointed times.
> But learn my lessons as I please myself. (3.1.16-20)

Bianca embraces completely Tranio's advice, falling to her studies as her stomach serves her (1.1.38). From her words in 3.1, it is clear that she is at least as headstrong as Katherina, and it is significant that even much later Bianca still does not even know that there is such a thing as a "taming school" (4.2.55). Since Petruchio has whisked Katherina off before the wedding reception has ended, Baptista instructs Lucentio (Tranio) to "supply the bridegroom's place" and tells Bianca to "take her sister's room" (3.2.251-252). On the surface, Baptista is trying to ensure that his guests will enjoy a wedding feast, as he had promised. Beneath the surface, however, there is a hint that Bianca will not only move into Kate's place at the table, but that she will begin to act like Kate. In the final scene it is revealed that Bianca has truly "taken her sister's room."

Once he arrives at his own home, Petruchio pursues a further element of his design to tame Kate. The courtship scene highlighted the power and the importance that words must have in any educational program. Words, however, do not work alone. As the Proverbs consistently show, the word works hand-in-glove with the rod: the rod and reproof give wisdom (Proverbs 29:15). Teachers and education officials the world over have rediscovered this ancient truth in recent years. They have realized that it is impossible to impart knowledge, to remake the world through words, if there is no discipline. A disorderly, disrespectful, completely unstructured classroom is a classroom where no real education can take place. Bianca's training proceeds as she pleases; she decides what she studies and when; she is never required to do anything against her will. Petruchio has a different plan for Kate. She will undergo a discipline of pain, one that Petruchio hopes will produce a wife who accepts his authority and lives by his word. Here again, it is helpful to compare Petruchio's training of Kate to Christ's edification of the Church. The Reformers and their disciples came to the conclusion that the Church was not only marked by true teaching, by the Word, but also by the exercise of Discipline, by the Rod.

Petruchio's "discipline of pain" has two elements. Peter, one of Petruchio's household servants, recognizes that "He kills her in her own humor" (4.1.168), that is, he tames the shrew by out-shrewing her. Petruchio "kills her in her own humor" by attacking everyone around him—except Kate. When Kates horse stumbles on the way home from the wedding and throws Kate into the mud, Petruchio gets mad at Grumio. When they are served their first meal at home, Petruchio complains that it is burned and throws it around the room. His tantrums perhaps frighten Kate; how would you like to sit down to eat with someone who may overturn the table at any moment? Besides, as we mentioned above, his behavior offers Kate a glimpse of her own conduct by playing her role in a greatly exaggerated way. Whatever Petruchio's intentions, one of the results is that Kate begins to defend the servants from Petruchio (4.1.141, 156-157). Petruchio has maneuvered Kate so that, instead of being an attacker, she becomes a defender of those who are unjustly attacked. She feels the pain of being the object of attack.

Petruchio also disciplines by requiring her to abstain from meat and sleep:

> Thus have I politicly begun my reign,
> And 'tis my hope to end successfully.
> My falcon now is sharp and passing empty,
> And till she stoop she must not be full-gorged,
> For then she never looks upon her lure.
> Another way I have to man my haggard,
> To make her come and know her keeper's call:
> That is, to watch her, as we watch these kites
> That bate and beat and will not be obedient.
> She ate no meat today, nor none shall eat.
> Last night she slept not, nor tonight she shall not.
> As with the meat, some undeserved fault
> I'll find about the making of the bed,
> And here I'll fling the pillow, there the bolster,
> This way the coverlet, another way the sheets.
> Ay, and amid this hurly I intend
> That all is done in reverent care of her.
> And, in conclusion, she shall watch all night,
> And if she chance to nod I'll rail and brawl,

And with the clamour keep her still awake.
This is a way to kill a wife with kindness. (4.1.175-197)

Petruchio borrows imagery from falconry. During Shake-speare's day, falcons were trained to hunt, and falconry was a favorite sport of kings and nobles. To tame a falcon, and make it responsive to the master's voice, you deprive it of sleep and food. Petruchio wants to make Kate "stoop." This is also a term from falconry; a falcon "stoops" when it dives at a lure. Petruchio wants his "falcon" to "stoop" in another sense: he wants her to become submissive and obedient to him. He wants her to "know her keeper's call," to accept and live by his word. There is also a hint that Petruchio is training Kate to "hunt," a hint perhaps picked up in the final scene of the play.

There is probably some biblical imagery in the fact that Kate is not allowed to come to the table until she is willing to bow her knee to her husband. In the Church, food is a means of discipline. Church members who sin gravely and refuse to repent should not be allowed to come to the Lord's table. If they turn, if they are transformed and again accept the word of the Lord, they are received to the table again. Petruchio imposes the same discipline on Kate. On the wedding night, he does not allow her to eat, on the pretext that the food is unfit. By denying her food, Petruchio teaches Kate to "en-treat"; for the first time in her life, she does not demand but asks. She begs Grumio for some food: "I, who never knew how to entreat, nor never needed that I should entreat, am starved for meat, . . . I prithee go and get me some repast" (4.3.7-9, 15). When Petruchio brings her some food, she com-plains that it is "cold as can be," and Petruchio begins to take it back:

> *Petruchio:* Here, love, thou seest how diligent I am,
> To dress thy meat myself, and bring it thee.
> I am sure, sweet Kate, this kindness merits thanks.
> What, not a word? Nay, then, thou lov'st it not,
> And all my pains is sorted to no proof.

Here, take away this dish.
Katherina: I pray you let it stand.
Petruchio: The poorest service is repaid with thanks,
And so shall mine before you touch the meat.
Katherina: I thank you, sir. (4.3.39-47)

Petruchio's falcon is beginning to stoop. Instead of demanding and ranting and getting her way, she is learning to respond to her husband's word, to pray for his gifts, and give thanks when she receives.

Petruchio educates by the discipline of food and sleep, and at the end of 4.3, clothing becomes the focus of his politic reign. Petruchio shows Kate a new gown but complains to the tailor about every detail and finally sends it back. He shows her what she shall have, but then forces her to wait until he is ready to give it to her. Again, part of Petruchio's point is to give Kate an object lesson: She will receive the clothing of a gentle woman only when she has become gentle (4.3.70-71). He is also reinforcing his insight that a change of clothes is not the same as a change of character. It would be easy for Petruchio to achieve a kind of peace and stability by giving Kate whatever would please her. This may cover over her shrewishness by filling her with a kind of satisfaction. But giving her the clothing of a gentlewoman would not make her gentle. Petruchio is looking for a deep and real conversion; only then will he clothe his new wife in new clothes. Petruchio knows that a shrew dressed in a fancy gown is still a shrew. This is the point of his lecture on the value of clothing:

> 'tis the mind that makes the body rich;
> And as the sun breaks through the darkest clouds,
> So honour peereth in the meanest habit.
> What, is the jay more precious than the lark
> Because his feathers are more beautiful?
> Or is the adder better than the eel
> Because his painted skin contents the eye?
> O no, good Kate; neither art thou the worse
> For this poor furniture and mean array. (4.3.169-177)

Until she has passed through her training period, she is not yet ready for garments of glory and beauty. Until she stoop, she will not be full-gorged.

"Killing her with kindness" seems an odd way to describe Petruchio's treatment of Katherina. "Killing" sounds right, but "kindness"? This phrase, however, highlights two fundamental elements of the taming. First, Petruchio, as we have seen, will not be satisfied with a superficial transformation, with a change of clothing. He knows that if wild Katherina is to become a household Kate, the old Katherina must die to make room for a new creature. Depriving Katherina of food and sleep leads her through a kind of death, and toward a renewing resurrection. The entire episode in Petruchio's home is like a descent into hell; Kate is forcibly separated from her family, forced to travel through freezing weather, deprived of comforts and basic necessities. As in Dante's *Divine Comedy*, the passage through hell is a necessary part of the journey toward Paradise. Second, however cruel Petruchio's antics, it is still true that he loves his bride. It would hardly be loving for Petruchio to permit Kate to continue in her original destructive and self-destructive course, a course that has isolated her from her father and sister and from the whole community of Padua. Making allowance, as we always must, for the comic, fairy-tale tone of the play, Petruchio's method is well described as "tough love," as "severe mercy."

Petruchio's discipline of pain, his discipline by food, sleep, and clothing, finally bears fruit in 4.5. On their way to visit Kate's family, Petruchio refuses to go on until she agrees with the way he describes the world, until she consents to be guided by his word rather than by her senses and her own reason. Finally, Kate stoops and accepts Petruchio's mad description of the world:

> *Petruchio:* Come on, a God's name, once more toward our father's. Good Lord, how bright and goodly shines the moon!
> *Katherina:* The moon? The sun; it is not moonlight now.

> *Petruchio:* I say it is the moon that shines so bright.
> *Katherina:* I know it is the sun that shines so bright
> *Petruchio:* Now by my mother's son, and that's myself,
> It shall be moon, or star, or what I list,
> Or e'er I journey to your father's house. . . .
> *Katherina:* Forward, I pray, since we have come so far,
> And be it moon, or sun, or what you please;
> And if you please to call it a rush-candle
> Henceforth I vow it shall be so for me.
> *Petruchio:* I say it is the moon.
> *Katherina:* I know it is the moon.
> *Petruchio:* Nay, then you lie. It is the blessed sun.
> *Katherina:* Then, God be blessed, it is the blessed sun,
> But sun it is not, when you say it is not,
> And the moon changes even as your mind:
> What you will have it named, even that it is,
> And so it shall be so for Katherine. (4.5.1-22)

Kate's statement that the moon changes as Petruchio's mind refers to the belief that the moon was responsible for madness (the Latin *luna*, "moon," is the root of the English words "lunacy" and "lunatic"). This reference gives her words a light-hearted, even ironic tone, but what has happened is profound and serious: Kate repeats Petruchio's names for the world; she consents to live in the reality he describes. Because Kate has stooped, Petruchio's word-world has become flesh; it has become real for the two of them. Because she has stooped, she is on her way to being changed from mad Katherina to super-dainty Kate, the prettiest Kate in Christendom (2.1.186-187).

The debate about sun and moon takes on an added significance when we see it in the light of what happens at the end of 4.3. There, Petruchio tells Kate to prepare for a trip to her father's house. Kate contests Petruchio's claim that it is "seven o'clock," saying instead that it is "almost two." Petruchio insists that "It shall be what o'clock I say it is" (4.3.192), and calls off the trip. Hortensio, who has come to visit Petruchio exclaims, "Why, so this gallant will command the sun" (4.3.193). In scene 5, Kate confesses that, so far as she is concerned, Petruchio is lord of the sun, the moon, of all time.

Petruchio has accomplished a great deal by getting Kate to agree privately to name the world as he does. But he is not satisfied until she has been tested publicly, until she is willing to put Kate on public display. When they meet Vincentio, Petruchio calls the old man a "gentle mistress" and "lovely maid" (4.5.27, 33). Kate no longer merely passively accepts Petruchio's word but actively contributes to the world he creates. She goes beyond Petruchio's description and starts playing Petruchio's game with her own ingenuity and wit; Vincentio is not merely a young woman but a "budding virgin, fair, and fresh, and sweet," a young woman who will make happy the man she marries (4.5.37-41). Kate's submission does not stifle her creativity. Instead, it is precisely by stooping, precisely by accepting Petruchio's word-world, that she is freed to enter into a partnership with Petruchio in the creation of a new world. Petruchio has not only remade the world for Kate but has turned Kate into a creative rather than a destructive force. Again, there is a profound Christian truth here: When we have accepted the Lord's Word as truth, our creative powers are freed and we become co-builders with Christ of a new creation.

The sun imagery reappears in the scene with Vincentio. When Petruchio corrects her by saying that Vincentio is an old man, Katherina apologizes, explaining that the sun got in her eyes and made everything look young and green. Like Benedick and Beatrice in *Much Ado*, she has learned to look at the world through new eyes, through eyes given her by another, through eyes dazzled by the one who commands the sun. And with the sun in her eyes, all the world looks green, fresh, new.

Review Questions.

1. How does Petruchio dress for his wedding? Why? How does he act during the wedding?

2. Describe Bianca's education. Why is it significant that

she has never heard of a "taming school"?

3. In what sense does Bianca "take her sister's room"?

4. Why does Petruchio constantly attack his servants? How does Kate react?

5. Explain the double meaning of "stoop."

6. Why is it significant that Petruchio refuses to let Kate eat or sleep?

7. What does Petruchio do with Kate's new clothes? Why? How does this fit with larger themes in the play?

8. How does Kate show that she has become submissive to Petruchio?

9. Does Kate's submission stifle her liveliness and creativity?

10. Explain the "sun" imagery in the last part of Act 4.

Thought Questions.

1. Hortensio calls Bianca the "patroness of heavenly harmony" (3.1.5). What does he mean? With whom he is contrasting Bianca? In the light of the end of the play, what is ironic about his words?

2. Who is the "old pantaloon" that Lucentio is trying to "beguile"? (3.1.35-36). Why is it significant that Lucentio's rival is "old"? How does this fit with other references to conflicts between old and young?

3. What is Bianca really doing as she "studies" music and Latin? (3.1). What does this tell us about Bianca? What does it say about the "educational method" that she uses? Does she prefer Ovid or Aristotle?

4. How does Katherina feel when Petruchio is late to the wedding? (3.2.8-20). Is she relieved? Disappointed? Why?

5. Why does Petruchio criticize his serving men? (4.1.109-112). How does this parallel his plans to tame Kate?

6. Grumio comments on the ragged clothing of the servingmen (4.1.117-123). How does this fit into the play as a whole?

7. What agreement does Tranio make with Hortensio?

(4.2.11-43). How is Hortensio being duped?

8. How does Tranio persuade the "Pedant" to impersonate Lucentio? (4.2.72-121).

9. How does Katherina treat Grumio when he refuses to give her meat? (4.3.31-35). What does this say about the progress of her training?

10. What does Hortensio do after he has given up courting Bianca? What does he say he has learned from Petruchio? (4.5.77-79). Has he learned his lessons at the taming school?

Lesson Four: Act 5

5.1 is an unmasking/recognition scene. The climax of the romantic subplot involving Lucentio and Bianca has been set up by a series of disguises. Lucentio, disguised as Cambio, has been courting Bianca while pretending to teach her Latin. Tranio, disguised as Lucentio, has been bargaining with Baptista for Bianca's hand in marriage. He has found an anonymous Pedant who impersonates Lucentio's father, Vincentio, and gives Baptista assurances that he has wealth enough for a suitable dowry.

The occasion for removing the disguises is the arrival of the real Vincentio in Padua; Vincentio is the one who can remove all the masks at a stroke. He knows who Tranio and Lucentio really are, and he certainly knows that the Pedant is not Vincentio. It is worth noting that the unmasking, the assigning of proper identities, is the task of a father. Vincentio confronts the Pedant who is impersonating him, discovers Tranio in Lucentio's clothes (and fears that Tranio has killed his son), and then Lucentio appears, now married to Bianca, to tell what has occurred. When the confusion has subsided, it seems that everything has come out for the best. Vincentio is none the worse for his bewilderment, and Lucentio has married the girl of his dreams. Everyone returns to his true identity, and is ready to live happily ever after. As Lucentio says, love is the power that has caused the various transformations:

> Love wrought these miracles. Bianca's love
> Made me exchange my state with Tranio,
> While he did bear my countenance in the town,
> And happily I have arrived at the last
> Unto the wished haven of my bliss. (5.1.112-116)

Lucentio's words apply in a much more profound sense to Kate and Petruchio than to himself and Bianca. Lucentio may have traded places with Tranio for love of Bianca, and Tranio may have agreed to the plan for love of Lucentio. As Petruchio pointed out at the wedding, however, changing clothes is much easier than changing one's self. As Petruchio has been demonstrating, love, so long as it is not mere feeling but the true and hardy love that is closely allied with discipline, has power to produce change of the heart.

With Petruchio having won over Katherina, and Lucentio securing the hand of Bianca, and all the characters reassuming their proper clothes and identities, the play could end with scene 1. If Shakespeare had merely been writing farce or a romantic comedy, scene 2 would be unnecessary. As it is, 5.2 is the climax of the play, for Shakespeare has further unmaskings to perform. The characters are wearing their proper clothes but some are still disguised, and it is time for their true colors to be revealed. Shakespeare has to this point followed the course of two courtships, and in contrasting the courtships has brought out contrasts between various methods of education. Now it's time to see the results. Now it's exam time.

The occasion for the final test is the wedding feast of Lucentio and Bianca. Hortensio's new wife, called only "Widow," says to Petruchio, "He that is giddy thinks the world turns round" (5.2.20). When Kate demands an explanation, the Widow replies: "Your husband, being troubled with a shrew, measures my husband's sorrow by his woe" (5.2.28-29), an ironic comment since there is every reason to believe that the Widow is already making Hortensio's life miserable. Kate and the Widow exchange bitter remarks, with their husbands egging them on. (Petruchio's "To her, Kate" [5.2.33] reminds us that he trained Kate like a falcon; he's prepared her to be a huntress.) When the women retreat, Petruchio proposes a bet with Lucentio and Hortensio; each of the three husbands will summon his wife, and the winner will be the one whose wife responds. Not only is Katherina the only one to appear, but, on Petruchio's instructions, she fetches the others (shades of that falcon again) and lectures them on their duties toward their husbands (5.2.136-179). Bianca, at last, is unveiled as the stubborn young woman she has always been. Meanwhile, Kate, by both her words and her actions, demonstrates that the shrew has been tamed and that her marriage is a strong and happy one.

Some students of the play have suggested that Katherina does not mean what she says in her speech, but this is really not credible. First, her speech is filled with biblical allusions. It does need to be said that the Bible has a high view of woman's place in God's plan. Scripture reports on and celebrates many heroic women: Sarah, Deborah, Ruth, Esther, Mary. The New Testament insists that women are co-heirs with men of the gift of salvation (1 Pet. 3:7) and that in Christ men and women have the same standing before God (Gal. 3:27-28). Moreover, Christian men are not to be tyrants over their wives but take the self-sacrificing Christ as their model (Eph. 5:22-33). Having said that, Katherina's speech reflects a genuinely biblical truth in its emphasis on the man's headship over the woman: the husband is "lord" (5.2.146; 1 Pet. 3:6) and "head" (5.2.147; 1 Cor. 11:3; Eph. 5:23), who "cares for" the wife (5.2.147; Eph. 5:28-30), to whom a wife owes "true obedience" (5.2.153; Eph. 5:24). It is simply not believable that Shakespeare would mock such widely accepted Christian views of marriage, or treat them sarcastically.

The whole action of the play, finally, leads up to a scene in which Kate's new character can shine forth. Shakespeare has been developing a contrast between the soft and ineffective educational methods at work in Bianca's training and the severe but effective methods of Petruchio. The last scene unmasks Bianca as a shrew in dove's clothing. It is only fitting that the same scene should reverse the public image of Kate as well, revealing the new creation that has emerged under Petruchio's tutelage. That Kate responds to the "command," the word, of her husband also fits one of the major themes we have seen develop in the play.

J. Dennis Huston has given several reasons why Kate's appearance and speech provide a fitting climax to the play, and also defends the view of marriage that Kate's speech portrays:

> First, . . . at last the hero—here in the persons of Petruchio and Kate together—has succeeded in freeing the princess from the monster; and she appears in full regal splendor, striking all with wonder and embodying, in both her person and her behavior, the promise of new order in the kingdom. . . . Second, . . . this scene brings Kate the emotional satisfaction of effecting desires long felt but little acknowledged—to become the center of approving communal attention, to win the unqualified praise of her father, to see her sister misbehave and suffer public reprimand, and to gain a husband's admiring love. Third, and most important, it presents a revised version of Kate's original wedding celebration. . . . Kate is actively included in the feasting which celebrates social harmony, and here, too, her husband . . . turns all attention temporarily away from himself and toward her, revealing her as true bride rather than as a suffering victim. For in speaking of the duty that a wife owes her husband, Kate speaks also of the duty a husband owes his wife; she describes the mutual responsibility and trust necessary in any successful marriage.

Huston's last point is important. Kate does not describe marriage as a one-way street, in which the man tyrannizes his wife. In Kate's view, there is an order in marriage; the man is lord, head, and sovereign. But Kate also understands marriage as a partnership, in which the husband

> cares for thee,
> And for thy maintenance; commits his body
> To painful labour both by sea and land,
> To watch the night in storms, the day in cold,
> Whilst thou liest warm at home, secure and safe.
> (5.2.147-151)

Kate's view of marriage involves male headship, but it also reflects the theme of mutual submission (Eph. 5:21).

Petruchio knows that he is the "winner" (5.2.186-187), as much as Lucentio and Hortensio realize they have lost (5.2.181). But Petruchio's victory is not his alone. Both Petruchio and Kate have won. Petruchio has sculpted a wife through word and rod that is the envy of the whole assembly; Kate is still a woman of great energy and wit, but no longer employs that energy and wit in tantrums and rages but in praising, serving, supporting and defending her husband. He has not broken her spirit but directed it to a more appropriate end. For her part, Katherine has learned the value of self-control and caring about her husband. In submission to her husband's word she finds her truest freedom. His love has killed the old Katherina and his word has created a new Kate. When she kneels before Petruchio to place her hand under his foot, he raises her up to kiss her (5.2.180). By willingly, lovingly submitting to her husband, Kate finds herself lifted up to see him face to face. In her submission, she is exalted. Stooping, she is finally full-gorged.

Review Questions.

1. Explain the various disguises that set up the action in 5.1.

2. Whose arrival in Padua reveals the true identity of the various disguised characters? Why is he the best one to identify everyone?

3. Why doesn't the play end after 5.1? What is the purpose of 5.2? How is 5.2 similar to 5.1?

4. What does the Widow say to offend Katherina? Why are her words ironic?

5. What is Petruchio's wager?

6. What does Petruchio order Katherina to do to the other women?

7. What is Katherina's speech about? Explain how her speech describes marriage as a matter of mutual responsibility and trust.

8. Did Shakespeare intend Katherina's speech to be taken sarcastically? Why or why not?

9. List some of the biblical allusions in Kate's speech.

10. What happens when Kate offers to put her hand under Petruchio's foot?

Thought Questions.

1. What does Baptista think of the real Vincentio when he appears? (5.1.63). Who else has been described in this way?

2. Who finally identifies Vincentio? (5.1.90-91). Is he a reliable witness?

3. Explain the two senses of the word "fear" in 5.2.16-19.

4. What does Bianca mean with her reference to Gremio's "horn" (5.2.40-41). How does she treat the elderly Gremio? Why?

5. How does Bianca respond when Petruchio tries to draw her into a contest of wits? (5.2.43-48). What does this tells us about Bianca?

6. To what does Tranio compare Petruchio's relationship with Kate? (5.2.55-62). What is the pun on "deer" in line 56?

7. What is Bianca's response when Lucentio bids her come? (5.2.80-81). What is the Widow's response to Hortensio? (5.2.91-92). How does this show, as Petruchio says, that things get "worse and worse"?

8. According to Katherina's speech, how are a woman's heart and body similar? (5.2.165-168). Why are they as they are?

9. What does Katherina say is the source of Bianca's and the Widow's refusal to submit to their husbands?

(5.2.170-173). What have they not learned?

10. Petruchio says that Lucentio hit the "white" (5.2.186). What is the image? Hint: It has something to do with archery. Second hint: "Bianca" means "white."

Video Productions of *The Taming of the Shrew*

I reviewed one version of *The Taming of the Shrew*, starring Richard Burton and Elizabeth Taylor. Burton is an appropriately brash, bragging Petruchio, and Taylor is a physically as well as verbally violent Katherina. The film plays up the farcical aspects of the play, capturing its manic, swirling pace. During the courtship scene, Burton chases Taylor through a barn, Burton has to walk tight-rope-like along the roof line, and they fall together into a mound of cotton. Burton's Petruchio throws food around his house so effectively we suspect he's practiced at home. The few moments of tenderness are, however, very effective. After Kate's final speech, Petruchio looks on her with almost tearful admiration. When she bows to place hand under his foot, he takes her hand and lifts her up—a splendid little touch. The minor characters are good: Lucentio is every inch the smitten lover, for whom Tranio does all the hard thinking; Bianca is pretty, manipulative and coquettish; Baptista seems bewildered at the continual commotion in his house; Gremio and Hortensio are pure losers, as they are in the play. The only caution is that the film does play up some of the bawdiness of the play. There are some suggestive early shots. At worst, however, the film would be rated PG.

Suggested Paper Topics

1. Examine the clothing imagery in the play: in the Induction scenes, the exchanges of clothing, Petruchio's mad attire and his speeches on clothing.

2. Study the character of Kate, her relationship with her father and sister. Why is she a shrew? Does she really change? What does she feel toward Petruchio?

3. Discuss Petruchio's methods of taming Kate. Does he

hate women? Are his methods humane?

4. Explore the relations between the sexes as portrayed either in the Lucentio-Bianca or the Petruchio-Katherina courtship. Who is likely to have a happier marriage? Why?

5. Examine the animal imagery in the play, especially shrews, falconry.

6. Look up some of the allusions to Ovid, from his *Metamorphosis* or the *Art of Love*. What do these allusions contribute to the play?

7. Examine the comparisons of Petruchio to Hercules. Research the myths of Hercules to explain how Petruchio is like him.

8. Explore the theme of identity, transformation, and conversion. Pay special attention to the contrast between superficial disguises and real change.

9. Make a careful study of Kate's final speech. What picture of marriage does she give? Is it a Christian view?

10. Explore Petruchio's use of words, paying special attention to how he uses words to create an alternative world. Does this reflect a Christian view of language? Why or why not?

May I Be So Converted and See With These Eyes?
Much Ado About Nothing

One of the many remarkable things about Shakespeare is the astonishing diversity of his plays. Nearly everything in *Much Ado* is different from *Macbeth*, yet Shakespeare handles both with an equally sure hand. Most obviously, *Macbeth* is a tragedy, while *Much Ado* is a comedy. The settings of *Macbeth* and *Much Ado*, moreover, could not be more different. Macbeth was king of cold, dark Scotland. In Orson Welles's film version of *Macbeth*, the play is set in wet, black, cave-like castles or underground, in a kind of hell. *Much Ado* takes place in warm, sunny Italy. Kenneth Branagh's recent film version, in which much of the action takes place out of doors, captures the Edenic flavor of the setting. The air in Macbeth's Scotland is filthy, but the air of Messina, the Italian villa where *Much Ado* takes place, is clean and clear.

The two plays depict different arenas of human life and activity. *Macbeth* is a political play, concerned with power and violence; the only active woman character is Lady Macbeth, but she is, at least in the early portions of the play, more masculine than her husband. *Much Ado* is not concerned with the world of politics. There are soldiers in the play, but war is behind them and they are on holiday; there are princes, governors and counts in the play, but they do not spend their time fulfilling the duties of their offices. This play focuses on love, romance, and courtship.

Structurally, *Much Ado* is similar to *The Taming of the*

Shrew. In both plays, Shakespeare depicts parallel courtships. One of the courtships—in *Much Ado*, the romance of Claudio and Hero—is a conventional romance between a sweet and silent woman and a dashing and smitten man. The other courtship (Beatrice and Benedick) is the opposite, characterized by sharp, violent exchanges of wit. By depicting the development of these two courtships through the play, Shakespeare invites us to compare the two, and ask the question, Which is preferable? Which style of courtship is the more stable basis for a lasting love? In addition to portraying contrasting courtships, the play turns on contrasting deceptions. Don John, the bastard prince, deceives Claudio so that he renounces Hero at the first wedding; he deceives in order to destroy. Don Pedro, his half-brother, also uses deception, but for benevolent ends: He uses trickery to bring Beatrice and Benedick to a "mountain of affection the one with the other" (2.1.382-383).

It will be helpful to say a word or two about the title of this play. The word "nothing" is, as Harold Goddard points out, a significant one for Shakespeare. Goddard suggests that we think of it in pictorial terms. Draw or imagine a circle. The inside of the circle represents what actually is the case, what is actually true and what has actually happened. List some of those things on the inside of the circle: the date and place of your birth and your parent's names, World War II and the war in Bosnia, the name of your church and the book of Job. The outside of the circle represents those things that might conceivably have happened, but did not. Outside of the circle are all the possibilities that are not actually the case. Suppose you were born in the United States; that would be inside the circle. But you could have been born in a poor neighborhood of Calcutta, India; that would be outside the circle. Suppose you have been raised in a Christian family; but you could have been born in the middle of China, in a place where no one has ever seen a Bible. It was not logically impossible for George Bush to have been elected president in 1992, but he was not. Goddard says that in Shakespeare's terminology, the outside of the circle is the realm of "nothing."

Now, draw arrows that point from the things outside the circle toward the inside of the circle. These arrows represent the important point in the diagram: Reality—what is inside the circle—is constantly shaped and influenced by "nothing"—what is outside the circle. We hope for things, and therefore act in a certain way based on those hopes, but they may not come to pass. Here is a boy who hopes to play professional basketball, and spends countless hours training and practicing. In the end, it turns out that he is too small or too slow to compete in the NBA; the boy's life has been shaped in fundamental ways by unfulfilled hopes, by what is not really the case, by "nothing." Similarly, we fear things, and act to avoid them, but they never happen. Here is a girl who fears an upcoming test, and makes herself sick with worry, only to discover that the test is easy; the week before the test was a living hell, but it was so not because of anything real but because of "nothing." The choices we make in life are constantly being molded by possibilities, by hopes and dreams and fears, that never become actual. The inside of the circle is constantly being hit with slings and arrows from the outside.

Much Ado is greatly concerned with how "nothing" influences the way people live their lives. Characters in the play make decisions in response to rumors, lies, tricks, deceptions, and masks. They frequently act on the basis of what they believe is true, on the basis of their fears and hopes, but in the end many of these fears and hopes prove baseless. Their lives are shaped by beliefs that are not true; their choices and actions are molded by "nothing."

There is another aspect to this as well. There is a pun in the title of the play. In Elizabethan English, the word "nothing" would have been pronounced like "noting," and "noting" in Shakespeare's day had the meaning of "eavesdropping" or "overhearing." The play moves forward by what characters "note." Don John embarks on his plot to deceive

Claudio when one of his henchmen overhears the Prince making plans to court Hero on Claudio's behalf. Benedick and Beatrice fall in love with each other when they overhear staged conversations about their love. Claudio turns against Hero because he eavesdrops at her window and thinks he sees her with another man. Dogberry's watchmen discover the plot by overhearing a conversation between Borachio and Conrade. The theme of "noting" is related to the imagery of "masks" used throughout the play. The Prince proposes to Hero at a masquerade, where everyone's identity is hidden, and Hero is again veiled at the final wedding scene. In addition to literal masks and veils, the characters wear figurative masks, hiding their true intentions and personalities behind tricks, deceptions, and facades.

These two meanings of "nothing/noting" are obviously related. The play shows us characters whose lives are shaped by "nothing" and this "nothing" comes to them through "noting." The characters make much ado about nothing because they have spent their time making much ado about noting.

A final overall theme is the relation of wit and folly. The main characters of the play are from the ruling classes of Italian society. They believe they are in control of their world. They are the "wisdoms" who believe they can distinguish truth from falsehood. In fact, the "wise" are constantly making mistakes, errors in judgment, and miscalculations. It takes a group of "shallow fools," Dogberry and his watch, to uncover the plot against Claudio and Hero and to make things turn out right. Shakespeare is poking fun at those who think they rule the world, and in so doing he reflects the paradoxical Christian theme of wisdom and folly. Paul said that the "wisdom of this world" is foolishness before God, and that the foolishness of God is wiser than the wisdom of the world (1 Cor. 1:18-25). In *Much Ado*, the most successful characters are those who navigate through the world of noting/nothing by means of a trusting wisdom that many would consider foolishness.

Lesson One: Acts 1.1-2.1

Act 1 introduces the characters, their relationships in the past, and their various attitudes toward love and romance. The play opens with a messenger announcing the arrival of the regiment of Don Pedro, Prince of Arragon, for a holiday at Messina. A careful reader will notice that Don Pedro's latest war has been against his half-brother, the illegitimate Don John. When he welcomes the soldiers to Messina, Leonato, the governor, mentions that Don John has been "reconciled to the prince your brother" (1.1.161-162), and Don John himself later blames Claudio, who fought heroically in the war, for being the cause of his overthrow (1.3.67-68). This explains Don John's hatred for Claudio and his desire to spoil Claudio's marriage.

The military background to the play is significant. *Much Ado* draws a contrast between how men act as soldiers and how they act as lovers. Claudio tells Don Pedro that before the recent military action he looked on Hero with a soldier's eye. Now that the victory is won, he is ready to "drive liking to the name of love" (1.1.309), and he goes on to contrast the "rough" task of war with the "soft and delicate" desires of love (1.1.312). Wartime is time for action and violence; peacetime is for love.

More subtly, there is a contrast between how war and love variously affect the soldiers' relationships with one another. During wartime, soldiers necessarily develop a deep comraderie and strong loyalty toward their Prince. No battle is won unless soldiers work together and obey the orders of their commander. Benedick and others fear marriage and love because they will split up the "men's club" atmosphere that had developed during the war. Romance will turn the men into rivals rather than brothers fighting together. When he believes that Don Pedro has betrayed him by courting Hero for himself, Claudio expresses this fear: "Friendship is constant in all other things, save in the office and affairs of love" (2.1.183-184). Men, in Claudio's view, are loyal, trustworthy, friendly, courteous, kind—perfect Boy Scouts!—

until women get in the way. In fact, the fear that the pursuit of love will turn men into rivals is well-grounded. As we shall see below, one of the tests of genuine love is a man's willingness to break ranks with the regiment, the men's club, and take his place at the side of his beloved. In biblical terms, the test of true love is a man's willingness to leave old relationships behind and cleave loyally to his beloved.

While Shakespeare contrasts war and love, he also brings out some of the similarities. Military images and metaphors are used to describe, especially, the courtship of Beatrice and Benedick. In Beatrice's first speech about Benedick, she says that he once challenged Cupid to an archery match; love is compared to a contest of military prowess (1.1.39-45). Leonato refers to the "merry war" and "skirmish of wit" that Beatrice carries on with Benedick (1.1.62-65). The use of military metaphors for courtship and love is intended partly for comic effect. But Shakespeare evidently has more serious points to make as well. On the one hand, the plays causes us to wonder if Claudio has really been able to leave behind the "rough" task of war when he begins to court Hero; war seems to have turned him into a perfect cad. Relationships between men and women, on the other hand, even more than relationships between men and men, and women and women, always have an element of battle. A smooth and easy relationship is likely a shallow one. Far from condemning the tension and strife of courtship, Shakespeare seems to revel in it. He favors a merry war of words, a skirmish of wits, to the witless silence of some lovers.

The opening scene provides background to the relationship of Benedick and Beatrice. On the surface, the opening scene tells us only that Beatrice and Benedick quarrel and tease each other constantly. Beatrice asks the messenger about Benedick's performance in the recent war, using insulting names and complaining of Benedick's faithlessness and lack of skill in battle (1.1.30, 39-45, 73-78). More is here than may appear at first. Though Beatrice mocks Benedick, her first thought is to ask about him; for a woman who claims to despise Benedick, she is terribly interested in his performance in the war.

Moreover, when she says that Benedick is never faithful to anyone for long (he "wears his faith but as the fashion of his hat—it ever changes with the next block" [1.1.76-78]), she sounds like a wounded lover. When the soldiers present themselves at Messina, Benedick and Beatrice resume their banter. After mocking Beatrice sharply for the speed of her tongue (1.1.147-49), Benedick calls an end to the skirmish. Beatrice responds, "You always end with a jade's trick. I know you of old" (1.1.150-151). A "jade" is a worn-out horse who drops out of a race before the finish line; Beatrice knows from "of old" that Benedick will drop out when things get tough. Hints in the first scene that Beatrice and Benedick were once attracted to one another are confirmed during the masquerade scene, where Beatrice implies that Benedick was once unfaithful or false to her (2.1.288-92). Benedick and Beatrice fight and quarrel with each other partly to protect themselves. They have been wounded by love in the past, and they avoid further pain by keeping each other at a distance and by covering their attraction under a mask of wit.

The opening scene also introduces the various character's view of the nature of romance and love. There are two dimensions to Claudio's love for Hero. On the one hand, Claudio's is a classic romantic love. In the romantic view of love, the man elevates the woman into something more than human. The romantic views his beloved not so much as a person as the embodiment of some higher principle. She is so exalted that she is unapproachable, heavenly, spiritual. As a result, in classical romance, the man does not really want fulfillment of his love. To consummate his love would mean getting married and having to cope with the grind of daily life together. Marriage is much too earthy for the romantic. The romantic revels in obstacles. He wants to suffer feelings of love without allowing love to come to fruition in a permanent, covenanted relationship. As a romantic lover, Claudio falls in love with Hero nearly at first sight, before she has said anything. (In fact, Hero says little throughout the play; notice especially how seldom Claudio and Hero talk alone together.) Though Claudio admits that he has barely noted Hero before, he now thinks that she is a jewel that all the world cannot buy (1.1.187), the "sweetest lady that ever I looked upon" (1.1.194-195).

That reference to Hero as a "jewel" points to a different side of Claudio's attraction to her. In Shakespeare's day, women were often treated as no better than commodities to be examined, bought, and sold by men. It is reported that Thomas More (the saint!) required his daughter to take off her clothes so that a prospective husband could examine her naked. Fathers arranged marriages for their daughters that would help them advance socially and politically, without regard to the desires or best interests of their daughters. That Claudio's interest in Hero is commercial as well as romantic is shown during his conversation with Don Pedro at the end of Act 1:

> *Claudio:* Hath Leonato any son, my lord?
> *Don Pedro:* No child but Hero; she's his only heir.
> (1.1.303-304)

Don Pedro, without waiting for Claudio to spell it out, knows that Claudio is asking about the material rewards of marrying Hero.

Though they seem to be polar opposites, these two aspects of Claudio's love for Hero are really two sides of the same coin. Romantic and commercial views of women share a basic similarity: neither the romantic nor the commercial view treats a woman as a person. The romantic sees the woman as a spiritual principle; the commercial view treats the woman as a commodity, as if women were merely ornaments to adorn their men. Both are inherently misogynist, based on hatred of women, a refusal to treat women as women, as fellow humans sharing God's image.

"Love" based on romantic exaltation of women or on commercial demeaning of women is fragile. A man who believes his beloved to be the ideal of perfection cannot tolerate any hint of imperfection. This is one reason why the romantic does not want to get too close to his beloved; deep down, he knows that if he gets too close he will discover blemishes and imperfections. As we see below, when Claudio learns of Hero's supposed imperfections, his professed love turns to rage and hatred. Romantic love spiritualizes the woman, treating her as a disembodied principle. When confronted with (false) reports of Hero's very physical love for another man, Claudio's romantic image of Hero is destroyed; she is not, Claudio thinks he learns, as spiritual as he believed. She is no longer a jewel; she's a rotten orange. Erecting love on a commercial basis is equally unstable. If a man enters marriage as a social or economic convenience, then any whiff of scandal is disastrous. If a man's purpose in getting married is to be well-regarded and to advance in society, a marital scandal that harms his social standing will destroy the very purpose of the marriage.

The fragile nature of Claudio's love is manifested in his conversation with Benedick about Hero (1.1.168-210). Claudio is intent on getting Benedick's approval. Benedick, however, does not oblige. Benedick "can see yet without spectacles" and to him Hero is too short, too dark, too little (1.1.177-182, 196-201; note the relationship between love and sight, which we shall see again). When Don Pedro praises her, Claudio thinks he is joking. Why is Claudio so intent on getting his fellow soldiers' approval?

First, Claudio's uncertainty is a sign that his main attachment is still to the men's club of the regiment. He is not confident enough of his own judgment to choose Hero without their consent. It is also possible that he wants to be able to show Hero off, to be the envy of every man in the company. If Hero is not attractive to the other men, he will not be able to display his jewel. Finally, the dynamics of the situation are illumined by what the French critic Rene Girard calls "mimetic desire." According to this theory, we desire things not because they are desirable in themselves, but because we imitate other people who desire them. We "mimic" the desires of others, and therefore our desires are "mimetic." While many of Girard's conclusions are questionable, he is describing something real. The whole advertising industry is built on the assumption that people will want things if they see other people—especially "cool" people like sports heroes and movie stars—wanting them. Claudio's desire for Hero is mimetic. If Hero is not desirable to anyone else, he reasons, perhaps I should think again about my own desire.

Whatever we might think of Beatrice's manners, it is evident that she will not fall into the trap that Hero does, apparently without protest. No one could possibly think of Beatrice as a priceless jewel; she's too sassy and sharp for anyone to think she is an embodiment of a higher, spiritual principle. She is equally unwilling to be turned into a commodity. Given her status and her times, her only defense against being romanticized or being bought and sold is her wit and the strength of her will to resist. And she uses these to good effect first in putting off marriage, and then in getting love on her own terms. Shakespeare prefers a woman of wit, will, and strength, one who refuses to be treated as a piece of meat for male consumption.

Though Beatrice says that men are "made of earth" (2.1.63-64), she is not a man-hater. There are moments when she seems to long for marriage. At the same time, she fears some of the consequences. She realizes that marriage means that she gives up a measure of her independence, and she believes that marriage means that she will be "overmastered" and subordinated. Perhaps she fears she will end up like Hero: a silent ornament and appendage to a dull man. Her brief speech on marriage in 2.1.76-84 gives expression to her concerns. She sees the development of a courtship as a series of three steps: wooing, wedding, repenting. Each stage of the relationship is similar to a dance step: wooing is a jig, fast and hot; the wedding is a stately measured dance; then the rest of life is a cinquepace of repentance. The cinquepace is a fast dance; Beatrice may be implying that married people spend their lives frantically trying to please the other or frantically trying to get out of marriage. In any case, there is surely a pun on cinquepace and "sink pace." Marriage, in Beatrice's view, begins as a rapid dance that moves slower and slower until the married person sinks into the grave.

Benedick begins the play as a confirmed bachelor. Why is he so dead-set against marriage? Why is he so upset when Claudio is ready to get married and settle down? Benedick's fear of marriage becomes clearer if we investigate the pervasive imagery of horns in the first scene. Horns mark a man who has become a "cuckold," and a cuckold is a man whose wife commits adultery behind his back. The folklore of Shakespeare's day had it that a man who has been "cuckolded" grew horns. When Claudio tells Benedick he is in love and wishes to marry Hero and Benedick asks, "hath not the world one man but he will wear his cap with suspicion" (1.1.204-206), the cuckold imagery is in the background. Benedick implies that men wear caps to hide the horns of the cuckold, and he wonders if there are going to be any unmarried men left who will not have to hide a cuckold's horns. Don Pedro says that just as the savage bull bears the yoke, so also Benedick will bear the yoke of marriage, but Benedick replies, "if ever the sensible Benedick bear it, pluck off the bull's horns and set them in my forehead" (1.1.270-272). The implication of these various comments is that to be married is to be a cuckold. To be married, to pledge your faith to a single woman, is set yourself up for betrayal. Benedick and the other men display a continual fear that, if they marry, their wives will be unfaithful to them. Their assumption is that women are unreliable and faithless.

Linked with this fear of becoming a cuckold is what we noted above: the fear of breaking up the comraderie of the company of soldiers. Benedick believes that if he desires a woman, other men will desire her also. This "mimetic desire" will turn the men into rivals. When two men desire the same woman, conflict is all but inevitable. Thus, when one man desires a woman, he is putting himself in a position to become a rival to another man. Love and marriage threaten to break down the bonds of male friendship that have held the company together during the war. Better not to love at all than to take this risk. Falling in love does indeed require a change in all previous relationships, as Benedick himself will soon discover to his dismay.

Review Questions.

1. Explain the structure of the play.

2. Explain the title of the play.

3. Where have Don Pedro and his company been prior to the beginning of the play?

4. Why is Don John angry with Claudio?

5. How are love and war different? How are they similar?

6. What is Claudio's view of love and marriage? What is the "romantic" view of love? What is the "commercial" view? How are they similar?

7. What is Beatrice's view of love and men?

8. Why does Benedick resist love and marriage? What does his resistance have to do with cuckoldry?

9. What kind of relationship do Benedick and Beatrice have? What is the history of their relationship?

10. What is "mimetic desire"? What are its results?

Thought Questions.

1. Beatrice compares Benedick's friendship to the "fashion of his hat" (1.1.76-78). There are several references to "fashion" in the play. How does the theme of fashion relate to the overall themes of the play?

2. Cupid is mentioned several times in the first two acts. Who is Cupid? Select one reference (for example, 1.1.39-45; 2.1.400-403) and explain what is meant by the allusion to Cupid.

3. Beatrice speaks of "the Benedick" as a disease that is

very expensive to cure (1.1.87-92). What does she mean? In the light of the rest of the play, how is this ironic?

4. Read carefully through the first exchange between Beatrice and Benedick (1.1.121-151). Put the dialogue into your own words to trace how each plays off the other's words.

5. In answering Claudio's question about Hero, Benedick contrasts his "simple judgment" to his "custom, as being a professed tyrant to their sex" (1.1.172-75). What does this imply about Benedick's claim to be a happy bachelor?

6. Why does Claudio ask Don Pedro to court Hero for him? What does this tell you about Claudio?

7. Don John says, "I cannot hide what I am" (1.3.13). Is this true? Why does Don John say this?

8. What advice does Beatrice give Hero in 2.1.56-60? What does this tell you about Beatrice's views on marriage?

9. Why is Claudio so ready to believe Don John when he says that Don Pedro is courting Hero for himself? (see 2.1.180-90).

10. Benedick says that Claudio acts like a blind man from whom a boy has stolen meat (2.1.206-208). What is the significance of calling Claudio "blind," and of saying his "meat" has been stolen?

Lesson Two: Acts 2.2-3.3

These fives scenes can be outlined as follows:

A. Evil deception, I (Don John's plan).
    B. Benevolent Deception, I ("Gulling" of Benedick)
    B. Benevolent Deception, II ("Gulling" of Beatrice)
A. Evil Deception II (Don John executes plan)

    Dogberry's watch uncovers Evil Deception

The deceptions (or "gullings") of Benedick and Beatrice are "sandwiched" between scenes dealing with Don John's deception. By arranging the scenes in this manner, Shakespeare invites us to compare and contrast the two deceptions and their perpetrators, Don Pedro and Don John. Both Don John and Don Pedro are deceivers; both use deception to manipulate and control those around them. The difference is obvious, however; Don John deceives in order to destroy love, while Don Pedro uses deception to bring a buried love to new life. The series of scenes ends with the first introduction of Dogberry, who will ultimately be the hero of the comedy, the one who ensures that the comedy does not turn tragic. Dogberry discovers Don John's plot on the night before the wedding, and therefore has information that would prevent a terrible series of events, but no one knows that Dogberry knows; in fact, Dogberry himself does not know that what he knows is important for others to know. In a play where everyone goes about eavesdropping and overhearing and noting, in a play where everyone seems to know everything that goes on, the key discovery goes unnoticed by everyone—except the shallow fool, Dogberry.

The conversation between Don John and his henchman, Borachio, in 2.2, has several subtle twists that reveal underlying themes of the play. Don John has been lamenting the failure of his plot to turn Don Pedro and Claudio against each other at the masquerade, and together with Borachio he makes plans for a more elaborate deception. When Borachio tells Don John that he can visit Margaret, Hero's maid, at any time, Don John is puzzled:

Don John: What life is in that, to be the death of this marriage?
Borachio: The poison of that lies in you to temper.
(2.2.19-22)

Don John wants to kill Claudio's marriage. The means to achieve this goal will be "poison." The reference to poison, as often in Shakespeare, is related to imagery of serpents, and ultimately refers to Satan; Don John is the serpent in the

Edenic world of Messina, and he is seeking to destroy the harmony and bliss of Claudio and Hero as Satan corrupted the marriage of Adam and Eve. Literally, the poison will be the deception he is planning. Like the serpent in the garden, Don John seeks to kill by lies. Like Satan, he is a murderer and a liar (Jn. 8:44).

Borachio says that the poison must be "tempered" or prepared. The event that is the basis for the deception—Borachio's meeting with Margaret at Hero's window—has literally nothing to do with Claudio or Don Pedro; Borachio and Margaret are not innocent, but Claudio has no reason to be interested in their actions. For this event to become poison to kill a marriage, the event must be tempered by deception. Only if Claudio can be persuaded that Hero is meeting with another man on the night before her wedding will he begin to make "much ado about nothing." It is not the event itself that kills the marriage; it is not even Claudio's witnessing of the event that kills the marriage. What threatens to kill the marriage is the combination of the event with a false interpretation. When our view of the world is shaped by poisonous lies, and when we act on those deceptions, the product, as Eve discovered, is death.

Throughout the conversation of Borachio and Don John, there is a constant emphasis on "seeming" and "semblance." Don John wants to make it seem that Hero is unfaithful. The idea that things are not always what they appear is commonplace. Everyone knows that our eyes can deceive us. In *Much Ado*, however, the situation that Shakespeare has created is more complex than this. Think of a ball like an onion, with several layers over a central core. The outside layer is red; when you peel away the outside layer, you come to a blue layer, and you say, "Ah ha! The ball is really blue." If you stop there, you would be deceived, because once you peel away the blue layer, this ball turns out to be red after all. Just as you have to peel away several layers to find out the real color of the ball, so in *Much Ado*, appearances and deceptions are several layers deep. To get to the truth, the characters have to penetrate several layers of falsehoods.

Claudio looks at Hero's appearance, and concludes she is a maid, a virgin. Because of Don John's deception, he believes that he has peeled away the deceptive outer layer, the layer of seeming, and now sees Hero for what she really is—a prostitute visited by a stranger on the night before her wedding. Hero seemed to be a maid, but as it turns out, she is not. Claudio thinks he has learned that appearances can be deceiving. What has really happened is that he has missed the truth and now believes a lie. He has learned that appearances can deceive; but he has not learned that apparent deceptions can also be deceiving. Claudio has yet to learn that what someone tells us is false may turn out to be true. He peeled off the outer layer, but the underlying layer is false. In fact, the outer layer was true to begin with. Hero is not, as Claudio comes to believe, wearing the disguise of a maid; she *is* a maid. Thinking he is ripping the mask from Hero, Claudio is really tearing at her face.

Layers of appearance and deception make it exceedingly difficult to arrive at the truth. When we think we are wise enough to see through a disguise, we may only be seeing another disguise. When we see through one lie, and believe we have come to the truth, we may be really believing another lie. Shakespeare seems to be telling us that we can never really know the truth about anything, because someone might be deceiving us. It may seem Shakespeare is an advocate of skepticism, the view that we can never know anything. (Philosophers will tell you that skepticism is self-contradictory; the answer to someone who says, "We can never know anything for certain" is simply, "Do you know that for certain?")

Shakespeare, however, is no skeptic. But how does he suggest that the dilemma be resolved? Part of the solution is to recognize that seeing is not the most basic aspect of knowing. This is brought out in the "Gulling" scenes. Benedick's monologue before his "Gulling" summarizes a key theme of the play. Benedick describes at length the change that has overtaken Claudio since he has fallen in love with Hero (2.3.6-23). He has been transformed from a soldier into a lover, a change that, Benedick thinks, is all for the worse. To Benedick, the transformation seems complete. Claudio once mocked lovers, but is now subject of his own mockery. His tastes in music have changed: once he listened only to the drum and fife, to martial music, but now he wants the tabor and pipe and the lute—instruments suitable to women and lovers. (Benedick, still a soldier through and through, has no taste for the lute, which he says is only sheep's guts, 2.3.62-63.) Claudio once was interested in armor, but now he goes about in a new doublet and wears the latest in fashion. Claudio once spoke plainly, but now his speech is a "fantastical banquet" of words.

In Benedick's mind, to become a lover is to cease to be a man. This is true not only because a man in love attends to the softer, more tender things of life, rather than the hardy life of a soldier in the field. It is more profoundly true because a man in love is beloved by a woman, and to be loved by someone else means being passive. Being loved means being acted upon rather than acting. For Benedick, being passive is a feminine trait. True men are soldiers, always acting and never being acted upon.

Benedick's description of Claudio is crucial to the play's conception of true love and helps us resolve the dilemma that arises from the problem of multiple layers of lies. After enumerating the changes in Claudio, Benedick asks, "May I be so converted and see with these eyes?" (2.3.23-24). The irony of the question is sharp; within moments, Benedick will undergo a transformation far more complete than anything Claudio has dreamt of. But the way Benedick characterizes falling in love is fundamental: To fall in love is to be converted, to be totally changed from head to toe, to take a new position in the world, to look at the world through new eyes. And this is precisely what happens to Benedick. After he has become convinced that Beatrice is in love with him, she is sent to call him to dinner. They have the following exchange:

> *Beatrice:* Against my will I am sent to bid you come in to dinner.
> *Benedick:* Fair Beatrice, I thank you your pains.
> *Beatrice:* I took no more pains for those thanks than you take pains to thank me. If it had been painful, I would not have come.
> *Benedick:* You take pleasure, then, in the message?
> *Beatrice*: Yea, just so much as you may take upon a knife's point and choke a daw withal. You have no stomach, signior. Fare you well. [Exit]
> *Benedick:* Ha! "Against my will I am sent to bid you come in to dinner." There's a double meaning in that. (2.3.255-268)

Beatrice has not changed a whit, and there is no double meaning in her words. She is the same "Lady Tongue" whom Benedick earlier said he could not stand to be close to. What has changed is Benedick. Since he is now in love, he sees everything in a new light. Beatrice is unchanged, but Benedick has been converted. Seeing now is not the most fundamental thing, since appearances can deceive; the most fundamental thing is being converted. What and how we see depends on whether or not we have been converted.

By comparison with Benedick's total conversion to love, Claudio's is superficial in the extreme. Claudio's tastes in music and clothes may have changed, but he does not see things through the eyes of one converted to love. When he sees Don Pedro wooing Hero, he thinks he has been betrayed. When he sees Borachio going to Hero's window, he immediately thinks the worst, and makes plans to shame Hero publicly. Because he has not undergone a real conversion to love, because his love still depends on what he sees, Claudio's eyes are easily guided by appearances, lies, and deceptions. Benedick will not be misled by "seeming" because at a basic level he does not depend on seeing. At a basic level, his seeing depends on his conversion to love.

The scene of Benedick's "gulling" enriches the play's depiction of the relations between love and sight. In order to

convert Benedick, Don Pedro, Leonato, and Claudio do two
things. First, they tell the truth. As Don Pedro says, Beatrice,
in spite of herself, really does have an interest in Benedick.
And Don Pedro and the others are correct when they discuss
Benedick's faults, particularly his pride and "contemptible
spirit" (2.3.187-188). Though Don Pedro's plot is a deception, it is a deception that gets to the truth (unlike Don John's).
Second, the plotters let Benedick know that he is beloved. He
believes himself to be loved before he responds by choosing
to love Beatrice in return. Benedick is converted to love when
he hears the report of Beatrice's love for him. Faith in the
love of another comes before love. There is good theology
in the scene: as John says, we love God because He first loved
us (1 Jn. 4:19) and Jesus said, Blessed are those who have not
seen and yet have believed (Jn. 20:29).

When Benedick hears the plotters' conversation, he is con-
victed of his faults and repents. Benedick recognizes the truth
in their rebuke, and he resolves to change for the better. In
the next scene, he has shaved his soldier's beard and in a later
scene he is attempting to write a love sonnet to Beatrice. He
thinks of the mockery he will have to endure when others
learn of his change of heart, and tries to prepare responses
(2.3.231-54). But all the responses that he plans are no more
than jokes. In fact, he is not in love with Beatrice simply because he has outgrown adolescent tastes, nor because he is
convinced the world must be peopled. He loves Beatrice because he has been converted.

The gulling of Beatrice is similar to that of Benedick. 3.1
contains the first and nearly the only extended speeches by
Hero, and she makes the most of the opportunity. Like Don
Pedro, Claudio, and Leonato, Hero is only pretending to
pretend. In fact, her censures of Beatrice show her true feelings. As with Benedick, Beatrice is censured and rebuked
mainly for her pride and scorn of others. And like Benedick,
Beatrice is converted because she learns of another's love for
her; her love is a response to a report that she is beloved. She
repents and promises to return Benedick's love. Truth,

disguised as a deception masquerading as truth, sets her free.

After the two plots—Don John's and Don Pedro's—have been set into motion, Dogberry is introduced for the first time. Dogberry's role in the play provides the other part of the solution to the problems of seeing and seeming, appearance and deception, and knowing the truth. On the surface, Dogberry serves a comic purpose. His instructions to the watch illustrate his basic lunacy. If they see someone suspicious, Dogberry tells them, they should order him to stand, but if he does not stand, they should let him go. If they see a thief, they should be suspicious, but since spending time with thieves might corrupt them, the watch should not try to capture thieves. The watch needs to be quiet, and since people are quiet when they are asleep, the watch is free to sleep through the night (3.3.1-102). I don't know about you, but I would not sleep securely in Messina with Dogberry on the watch.

In two important ways, however, Dogberry contributes to the development of the larger and more serious themes of the play. First, he misuses language constantly. He always says precisely the wrong word. He threatens wrongdoers with "everlasting redemption" (instead of damnation, 4.2.59-60) and asks Borachio why he does not suspect (instead of respect) the office of constable (4.2.77-78). His malapropisms make Dogberry funny, but they also take to a comic extreme a tendency that everyone in the play shares to one degree or another. Communication in Messina is constantly being tangled. The plot moves along through a series of mistaken interpretations. People overhear, but hear wrong; people see, but mistake what they see; people speak, but they do not speak the truth; Benedick and Beatrice overhear conversations that are supposed to be deceptive, and believe them. Dogberry is a perfect hero in a world like this: He is a man who says the very opposite of what he means. But his mangled words become the means of restoration.

Second, though Dogberry is, on the surface, an utter fool, this shallow fool turns out to be more discerning than

the wisdoms of Messina. Dogberry and his watch (acciden-
tally, to be sure) expose the deceptions that misled the wise
and powerful. The "wisdoms" of the play spend their time
and energy trying to deceive and manipulate and control each
other. Dogberry makes no effort to control things; he takes
life as it comes, and tries to fulfill his duties (insofar as he
understands them), and ends up a hero. He has a blunt, dumb
honesty and simplicity that is lacking in many of the other
characters. When he tells the Sexton during the examination
scene to "Write God first" (4.2.21), he shows he has his pri-
orities in order. Though presented in a comic light,
Shakespeare is suggesting that a proper kind of foolishness is
the key to true wisdom. Dogberry is a "fool" with too much
simple honesty to be deceived by appearances.

Much Ado poses the problem of how one can be confident of any knowledge in a world full of appearances, disguises, and outright deceptions. Shakespeare does not provide a logically airtight answer to this dilemma. The play does
not offer any philosophical formulas for discovering the truth.
Instead, the play suggests that the key to discerning between
truth and falsehood, to penetrating the lies and disguises, is a
wisdom founded on faith, love, and humility.

Review Questions.

1. Explain the significance of the order of these five
scenes.

2. How are Don John and Don Pedro similar? How are
they different?

3. How does Don John describe his plot to deceive
Claudio? What is significant about this description?

4. How does *Much Ado* illustrate the truism that "appearances can be deceiving"? How does Shakespeare show the
complexities of appearance and reality?

5. How does Shakespeare resolve the problems of appearance and reality in *Much Ado*?

6. Why does Benedick think it unmanly to be in love?

7. How does Benedick describe falling in love? How

does this description apply to Claudio? How does it apply to Benedick himself?

8. What do Benedick's friends say to make him fall in love? What does Hero say that makes Beatrice fall in love with Benedick?

9. What kind of character is Dogberry?

10. How does Dogberry fit into the themes of *Much Ado*?

Thought Questions.

1. How does Borachio suggest that Don John appeal to Don Pedro? (2.2.21-26). Why does Borachio suggest this kind of approach? Compare this with Don John's words in 3.2.116-118.

2. Where do the gulling of Benedick and Beatrice take place? (2.3.3-4; 3.1.5-13). What is significant about this setting? Compare with 3.3.158-161.

3. Benedick says he prefers a "horn" to the lute (2.3.61-64). In the light of what we saw in the first lesson, why is this noteworthy?

4. Why did Shakespeare include the song before the deception of Benedick? (2.3.65-77). How does the song reflect what's going on in the play?

5. What does Don Pedro expect to happen to Beatrice and Benedick when they finally meet? (2.3.220-226).

6. Hero says that Cupid's arrow "only wounds by hearsay" (3.1.21-23). What does she mean by this? How does this fit with the depiction of love elsewhere in *Much Ado*?

7. While "gulling" Beatrice, Hero tells Ursula that she will try to keep Benedick from loving Beatrice by staining her with slanders (3.1.82-86). In the light of what happens to Hero, what is significant about these lines?

8. What does Claudio plan to do after his wedding? (3.2.1-4). What does this say about Claudio's love for Hero?

9. Summarize Dogberry's instructions to the watch (3.3.1-102).

10. With Dogberry's watch listening, Borachio and

Conrade have a conversation about fashion (3.3.116-174). What do they say about fashion? What do the members of the watch think they are talking about?

Lesson Three: Act 4

Again, it will be helpful to look at the overall structure of this act, since we see here the same rhythm that appeared in the earlier series of scenes:

A. Evil Deception Consummated: Marriage killed
B. Benevolent Deception Consummated: Benedick and Beatrice confirm love
    Dogberry unravels the plot

Interestingly, the fulfillment of the two deceptions are directly linked. The death of Claudio's marriage (the goal of Don John's plot) leads immediately to the conversation of Beatrice and Benedick where they profess their love for each other (the goal of Don Pedro's plot). Without Claudio's rejection of Hero, Beatrice would have had no occasion to test Benedick's love.

When we examined *Macbeth*, we discussed the symbolism of the feast. A feast setting signifies joy, fellowship with one friends, enjoyment of the fruits of the earth. The feast shows the world as it ought to be. Wedding scenes, as we learned in *Henry V*, play a similar role in drama and literature. A wedding is not only the union of a particular man with a particular woman, but also a sign of something larger. A wedding unites not only the couple getting married, but it is also a kind of union of opposites (a man and a woman). Weddings signify reconciliation and resolution of conflict and differences (as do courtroom scenes). Weddings also signify new beginnings, the beginning of a new world. This is literally true. The world is changed forever by a wedding. Before a wedding, we have a single man and a single woman; after the wedding we have a couple, a family. Something exists afterwards that did not exist before the wedding. Where there was one, now there are two; and, because the man and woman become one flesh, where there were two, there is now one.

When we look at the wedding in biblical perspective, its significance is enhanced. Weddings are often Edenic settings. The man is a new Adam, the woman a new Eve, and the family that is created by the wedding is called to be a new creation. A wedding is a restoration of the fallen world. Being a recapitulation of creation, a wedding points to the recreation of the world at the end. The Bible teaches that when Jesus returns, the wedding feast of the Lamb, Jesus' spiritual marriage to His bride, the Church, will be consummated and harmony and reconciliation will reign over the entire creation. This is the way the world ends—with a wedding.

Against this background, we can see that the first wedding scene in *Much Ado* is not a typical wedding. Benedick has it right: As Claudio viciously denounces Hero, Benedick says with comic understatement, "This looks not like a nuptial" (4.1.69). Instead of the union of opposites, Claudio and Hero are separated. Instead of new life, the scene ends with Hero undergoing a kind of death. Instead of joy, delight, and vows of faithfulness, there is anger, anguish, and accusations of betrayal. The first wedding is a hellish, demonic parody of a wedding. There is a serpent in the Eden of Messina, and his lies make the wedding a disaster. Far from producing a new creation, the wedding leaves Messina a damaged and fallen world.

In his behavior at the first wedding, Claudio reveals the shallowness of his "conversion" to love. Matthew tells us that when Joseph found Mary was pregnant, he desired to put her away quietly (Mt. 1:19). Claudio is anything but quiet about Hero's supposed sins. If this is how Claudio acts after putting aside the rough task of war and devoting himself to the soft and delicate affairs of love, I'd hate to see him on the battlefield! War has—permanently it appears—turned

Claudio into a fighting animal. Even before he sees any evidence, he is ready to humiliate Hero publicly (3.2.125-127). His behavior indicates his feelings had less to do with love for Hero than for something else. He acts like a man who has been cheated in a bargain: When he throws Hero back to Leonato, he calls her a "rotten orange" (4.1.34). Claudio thought he was getting a jewel, but now he believes the jewel is phony; he has treated Hero as a commodity from the beginning, and now when she proves unsatisfactory, he wants his money back. Having thought of Hero as a piece of meat, Claudio is enraged when she turns out to be spoiled.

Claudio's reaction also grows out of his romanticized view of Hero. He has idealized Hero so much (the jewel that the world cannot afford to buy) that any hint of imperfection brings her crashing down from her pedestal. Claudio reacts as he does, moreover, because his own honor has been offended. He is most concerned with how Hero's sins will reflect on him. This, in fact, is how Don John appeals to Claudio when he begins the deception: "If you love her [after seeing what I show you], tomorrow wed her. But it would better fit your honor to change your mind" (3.2.116-118). Claudio is a count, and a count has to protect his reputation. If he receives damaged merchandise, his honor turns to shame. Hero's infidelities will make Claudio look bad and make him a laughing stock; he will sprout the horns of the cuckold and have to go about in a cap. And for the wisdoms of Messina, looking bad is perhaps the worse thing of all.

When I taught *Much Ado* in the winter of 1994, one of my students perceptively asked this question: If Claudio thinks that another man is after his fiancé, why doesn't he go after the other guy? Why does he attack Hero, rather than her supposed lover? There are two answers to this question. First, Claudio's reaction shows that he had the same bias against marriage and women that Benedick had. Benedick, we saw above, believed that being married amounted to being

a cuckold; if a man settles on one woman, he is in danger
of being betrayed because women are untrustworthy.
Claudio's assumptions about women set him up for Don
John's deception. "That's just how I expect women to behave" summarizes Claudio's reaction to Don John's "revelation."

Second, Claudio's reaction shows where his loyalties lie.
He does not side with Hero and does not attack Hero's supposed lover because his allegiance is more with the men of
Messina than with his fiancé. He has made some superficial
changes in his tastes and behavior, but when a crisis hits, he
still sides with his army buddies. He has not taken up the
new position that love requires of him. It is interesting in this
respect to notice that Claudio, even after he is engaged to
Hero, spends almost no time with her. They never have a
conversation alone. Instead, Claudio spends the few days before his wedding sporting with Don Pedro and the other
men. He has not made the break necessary for true love; he
has not been willing to leave his old life and cleave to his wife.
He has not truly been converted to love.

Claudio has not learned the proper relationship between
love and sight. When he sees Hero blush at his accusations,
he thinks she is only putting on an act: she only "seems" to be
a maid (4.1.35-40). Friar Francis, by contrast, looks at the
same blushes and interprets them as signs of Hero's innocence (4.1.157-172). Claudio thinks that his sight has
pierced through Hero's mask of virginity and now he can
see that she really is a "rotten orange." But he sees things this
way because he has believed Don John's lie. Claudio's trust in
the "serpent's" deception leads Claudio to misinterpret everything. His trust in Don John's lie tempers the poison that
kills his marriage.

Leonato's reaction to Don John's accusation is similar to
Claudio's (4.1.123-144). Believing Claudio and Don Pedro,
he laments that he ever had a daughter. His sight is so blinded
by the lie that even when he is presented with evidence of
Hero's innocence, he turns it into evidence of guilt. Don

Pedro says that Borachio confessed to visiting Hero's apartment at night "a thousand times" (4.1.95-96). But Beatrice has slept in the same room with Hero for an entire year, save only the night before the wedding (4.1.150-151). When Leonato hears that Beatrice was not with Hero the previous night, he erupts with, "Confirm'd, Confirm'd!" (4.1.152). In fact, Beatrice's testimony shows that Borachio is lying; if Borachio visited Hero "a thousand times," Beatrice would surely have noticed! Leonato, like Claudio, does not let love guide his sight. His sight is darkened by the lie.

Once again: Sight is not the most fundamental thing; the most fundamental thing is conversion, belief, faith. What we see will be determined either by love that arises from faith or it will be determined by the lie.

The first wedding scene is filled with imagery of nakedness, shame, and covering. Shame is induced by exposure; we feel shame when we are unmasked and stripped of our defenses and pretenses, when people see us for what we really are. Claudio says that Hero has covered her wantonness in a show of virginity and innocence. Leonato says that death would be the best "cover for her shame" (4.1.118). When the Friar suggests his plan, Leonato objects that he is covering with excuse that which appears in proper nakedness (4.1.176-177). In fact, what Claudio and Leonato think is the truth is really a cover, a deception. There is literally "nothing" to be exposed, uncovered, unmasked. Hero is a completely innocent victim. Quite literally, Claudio and Leonato make "much ado about nothing"

Friar Francis finally comes up with a plan to transform the tragic death of Claudio's and Hero's marriage into resurrection. His advice, however, sounds odd coming from a priest. He suggests that everyone pretend that Hero is dead. He hopes that the news of Hero's death will make Claudio regret his heartless denunciation, on the theory that we desire things more when they are absent than when they are close by (4.1.202-245). As we have seen, the action of the whole play moves forward by deceptions, so the Friar's

scheme is dramatically fitting. It is similar to the interpretation
that some in the early Church gave to the work of Jesus. They
taught that the cross was a great deception of Satan. Satan
believed he would be victorious if he incited Judas, the Jews,
and the Romans to kill Jesus. But Satan was tricked; God
turned Satan's evil plan into good by saving sinners through
the cross. Satan, the great deceiver, was undone by a divine
deception. The idea in *Much Ado* is similar: the effects of an
evil deception are undone by a benevolent deception.

The Friar's plot has biblical overtones in another way as
well. His plan is that, once Claudio has been brought to regret
his sins, Hero will be restored to life. As Friar Francis puts it,
"Come, lady, die to live" (4.1.255). The effects of the
"serpent's" poisonous lies will be remedied by the Hero's death
and resurrection. The Christian imagery goes further. The bride
(an image of the Church in Scripture) is humiliated and rejected because of the serpent's lies; but that does not mean
that the wedding feast is canceled. Friar Francis encourages
Hero with, "This wedding day perhaps is but prolonged. Have
patience and endure" (4.1.255-56). Through death and resurrection, there is hope for a fallen world—hope that the spoiled
wedding will be followed by a genuine wedding feast, hope
that harmony, reconciliation, and peace will one day reign,
hope that sorrow will be turned to joy.

Don John's evil deception has successfully killed the marriage (though Don John, like Satan, did not count on a resurrection!). At the same time, the combination of Claudio's rejection of Hero and Don Pedro's benevolent deception has
brought Benedick and Beatrice to a "mountain of affection,
the one with the other." When the other wedding guests have
gone, Benedick and Beatrice remain behind for their first conversation since they were "tricked" into falling in love.

Beatrice and Benedick have just witnessed a wedding
that made a mockery of marriage. They have seen the destructive potential of falling in love. They know what they are
risking when the profess love; they are risking betrayal, anger,

hatred, death. But they profess their love for each other anyway. In the light of the wedding fiasco, their simple exchange of affection is wildly daring and deeply moving. How well Benedick puts it: "I do love nothing in the world so well as you. Is not that strange?" (4.1.270-271).

True to form, Beatrice will not settle for a mere profession of love. Though she is in love with Benedick, she does not allow herself to become a passive partner, as Hero is. When Benedick asks what he can do to demonstrate his love, she says, simply and chillingly, "Kill Claudio" (4.1.292). Why does she demand this? Obviously, at the moment she is angry, and, certain as she is of Hero's innocence, wants Claudio to pay for his slander. Shakespeare captures the violence of her anger and her frustration at her helplessness: "O God, that I were a man! I would eat his heart in the marketplace" (4.1.309-310). But there is more going on than a momentary burst of passion. Beatrice knows that talk is cheap. Professions of love are a dime a dozen. She "knows" Benedick "of old" and knows that he changes his friendships like the fashion of his hat. She's right. Benedick's first reaction is to backpedal. If loving Beatrice means he has to kill Claudio, he needs to think twice (or more) about loving Beatrice. "We'll be friends first," he says lamely (4.1.300).

What Beatrice wants is for Benedick to demonstrate by his actions where his loyalties really lie. We have seen that, when push came to shove, Claudio sided with the men of Messina against Hero. Beatrice believes that, if Benedick's love is genuine, it must lead to a break with the old military life and military friendships. Killing Claudio is a radical break, to be sure. Essentially, though, Beatrice is demanding that Benedick "leave and cleave." She demands that he treat her enemies as his enemies. She is demanding that he provide evidence that for him love really means a conversion, that he really intends to assume a new position in the world, with the new loyalties, new battles, new enemies, and new tasks that come with it. She wants Benedick to demonstrate that he is not like the other men of Messina, for whom

> . . . manhood is melted into courtesies, valor into compli-
> ment, and men are only turned into tongue, and trim ones
> too. He is now as valiant as Hercules that only tells a lie and
> swears it. (4.1.322-326)

The men of Messina are full of words, but unwilling to risk
the loss of friendship by taking a stand against evil. A true
man is willing to break with other men for right and for the
defense of his beloved. Beatrice wants Benedick to show that
he is a true man. For Beatrice, a man's task is to guard and defend and avenge women. Though she makes this point with
great violence, her point is well taken. Claudio is an attacker
and abuser of women; he uses his superior strength and position to humiliate Hero. Beatrice wants Benedick to use his
strength and position for the opposite task.

Benedick understands the seriousness of her demands.
These are demands that Claudio has never met; he certainly
did not treat Hero's enemies as his own. Benedick knows
that he risks a great deal. He stands to lose not only his (current) best friend, but also his position among the soldiers of
Don Pedro's company (5.1.190-192). Despite these risks,
Benedick, after hesitations and comic backpedaling, finally
accepts Beatrice's terms. He will demonstrate his love by
challenging Claudio. His will make good his conversion not
only by words and faith, but by works.

Review Questions.

1. What is the significance of the structure of Act 4?

2. How do the plots of Don John and Don Pedro contribute to the love between Beatrice and Benedick?

3. What does a wedding signify? How does the first wedding of Claudio and Hero compare with an ideal wedding?

4. Why is Claudio so violently angry at Hero?

5. Why doesn't Claudio direct his anger at Hero's supposed lover? What does this tell you about the nature of
Claudio's love?

6. How is the imagery of nakedness, covering, and shame
used in the wedding scene?

7. How does Friar Francis propose to revive Claudio's marriage? Explain how his plan fits with the rest of the play.

8. Why is it significant that Beatrice and Benedick profess love for one another immediately after the first wedding?

9. Why does Beatrice want Benedick to kill Claudio?

10. What is Beatrice's opinion of the men of Messina?

Thought Questions.

1. Explain the exchange between Claudio and Don Pedro in 4.1.24-33.

2. To which goddesses does Claudio compare Hero? (4.1.58-63). What is the significance of the comparison?

3. What does Claudio conclude about beauty from this episode with Hero? (4.1.102-110).

4. What is the thrust of Leonato's speech in 4.1.123-144, when he thinks that Hero is guilty?

5. Friar Francis tells Leonato, "on this travail look for greater birth" (4.1.215). What does he mean by this?

6. What does Friar Francis say is the worst that might happen if Leonato follows his advice? (4.1.242-245).

7. Whom does Beatrice call "Count Confect"? (4.1.319). What does she mean by this?

8. In his conversation with Beatrice, Benedick says that no sauce can be devised that will make him eat his words of love (4.1.282-283). Is this true?

9. Lady Macbeth urged her husband to kill King Duncan, and Beatrice demands that Benedick kill Claudio. Is Beatrice another Lady Macbeth? How are they similar and different?

10. Earlier in the play, Benedick called Beatrice "Lady Tongue." What did he mean? What does Beatrice mean when she charges that the men of Messina have "turned into tongue, and trim ones too" (4.1.323-324)?

Lesson Four: Act 5

Through Acts 2-4 there is a regular rhythm to *Much Ado*, an almost waltz-like beat: deception, deception, DOGBERRY, deception, deception, DOGBERRY. In the first cycle, we have several scenes concerning deception, then Dogberry appears. In act 4, the twin deceptions come to their climaxes in contrasting scenes—the wedding scene and the scene in which Benedick and Beatrice profess their love—and then Dogberry appears again in the hilarious examination scene (4.2). In Act 5, we have a similar pattern. The deceptions and plots have led to a volatile situation. At the beginning of the final Act, Leonato and Antonio confront Don Pedro and Claudio. The two old men are ready to fight for the honor of Hero, but are persuaded to leave. Immediately after they leave, Benedick arrives to challenge Claudio. The lies and deceptions are leading to violence. Nowhere does *Much Ado* come so close to falling into tragedy. Just when things are getting heated up, who should appear but Dogberry? As in his previous appearances, he comes on the scene just in the nick of time to make sure that everything turns out happily. From this point on, the slope of the play's story line is constantly upward. Dogberry's revelations about Hero's innocence bring Claudio and Don Pedro to a kind of repentance, another wedding is arranged, and hope that Messina can once again become Eden is restored.

Benedick's challenge of Claudio simply confirms what we saw in Act 4. It demonstrates the depth and sincerity of Benedick's love for Beatrice. He is truly converted, and now sees the world with new eyes because he has taken up a new position in the world. Before, he believed his place was next to his best friend Claudio; now, he takes his place with Beatrice, and treats Claudio as an enemy because he is an enemy of his beloved. He breaks with Claudio and with Don Pedro out of love for his lady. Love has converted him into a redeemer, an avenger of the wronged innocent Hero.

Claudio, by contrast, has hardly changed. He still considers his actions perfectly just and good. He shows contempt for Leonato, the man who would have been his father-in-law, and for Antonio, calling them "old men without teeth" (5.1.117). He dismisses Benedick's challenge; though he realizes that Benedick is "in most profound earnest" (5.1.198), he immediately goes on to compare Benedick to an ape (5.1.205-206). Both he and Don Pedro think that Benedick has left "off his wit" (5.1.203-204). They cannot conceive of any man in his right mind breaking with the company of other men and taking up the cause of an innocent woman; they cannot conceive of a man who is willing to leave and cleave. Friar Francis' plan has not worked. Claudio does not seem to miss Hero in the least, still another sign of how shallow his affection was to begin with.

When Claudio and Don Pedro learn from Dogberry that Hero was completely innocent and that they have been deceived, their repentance begins. Dogberry's words are like "iron" through Claudio's blood; for the first time since the first wedding, Claudio thinks of Hero with affection: "Sweet Hero! Now thy image doth appear in the rare semblance that I lov'd it first" (5.1.258-259). Their confession of wrong leaves something to be desired. Claudio says he "sinn'd not but in mistaking" (5.1.282-283), but he actually did much more than that. He could have been mistaken without denouncing and shaming Hero publicly. Still, Claudio and Don Pedro are truly sorry for the harm they have caused, and are ready submit to whatever penance Leonato might devise.

Confession and repentance are well and good. But something more than confession is needed to restore broken relationships. You not only need the sinner to confess wrongs, but you need to have someone to accept that confession and respond with compassion. Claudio puts himself at Leonato's mercy; had Leonato been so inclined, he could have made Claudio suffer dearly. Fortunately, Leonato is merciful. The "penance" that Leonato imposes is mild. Claudio must proclaim Hero's innocence as publicly as he denounced her for sin, and he must take Leonato's niece for his bride

(5.1.287-299). Mild though this penance is, it demands a serious response from Claudio, since he will have to live with the consequences for the rest of his life. It is a testimony to the sincerity of Claudio's repentance that he readily accepts Leonato's conditions. When his confession meets with what Claudio calls Leonato's "overkindness" (5.1.301), a new day begins to dawn for Messina. Confession meeting with compassion is the first step on the path back to Eden.

Scene 2 gives us the play's last glimpse of Benedick and Beatrice alone, and we can see both how their relationship has changed and how it remains the same. Clearly, their jokes and teasing do not have the same edge of cruelty they had in Act 1. They are now in love, and their words are gentle not cutting. No more will Benedick call Beatrice "Lady Tongue" or a "harpy," as he did at the masquerade. But—thank God— falling in love has not taken the vitality and spark out of these two characters. They are no longer bitter toward one another, but neither have they become silent lovers like Claudio and Hero. They still banter back and forth; there is still a playful roughness to their relationship. They are simply, as Benedick says, "too wise to woo peaceably" (5.2.75-76). Their liveliness has not been destroyed by love. Beatrice has not given up her individuality, her strong wit and personality. She has not allowed herself to become a commodity, a piece of meat. Because their strengths have been taken up and transformed (not canceled) by love, they can hope for a satisfying life together.

The second wedding scene is perfect in all the ways that the first wedding was damaged. The first wedding ended with Hero "dead," but during the second she is raised to life. At the first wedding, Claudio and Hero were torn asunder, but at the second they are reconciled and united. The first wedding was spoiled by a poisonous lie, but by the second wedding the lie has been exposed and rejected. In the first wedding, Hero was publicly denounced as a whore; in the second "another Hero" is vindicated as a "maid" (5.4.62-64). The second wedding also consummates the love of Benedick and Beatrice; the love they professed after the first wedding is permanently sealed with marriage vows. The double wedding ties together the two parallel courtships that have structured the play, even as it brings resolution to the parallel deceptions. Benedick said of the first wedding that it "looks not like a nuptial." The second wedding is everything a wedding is supposed to be: reconciliation of opposites, union, new life, a restoration of Eden.

For Eden to be truly restored, the old Adam has to die and be replaced by a new. In Act 5, Claudio finally becomes that new man. In the first wedding, he allowed the lie to dictate and guide his sight and his love. When he heard Dogberry's confirmation of Hero's innocence, he told Leonato to "dispose for henceforth of poor Claudio" (5.1.302-303), implying that he would experience a kind of death. Not only his bride, but Claudio himself must die to live. At the second wedding, fittingly, he is not allowed to see his bride until he has taken vows. He is blessed because he is one who does not see and yet believes and loves; he makes his wedding vows, professes his love, by faith not by sight. Finally, Claudio has begun to be genuinely and lastingly converted to love.

The play ends with Benedick giving two important instructions. During the second wedding, Don John has been chased down and captured, and has been brought in chains to Messina. Benedick promises Don Pedro to "devise thee brave punishments for him" (5.4.131). Then Benedick immediately adds, "Strike up, pipers" (5.4.131-132). It may seem cruel to talk about torture and dancing in the same breath; dancing outside a prison cell sounds like a scene from a horror movie, not a comedy. Shakespeare knows, however, that there are evil people in the world; there are serpents in Eden. And Shakespeare knows too that there is really no happy ending until those serpents are crushed. The dance can begin only when the serpent is captured, bound, and rendered powerless. There is no real peace and joy unless justice is done, no new Jerusalem until Satan is cast into the lake of fire.

Review Questions.

1. What is Claudio's attitude in his encounter with Leonato and Antonio? Does he regret what he did to Hero?

2. What does Benedick's challenge of Claudio tell us about Benedick?

3. How does Claudio react to the news of Hero's innocence? Does he make a satisfactory confession?

4. What does Leonato require of Claudio?

5. How have Beatrice and Benedick changed in the way they relate to one another? How are they the same?

6. How is the second wedding different from the first?

7. How does the second wedding tie up the various threads of the plot?

8. How has Claudio changed from the first wedding? In what way is Claudio's experience like Hero's?

9. Why is it important for Claudio to take his wedding vows before he sees his bride?

10. What are Benedick's final words? Why are they important?

Thought Questions.

1. What are Leonato and Antonio talking about at the beginning of 5.1? How do their viewpoints change through the course of the scene?

2. Don Pedro comments that Benedick "goes in his doublet and hose and leaves off his wit" (5.1.202-204). Why does he make this reference to clothing?

3. What charges does Dogberry bring against Conrade and Borachio? (5.1.219-224).

4. When Claudio hears Dogberry's report, he says, "I have drunk poison whiles he utter'd it" (5.1.253). Discuss this statement in the light of Borachio's earlier use of "poison" to describe Don John's plot to kill Claudio's marriage.

5. According to Leonato's statement in 5.1.271-272, what killed Hero? What does he mean by this?

6. What kind of attitude does Claudio display when he publicly mourns Hero (5.3)? What do his final words mean:

"And Hymen now with luckier issue speed's than this for whom we render'd up this woe"? How sorrowful does he seem?

7. What kind of character is Margaret? (5.2.1-25; see 3.4.1-94).

8. Benedick says that it is true that he "suffers love" (5.2.69-70). What does he mean? How does Beatrice answer him? (5.2.71-74; see 5.4.91-93).

9. Explain the exchange between Claudio and Benedick in 5.4.43-51.

10. Near the end of the play, Benedick says, "man is a giddy thing, and this is my conclusion" (5.4.109-110). What does he mean? Is this a fitting conclusion to the play?

Film Versions of *Much Ado About Nothing*

I have reviewed one video version of *Much Ado*, Kenneth Branagh's 1993 production, widely available for sale or rent. Branagh directed and starred in *Henry V* in 1989, along with his now-estranged wife, Emma Thompson. They play the roles of Beatrice and Benedick in *Much Ado* and are outstanding. The rest of the young cast tends to be rather wooden; Keanu Reeves is much better playing opposite a wired bus. The exception is Michael Keaton. Keaton takes some getting used to, but plays the constable Dogberry with a mix of sleaze, zaniness, and dumb honesty. In spite of the weakness of certain members of the cast, overall the film is excellent. As with *Henry V*, Branagh shortens some speeches and edits the play in other ways to make it more suited to the screen, but nothing and no one essential is left out. There is, however, one blatant error. The film inexplicably reverses scenes 5.2 and 5.3, making it appear that Benedick and Beatrice learn about Hero's vindication on the day after Claudio has led a multitude in mourning at her grave. Where have they been!?

Parents need to be aware that there are some questionable scenes. One of the opening scenes shows both men and women nude (mostly from the rear), as they frantically run around an Italian villa bathing and getting dressed. One of the central scenes of the play—in which Claudio thinks he sees his fiancé Hero in another man's embrace—is fairly explicit. (In the play, this scene is not actually shown, only talked about.) Also, some of Dogberry's comic violence is a bit intense. The film earned a PG-13 because of these scenes. Apart from these, the only possibly objectionable elements are certain bawdy Elizabethan puns and jokes.

Suggested Paper Topics.

1. Compare and contrast a pair of characters: Beatrice and Hero; Benedick and Claudio; Don Pedro and Don John. They can be discussed with respect to their views of love and marriage, their personality traits, how they change through the course of the play.

2. Discuss the imagery of horns throughout the play. How are "horns" related to cuckoldry, and how does this relate to the overall plot and themes of the play? Why is it significant that Benedick prefers the "horn" to the lute as a musical instrument?

3. Discuss how the pun in the title (nothing/noting) expresses some important themes of the play.

4. Discuss the use of deception, disguises, and appearances in the play.

5. Discuss Shakespeare's use of military imagery in the play, especially its use in relation to love.

6. There are many comments on "fashion" in the play. Discuss the various ways in which this idea is used, and how it fits with some of the other themes of the play.

7. Discuss the importance of Benedick's words "May I be so converted and see with these eyes?" for the play.

8. Compare and contrast similar scenes: the two "gulling scenes," the two wedding scenes.

9. Examine the character of Dogberry and his function in the play.

10. Explain the role of some lesser character: Margaret, Leonato, Friar Francis.